P9-EKE-986

WHERE THE BLUEBIRD SINGS
TO THE LEMONADE SPRINGS

WALLACE STEGNER

WHERE THE BLUEBIRD SINGS
TO THE LEMONADE SPRINGS

LIVING AND WRITING
IN THE WEST

Afterword by T. H. Watkins

THE MODERN LIBRARY

NEW YORK

2002 Modern Library Paperback Edition

Copyright © 1992 by Wallace Stegner

Biographical note copyright © 2000 by Random House, Inc.

Afterword copyright © 2002 by the Estate of T. H. Watkins

All rights reserved under International and Pan-American Copyright
Conventions. Published in the United States by Modern Library, an imprint of
The Random House Publishing Group, a division of Random House, Inc., New York,
and simultaneously in Canada by Random House of Canada Limited, Toronto.

MODERN LIBRARY and the TORCHBEARER Design are registered trademarks of
Random House, Inc.

This work was originally published in hardcover by Random House, Inc., in 1992 in slightly
different form.

Some of these essays were published in *Ford Times, Smithsonian* magazine, and the *Los Angeles
Times Book Review.*

"Thoughts in a Dry Land" was previously published in *A Western Harvest,* edited by Frances
Ring and published by John Daniel and Company, 1991.

Grateful acknowledgment is made to the following for permission to reprint previously published
material:

Alfred A. Knopf, Inc.: "Finding the Place: A Migrant Childhood" by Wallace Stegner from *Growing Up
Western,* edited by Clarus Backes, published by Alfred A. Knopf, Inc., in 1989. Reprinted by permission of Alfred A. Knopf, Inc.

Confluence Press: "Haunted by Waters: Norman Maclean" from *Norman Maclean,* edited by Ron
McFarland and Hugh Nichols, and "A Letter to Wendell Berry," originally published as "Wendell
Berry, a Placed Person," in a book on Wendell Berry edited by Paul Merchant, both by Wallace
Stegner. Reprinted by permission.

Doubleday, a division of Random House, Inc.: "Letter, Much Too Late" by Wallace Stegner from *Family
Portraits* by Carolyn Anthony. Copyright © 1989 by Wallace Stegner. Reprinted by permission of
Doubleday, a division of Random House, Inc.

University Press of Colorado: Introduction, adapted from "A Geography of Hope" by Wallace Stegner
in *A Society to Match Our Scenery.* Adapted and reprinted by permission of The University Press of
Colorado.

The University of Michigan Press: "Living Dry," "Striking the Rock," and "Variations on a Theme by
Crèvecoeur" from *The American West as Living Space* by Wallace Stegner (University of Michigan
Press, 1987). Reprinted by permission.

University of Nebraska Press: "George R. Stewart and the American Land," foreword by Wallace Stegner from *Storm* by George R. Stewart. Copyright © 1983 by the University of Nebraska Press.
Reprinted by permission of the University of Nebraska Press.

University of Nevada Press: "Walter Clark's Frontier," a chapter by Wallace Stegner from *Walter Van
Tilburg Clark: Critiques,* edited by Charlton Laird. Copyright © 1983 by University of Nevada Press.
Reprinted by permission of University of Nevada Press.

Wisconsin Humanities Committee: "The Sense of Place" by Wallace Stegner, originally published as a
pamphlet by the Wisconsin Humanities Committee. This essay was commissioned and published by
the Wisconsin Humanities Committee with support from the National Endowment for the Humanities. Reprinted by permission.

Yolla Bolly Press: "On Steinbeck's Story 'Flight' " by Wallace Stegner first appeared as an afterword in
Flight, a limited-edition book, published by The Yolla Bolly Press, Covelo, California, in 1984.
Reprinted by permission.

LIBRARY OF CONGRESS CATALOGING-IN-PUBLICATION DATA IS AVAILABLE

ISBN 0-375-75932-8

Modern Library website address: www.modernlibrary.com

Printed in the United States of America

4 6 8 9 7 5 3

WALLACE STEGNER

Wallace Earle Stegner, the award-winning novelist, biographer, historian, essayist, critic, environmentalist, and teacher who pursued the truths that lay behind the mythology of the American West, was born in Lake Mills, Iowa, on February 18, 1909. He grew up in countless boom-and-bust towns all over the West as his father shuttled the family through Saskatchewan, North Dakota, Washington, Montana, and Nevada before finally settling in Salt Lake City in 1921. Stegner entered the University of Utah in 1925 and started writing fiction while a graduate student at the University of Iowa in the 1930s. He began his teaching career at the University of Utah and later taught at both the University of Wisconsin and Harvard. From 1946 until his retirement in 1971 Stegner headed the prestigious creative writing program at Stanford, which has had a profound effect upon contemporary American fiction. Twice a Guggenheim Fellow, he was also a Senior Fellow of the National Institute for the Humanities as well as a member of the National Institute and Academy of Arts and Letters and the American Academy of Arts and Sciences.

Stegner made an auspicious literary debut in 1937 with *Remembering Laughter,* a rueful tale about an adulterous triangle in Iowa farm country that evoked comparisons with *Ethan Frome.* His next three novels—*The Potter's House* (1938), *On a Darkling Plain* (1940), and *Fire and Ice* (1941)—disappointed reviewers. But he enjoyed widespread popular and critical success with *The Big Rock Candy Mountain* (1943), a semiautobiographical chronicle of a nomadic family drifting through the West in search of an easy life that is always just out of reach. His other novels of this period include *Second Growth* (1947), a story about the conflict between puritanical values and modern morality in a New

England town, and *The Preacher and the Slave* (1950), a brilliantly imagined portrait of Joseph Hillstrom, the legendary outlaw and labor organizer who became a martyr following his execution for murder in 1915. After abandoning long fiction for more than a decade Stegner returned to novel writing with *A Shooting Star* (1961), the bestselling story of one woman's hard-won triumphs over the irrational drives that have brought her to the edge of doom, and *All the Little Live Things* (1967), the tale of a New York literary agent who retires to California only to be engulfed by the chaos of the 1960s.

Meanwhile Stegner gained a whole new readership with his probing works of nonfiction. In *Mormon Country* (1941) and *The Gathering of Zion: The Story of the Mormon Trail* (1964) he dramatically recounted the epic history of the Mormons. In *Beyond the Hundredth Meridian* (1954), a biography of naturalist and explorer John Wesley Powell, he presented a fascinating look at the old American West as seen through the eyes of the man who prophetically warned against the dangers of settling it. And in *Wolf Willow* (1962), a memoir of his boyhood in southern Saskatchewan, he offered an enduring portrait of a pioneer community existing on the verge of the modern world. *Saturday Review* judged *Beyond the Hundredth Meridian* and *Wolf Willow* "two of the most important Western books of the decade. . . . Both are so to speak geo-history, intensified, sharpened, made viable and useful by poetic insights and a keen intelligence." Stegner's enchantment with the West is reflected too in the essays collected in *The Sound of Mountain Water* (1969) and *One Way to Spell Man* (1982), two volumes that also voice his frontline views on wilderness conservation. As Wendell Berry observed: "Stegner is a new kind of American writer, one who not only writes about his region, but also does his best to protect it . . . from its would-be exploiters and destroyers."

Stegner was awarded the Pulitzer Prize for *Angle of Repose,* which came out in 1971. "*Angle of Repose* is a long, intricate, deeply rewarding novel," wrote William Abrahams in the *Atlantic Monthly*. "[It] is neither the predictable historical-regional Western epic, nor the equally predictable four-decker family saga, the Forsytes in California, so to speak. . . . For all [its] breadth and sweep, *Angle of Repose* achieves an effect of intimacy, hence of immediacy, and, though much of the material is 'historical,' an effect of discovery also, of experience newly minted rather than a pageantlike recreation. . . . Wallace Stegner has written a superb novel, with an amplitude of scale and richness of detail altogether uncommon in contemporary fiction."

"*Angle of Repose* is a novel about Time, as much as anything—about people who live through time, who believe in both a past and a future," remarked Stegner. "It has something to say about the relations of a man with his ancestors and his descendants. It is also a novel about cultural transplantation. It sets one man's impulse to build and create in the West against his cultivated wife's yearning for the cultural opportunities she left in the East. Through the eyes of their grandson (a man living today) it appraises the conflict of openness and change with the Victorian pattern of ingrained responsibilities and reticences; and in the entangled emotional life of the narrator it finds a parallel for the emotional lesions in the lives of the grandparents. It finds, that is, the present in the past and the past in the present; and in the activities of a very young (and very modern) secretary-assistant it reveals how even the most rebellious crusades of our time follow paths that our great-grandfathers' feet beat dusty."

Stegner enjoyed great critical acclaim for his next work, *The Uneasy Chair* (1974), a full-scale biography of Bernard DeVoto, the historian, novelist, and ferociously funny critic of American society. "[This] book is full of dramatic episodes and offers, from a special point of view, a battlefield panorama of the literary world from 1920 to 1955," said Malcolm Cowley. "[Stegner] is an ideal biographer for DeVoto. Their careers sometimes crossed. . . . Both were brought up in Utah. . . . and both, as Stegner says, were 'novelists by intention, teachers by necessity, and historians by the sheer compulsion of the region that shaped us.' " *Time* agreed: "*The Uneasy Chair* consistently goes beyond the limits of its subject to illuminate what it meant to be a writer in the America of the '30s, '40s, and '50s."

In 1977 Stegner won a National Book Award for *The Spectator Bird* (1976), in which he again depicted literary agent Joe Allston, the protagonist of *All the Little Live Things*. Likewise in *Recapitulation* (1979)

Stegner resurrected Bruce Mason, a character from *The Big Rock Candy Mountain,* to assess the course his life has taken. "This is Stegner's *The Sound and the Fury,*" said the novelist's biographer Jackson Benson. "Like the Faulkner novel, *Recapitulation* is a book about time and its multiplicity of meanings in human experience, about the history of a family in its decline." Stegner's last novel, *Crossing to Safety* (1987), traces the turbulent, lifelong friendship of two college professors and their wives. "A superb book," said *The New York Times Book Review.* "Mr. Stegner has built a convincing narrative, has made survival a grace rather than a grim necessity, and enduring, tried love the test and proof of a good life. Nothing in these lives is lost or wasted, suffering becomes an enriching benediction, and life itself a luminous experience."

Although Stegner is perhaps best known for his novels, he also garnered substantial acclaim and three O. Henry Awards for his short fiction. Over the years he published nearly fifty short stories in such magazines as *Harper's* and the *Atlantic Monthly.* Some were reprinted in the collections *The Women on the Wall* (1948) and *The City of the Living* (1956). In addition his work was often featured in editions of *Prize Stories: The O. Henry Awards* as well as the annual series *The Best American Short Stories.* "Stegner's short fiction is unparalleled for the clarity and depth of its human insights," remarked James Dickey. "This fact, coupled with the unobtrusive yet highly individual style that only he commands, places him among the masters by whom later practitioners of the form will be judged." Upon publication of *Collected Stories of Wallace Stegner* in 1990, Anne Tyler noted: "Wallace Stegner has been steadily enriching readers' lives for more than half a century. . . . His admirers will take him any way they can get him—novels, essays, biographies—but after sinking into these stories gathered from a 'lifetime of writing,' we can't help but mourn the passing of his short-story days. These stories are so large; they're so wholehearted. Plainly, he never set out to write a *mere* short story. It was all or nothing." George Garrett concurred: "Every story in Stegner's *Collected Stories* bears the indelible signature of an artist."

Stegner's final book, *Where the Bluebird Sings to the Lemonade Springs,* another collection of essays about the West, came out in 1992. The *Los Angeles Times Book Review* deemed it "the essential Stegner . . . the brilliant crystallization of his lifetime of thinking about the American West." Wallace Stegner died in Santa Fe, New Mexico, on April 13, 1993, of injuries resulting from a car accident. *Marking the Sparrow's Fall,* a compilation comprising many of his unpublished essays about the West, appeared posthumously in 1998. As the *Los Angeles Times* observed: "The reader of Stegner's writing is immediately reminded of an essential America. . . . a distinct place, a unique people, a common history, and a shared heritage remembered as only Stegner can."

CONTENTS

CONTENTS

For Mary,
who, like Dilsey, has seen the first and last,
and been indispensable and enspiriting all the way

IN THE BIG ROCK CANDY MOUNTAINS

In the Big Rock Candy Mountains
There's a land that's fair and bright
Where the hand-outs grow on bushes
And you sleep out every night;
Where the box cars all are empty,
Where the sun shines every day
On the birds and the bees
And the cigarette trees,
And the lemonade springs
Where the blue bird sings—
In the Big Rock Candy Mountains.

—HARRY MCCLINTOCK
The Big Rock Candy Mountains

ACKNOWLEDGMENTS

Most of the essays in this collection have appeared previously in magazines or in books:

Introduction, adapted from a lecture, "A Geography of Hope," delivered at the University of Colorado and published in *A Society to Match Our Scenery* (University of Colorado Press, 1991).

"Finding the Place: A Migrant Childhood," in *Growing Up Western,* edited by Clarus Backes (Knopf, 1989).

"Letter, Much Too Late," in *Family Portraits: Remembrances by Twenty Distinguished Writers,* edited by Carolyn Anthony (Doubleday, 1989).

"Crossing into Eden," in *Ford Times,* May 1989.

"Thoughts in a Dry Land," in *Westways* magazine, September 1972.

"Living Dry," "Striking the Rock," and "Variations on a Theme by Crèvecoeur," as a booklet, *The American West as Living Space* (University of Michigan Press, 1987).

"A Capsule History of Conservation," under the title "It All Began with Conservation," in *Smithsonian* magazine, April 1990.

"Coming of Age: The End of the Beginning," as "Out Where the Sense of Place Is a Sense of Motion," in the *Los Angeles Times Book Review,* June 3, 1990.

ACKNOWLEDGMENTS

"On Steinbeck's Story 'Flight,' " as an afterword to a fine-press edition of the Steinbeck story (Yolla Bolly Press, 1984).

"George R. Stewart and the American Land," as a foreword to Stewart's novel *Storm* (Lincoln: University of Nebraska Press, 1983).

"Walter Clark's Frontier," in *Walter Van Tilburg Clark: Critiques,* edited by Charlton Laird (Reno: University of Nevada Press, 1983).

"Haunted by Waters," in *Norman Maclean,* edited by Ron McFarland and Hugh Nichols (Lewiston, Idaho: Confluence Press, 1988).

"The Sense of Place," as a pamphlet for the Wisconsin Humanities Committee (Madison, Wisconsin: Silver Buckle Press, 1986).

"A Letter to Wendell Berry," in *Wendell Berry,* edited by Paul Merchant (Lewiston, Idaho: Confluence Press, 1991).

INTRODUCTION

Once I said in print that the remaining western wilderness is the geography of hope, and I have written, believing what I wrote, that the West at large is hope's native home, the youngest and freshest of America's regions, magnificently endowed and with the chance to become something unprecedented and unmatched in the world.

I was shaped by the West and have lived most of a long life in it, and nothing would gratify me more than to see it, in all its subregions and subcultures, both prosperous and environmentally healthy, with a civilization to match its scenery. Whenever I return to the Rocky Mountain states where I am most at home or escape into the California backlands from the suburbia where I live, the smell of distance excites me, the largeness and the clarity take the scales from my eyes, and I respond as unthinkingly as a salmon that swims past a rivermouth and tastes the waters of its birth.

But when I am thinking instead of throbbing, I remember what history and experience have taught me about the West's past, and what my senses tell me about the West's present, and I become more cautious about the West's future. Too often, when they have been prosperous, the western states have been prosperous at the expense of their fragile environment, and their civilization has too often mined and degraded the natural scene while drawing most of its quality from it.

So I amend my enthusiasm, I begin to quibble and qualify, I say, yes, the West is hope's native home, but there are varieties and degrees of hope, and the wrong kinds, in excessive amounts, go with human failure and environmental damage as boom goes with bust.

Visionary expectation was a great energizer of the westward move-

ment, and something like it still drives the rush to the Sunbelt. But exaggerated, uninformed, unrealistic, greedy expectation has been a prescription for disappointment that the West has carried to the corner drugstore too many times. Ghost towns and dust bowls, like motels, are western inventions. All are reflections of transience, and transience in most of the West has hampered the development of stable, rooted communities and aborted the kind of communal effort that takes in everything from kindergarten to graveyard and involves all kinds and grades and ages of people in a shared past and a promise of continuance.

The deficiency of community is as apparent in the cities as in the small towns—perhaps even more so. Western cities are likely to have an artificial look, and why not, since so many of them are planted in an artificial environment maintained by increasingly elaborate engineering. In *Californians: Searching for the Golden State,* James Houston asks what should be a preposterous question—"Suppose ten million people were living in a semidesert where there was not one adequate source of water closer than 200 miles?"—and answers it with a further leap into the preposterous. That semidesert is the Los Angeles metropolitan area, and not ten million but fifteen million people are living there. Five years of drought have not even slowed down the growth. But ten years would, and fifteen would stop it cold, and twenty would send people reeling back not only from Los Angeles but from San Diego, Albuquerque, Denver, Phoenix, Tucson, every artificial urban enclave. And the tree rings inform us that droughts of that duration have occurred. Every western city hell-bent for expansion might ponder the history of Mesa Verde.

Deeply lived-in places are exceptions rather than the rule in the West. For one thing, all western places are new; for another, many of the people who established them came to pillage, or to work for pillagers, rather than to settle for life. When the pillaging was done or the dream exploded, they moved on, to be replaced in the next boom by others just as hopeful and just as footloose. Successive waves have kept western towns alive but prevented them from deepening the quality of their life, and with every wave the land is poorer.

Other regions have recovered better from the impact of our high-energy civilization and our habit of liquidating the resources that support us. Vermont, for example, is a rugged country with a violent climate, but it *heals*. Clear-cut it, and it goes patiently and inevitably back to raspberry bushes and browse, then to Christmas trees and dense stands of maple, ash, beech, birch, and poplar seedlings, and then, when one is not looking, to woods. The West, vast and magnificent, greatly various but with the abiding unity of too little water except in its extreme northwest corner, has proved far more fragile and unforgiving. Damaged by human rapacity or carelessness, it is more likely to go on to erosion gullies and desertification than to restore itself.

Aridity has been a difficult fact of life for Americans to accept, and an even more difficult one for them to adapt to. For nearly a half century after Lewis and Clark, we avoided, or hurried through, the dry plains that Pike and Long called the Great American Desert and thought unfit for human habitation. But by the 1860s we were pushing the agricultural frontier out into Kansas and out into the Platte Valley, and were misled by a wet cycle into believing that settlement improved the climate, that rain followed the plow. By the 1880s, when a ten-year drought withered homesteaders at the edge of the semi-arid lands, we began to shift from witchcraft to technology, and attempted to engineer aridity out of existence by damming and redirecting the streams. (Most of the consequences of that enormous plumbing job are still to come, but they are coming.) Or, as a plumbing variation, we robbed Peter to pay Paul: we stole the Owens Valley's water to make the subdivision of the San Fernando Valley richly profitable to Los Angeles developers. We conducted water through the Rockies from the western slope to permit the continued growth of Denver. We pumped down the groundwater until the pumps threw sand.

In the dry West, using water means using it *up*. What we put to municipal or industrial use is not coming back into the streams to be available for irrigation, or if it does come back, it comes back poisoned. What is used in irrigation largely evaporates. The percentage that finds its way back to the streams is increasingly laden with salts, fertilizers, and pesticides. And everything we take out of the rivers for any purpose leaves less in-stream flow for trout, rafters, picnickers, herons, ducks, skinny-dippers, and TV cameramen photographing pristine America. You can literally dry up a stream if you have a prior right for a so-called beneficial purpose.

Confronted with the facts of unavoidable shortage that is bound to get worse, with the infeasibility of more dams, the oversubscription of rivers, the alarming lowering of the water table, the unpredictable periods of drought, boosters are likely to speak of "augmentation," and to suggest ever-greater engineering projects, roughly comparable to the canals of Mars, to bring water down to the dry country from the Columbia or the Snake or the Yukon, or to tow it as icebergs from Glacier Bay to let San Diego expand and the desert blossom.

Pipedreams. Arrogant pipedreams. Why should deserts be asked to blossom? They have their own intricately interdependent plant and animal species, including the creosote-ring clones that are the oldest living things on earth. The deserts were doing all right until we set out to reform them. Making them blossom is something we inherited from Isaiah. It is an idea dear to American, and especially Mormon, hearts, and it has had remarkable short-term successes. But it is open to all sorts of doubts when we look into the future even a hundred years. Historically, irrigation civilizations have died, either of salinization or of accumulating engineering problems, except in Egypt, where, until the Aswan Dam, the annual Nile flood kept the land sweet. And if there are no technical reasons why we cannot move water from remote watersheds, there are ecological and, I might suggest, moral reasons why we shouldn't. As a Crow Indian friend of mine said about the coal in his country, "God put it there. That's a good place for it." Lots of things have learned to depend on the water where it is. It would become us to leave their living space intact, for if we don't, we take chances on our own.

Sooner or later the West must accept the limitations imposed by aridity, one of the chief of which is a restricted human population. Western growth has a low ceiling, a fact that neither boosters nor hopeful in-migrants like to admit. From before it was even known, the West has been a land of Cockaigne, an Indian Valley Line where every day is payday, a Big Rock Candy Mountain where the handouts grow on bushes and the little streams of alcohol come trickling down the rocks. Ordinary people, making it by guess and by God, or not quite making it, are just as susceptible to dreams as the ambitious and greedy, and respond as excitedly to the adventure, the freedom, the apparently inexhaustible richness of the West. And the boosters have been there from the beginning to oversell the West as the Garden of the World, the flowing well of opportunity, the stamping ground of the self-reliant.

Sometimes it is hard to tell the boosters from the suckers. They may be the same people. There have been plenty of western buccaneers of the Marcus Daley/George Hearst stamp, and plenty of boosters, from Lansford Hastings and Sam Brannan to William Gilpin and William E. Smyth, the John the Baptist of irrigation. It is hard to escape the conclusion that many of them were deluded deluders, true believers, wishful thinkers, blindfold prophets, at once the agents, the beneficiaries, and the victims of the vast speculative real estate deal that is American and western history.

I know that historical hope, energy, carelessness, and self-deception. I knew it before I could talk. My father practically invented it, though he qualified more as sucker than as booster, and profited accordingly.

He was a boomer from the age of fourteen, always on the lookout for the big chance, the ground floor, the inside track. As a youth he tried the Wisconsin and Minnesota woods, but found only the migratory wage slavery that has always been one payoff of the American Dream. He tried professional baseball but wasn't quite good enough. In the 1890s he floated out to North Dakota on the tail end of the land rush, but found himself in the midst of a ten-year drought and ended up speculating in wheat futures and running a blind pig. If you believe that the world owes you not merely a living but a bonanza, then restrictive laws are only an irritation and a challenge.

When it became clear that Dakota's promises were indistinguishable from Siberian exile, my father dragged us out the migration route to the Northwest. His goal was Alaska, but again he was late: the

Klondike rush was long over; the survivors had struggled back. For a while he ran a lunchroom in the Washington woods, where the Seattle suburb of Redmond now is. The loggers cut down the trees and left the lunchroom among the stumps. By 1914 we were up in Saskatchewan, part of another land rush, where for a change we *would* be in on the ground floor, and make a killing growing wheat to feed Europe's armies.

We plowed up something over a hundred acres of buffalo grass, and for a while we were a wheat farm. Then, because Saskatchewan is part of the arid West and we were in Palliser's Triangle, one of the driest parts of it, we became a tumbleweed patch and a dust bowl. Then we were on the road again, first to Montana, then to Utah, ultimately to Nevada and California. Rainbows flowered for my father in every sky he looked at; he was led by pillars of fire and cloud. In Salt Lake City he fell in with some men who had a doodlebug that would reveal the presence of gold and silver in the earth, and my safety deposit box still contains, not as assets but as wry reminders, deeds to several patches of Nevada gravel and mountainside that my father firmly believed would one day make us rich.

While he waited for one of those bonanzas to pan out, he ran a gambling joint in Reno, an occupation symbolically right for him as for the West at large. Later, when he was close to down and out, and growing desperate, he did one last desperate and damaging thing: he managed to get an option on some land in southern California, and to make his payments and a fast buck, he hired a crew to cut down all its two-hundred-year-old oaks and sell them off as firewood. Finally, like Clarence King and many another gambler no worse and no better, he died broke and friendless in a fleabag hotel, having in his lifetime done more human and environmental damage than he could have repaired in a second lifetime.

Out of his life I made a novel, *The Big Rock Candy Mountain,* my first and most heartfelt commentary on western optimism and enterprise and the common man's dream of something for nothing. I took the title from the hobo ballad that Harry McClintock, "Haywire Mac," is supposed to have written in 1928, but that I heard my father sing long before that. That vagrant's vision of beatitude—of a place where the bulldogs have rubber teeth and the cinder dicks are blind and policemen have to tip their hats, where there's a lake of stew and of whiskey too, where the handouts grow on bushes and the hens lay soft-boiled eggs—summarized his unquenchable hope as it summarizes the indigenous optimism of the West. I suppose it is a proof of the incorrigibility of that spirit that when I began to look for a title for this book of essays about the West, I was drawn back to that same hobo ballad. What lures many people to the West always has been, and still is, mirage.

The essays in this volume, some of them personal, some of them concerned with the West as living space, some of them examinations of writers who have dealt with western themes and the tentative, just-forming western subculture, are not a systematic discussion of the characteristic western problems, but they are never far from those troubling concerns. There are plenty of people in the West—millions, probably—who still think like my father, and who approach western land, water, grass, timber, mineral resources, and scenery as grave robbers might approach the tomb of a pharaoh. We have learned too little and there are many more of us, with vastly magnified industrial power.

And yet I hope these essays do not say that western hopefulness is a cynical joke. For somehow, against probability, some sort of indigenous, recognizable culture has been growing on western ranches and in western towns and even in western cities. It is the product not of the boomers but of the stickers, not of those who pillage and run but of those who settle, and love the life they have made and the place they have made it in. There are more of those, too, than there used to be, and they know a great deal more, and are better able to resist and sometimes prevent the extractive frenzy that periodically attacks them.

I believe that eventually, perhaps within a generation or two, they will work out some sort of compromise between what must be done to earn a living and what must be done to restore health to the earth, air, and water. I think they will learn to control corporate power and

to dampen the excess that has always marked their region, and will arrive at a degree of stability and a reasonably sustainable economy
based on resources that they will know how to cherish and renew.
And looking at the western writers, not only the ones I will discuss
here, but all the new ones, the Ivan Doigs and Bill Kittredges and
James Welches, the Greta Ehrlichs and Rudolfo Anayas and John
Daniels, the Scott Momadays and Louise Erdrichs and many more, I
feel the surge of the inextinguishable western hope. It is a civilization
they are building, a history they are compiling, a way of looking at the
world and humanity's place in it. I think they will do it. The feeling
is like the feeling in a football game when the momentum changes,
when helplessness begins to give way to confidence, and what looked
like sure defeat opens up to the possibility of victory. It has already begun. I hope I am around to see it fully arrive.

PART ONE
PERSONAL

FINDING THE PLACE: A MIGRANT CHILDHOOD

I had no understanding of it while it was happening, did not comprehend either the deprivations or the advantages until acquaintance with other regions and older cultures began to define the terms of my identity for me, but from February 1909, when I was born on my grandfather's farm near Lake Mills, Iowa, to September 1930, when I boarded a bus in Salt Lake City to go "back east" to graduate school in Iowa, all the places I knew were western: North Dakota wheat towns, Washington logging camps, Saskatchewan prairie hamlets and lonely home-steads, and the cities of Seattle, Great Falls, Salt Lake, Holly-wood, and Reno, with a lot of country seen on the fly between them.

My father was a boomer, a gambler, a rainbow-chaser, as footloose as a tumbleweed in a windstorm. My mother was always hopefully, hopelessly, trying to nest. Like many western Americans, especially the poorer kinds, I was born on wheels. I used to think that I was shaped by motion, but I find on thinking it over that what most conditioned me was the two places where we stayed long enough to put down roots and develop associations and memories and friends and a degree of self-confidence. These were the village of Eastend, at the edge of the Cypress Hills in Saskatchewan, Canada, and Salt Lake City, Utah.

Nevertheless, the characteristic western migratoriness was not unimportant. Growing up culturally undernourished, I hunted the Big Rock Candy Mountain as hungrily as ever my father did, but his was a mountain of another kind. He wanted to make a killing and end up on Easy Street. I wanted to hunt up and rejoin the civilization I had been deprived of. So my wheels didn't stop rolling until, at the age of thirty-six, after several years of graduate school in Iowa and California and a decade of teaching in Illinois, Utah, Wisconsin, and Massachusetts, I arrived with my wife and son at Stanford and the house in the Coast Range foothills, within sight of the last sunsets on the continent, where we have lived ever since. Teaching at Harvard, which should have gratified my highest ambition, didn't fully satisfy because I didn't much like the place where Harvard was situated. I took the first opportunity that offered a chance to get back west.

The years since 1945 have been, in the main, happy, contented, and productive, but like all busy years, they tend to blur and flow together. It is the years when the West was pretty young and I was even younger, the years when a full round of the seasons was a seventh or eighth or ninth of my life instead of a seventieth or eightieth, that are indelible.

My first five years were constant motion, and what I retain of them is no more than flits and flashes, images on a broken film flapping through the projector: rare sun on the roof of our tent in the deep woods where now stands Redmond, Washington; the musty, buttery odor of the bread crusts distributed from a dishpan at mid-morning in the Seattle orphanage where my desperate mother stashed my brother and me for a while; the foreign smells and sounds of my grandfather's Norwegian-speaking house in Lake Mills when we retreated there in the winter of 1913; the bare benches and varnished wainscots of the railroad station in Weyburn, on the Canadian border, with stern men in red coats staring down from the walls.

Those are preliminaries. The real film begins in the summer of 1914 in the raw new non-town of Eastend, where the Frenchman River flows out of the Cypress Hills. That was the first place in my life where we lived more than a few months. I was five when we arrived, eleven when we left. The years during which I participated in the birth of that town were the shaping years of my life. I have never forgotten a detail of them.

Eastend when we arrived was the Z-X ranch house and a boardinghouse for the crews building the grade for a Canadian Pacific branch line down from Swift Current. Its history, which none of us knew, was short and violent. *Métis* winterers had not ventured into the dark and bloody hills, disputed ground among the tribes, until 1867. In 1869 the Hudson's Bay Company built a post on Chimney Coulee, above the present town; it lasted one season before it was destroyed by the Blackfeet. In the 1870s the Mounties built a patrol post, first on Chimney Coulee, then on the river, to keep an eye on the Sioux and Nez Percés who had fled north of the line after the Indian wars. And in the 1880s cattle had begun coming in from Montana, and had spread out over that noble range for twenty years. The terrible winter of 1906–07 put most of the outfits out of business. The Z-X was a remnant survivor, protected by its situation in the lap of the hills. Out of it our family and a dozen others carved a townsite.

Within a few weeks, when the rails were laid, the town grew by several derailed boxcars, old Pullmans, and a superannuated dining car. We lived the first winter in the dining car, considered pretty classy. Later we lived in a rented shack. After two years, my father built a house and a small barn down in the west end, on the river.*

The first year in Eastend was a chaos of experiences, good and bad. I caught lice from the half-Indian kids I played with and was fiercely shampooed with kerosene. I learned dirty words and dirty songs from the children of railroad construction workers and from Z-X cowpunchers. With other boys, I was induced to ride calves and lured into "shit fights" with wet cow manure in the Z-X corrals. Then or later I learned to dog-paddle, first in the irrigation ditch, later in the river, and I fished for suckers in the deep holes of the bends, and followed trails through willows that felt like authentic wilderness. Then or later we put .22 cartridges or blasting caps on the tracks ahead of approaching handcars or speeders, and once we got satisfactorily chased by the gandy dancers of the section crew. Around Christmas we all watched the first soldiers go off to the war, and then and afterward we had trouble with Canadian kids who said the United States was too yellow to get in the fight. They had a song for us:

> Here's to the American eagle
> He flies over mountain and ditch
> But we don't want the turd of your goddam bird
> You American son of a bitch

My brother, who was big for his age, and tough, fought every kid his size, and some bigger, in defense of America's honor. But we were ashamed, and we got an instructive taste of how it felt to be disliked for tribal affiliations that we hadn't really known we had.

*In the 1980s that house, now billed as one of the oldest houses in Saskatchewan, was bought by the local arts council under the leadership of Canadian writer Sharon Butala. Refurbished, repainted, and reroofed, it is being made into a refuge for writers who need a few months of total peace and quiet for finishing their books. I intend to haunt that house, just to keep track of what goes on.

The town grew around us, and incorporated us, and became our familiar territory: Main Street with its plank sidewalks, its drug and grocery and hardware stores, its Pastime Theater, its lumberyard, its hotel and bank; Millionaire Row with its four or five bungalows with sweet peas and nasturtiums in their yards; Poverty Flat, where the two Chinese and some *métis* had shacks.

The people we knew were of many kinds: *métis*—French-Indian halfbreeds—left over from the fur trade days; Texas and Montana cowpunchers left over from the cattle period; and a stew of new immigrants, Ontario men, cockneys fresh from another East End, Scandinavians moving up the migration route from the Dakotas to the Northwest, a few Jews, a Syrian family, a couple of Chinese, a Greek. Mark Twain, confronted by a colorful character, used to say, "I know him—knew him on the river." I could say, almost as legitimately, I know him—knew him in Eastend.

A young frontier gathers every sort of migrant, hope-chaser, roughneck, trickster, incompetent, misfit, and failure. All kinds passed through our town, and some stayed, or were stuck. Our first doctor was a drifter and a drunk who finally died of eating canned heat. Our only dentist came through once a year, and in a week's stay did more harm than an ordinary dentist could have done in a decade. Our religious needs were served by two institutions: the shack-chapel and itinerant priest who took care of the *métis,* and the Presbyterian church with resident pastor who took care of everyone else. The Scandinavians, Germans, Ontario men, Englishmen, and run-of-the-mine Americans, even the Syrian grocer and his family, became Presbyterians because that was where the principal social action was. The Jewish butcher, the cowpunchers, the two Chinese who ran the restaurant, and the Greek who took over from them—all without families—remained refractory and unassimilable.

When we arrived, and for a couple of years thereafter, the Frenchman River provided a habitat for beaver, muskrats, mink,

weasels, sandhill cranes; in the willow breaks were big populations of cottontails and snowshoe hares preyed on by coyotes
and lynxes. On the long, mainly roadless way to the homestead
down on the Montana line—two days by lumber wagon with
the cow tied behind, one day by buckboard (we called it a
democrat), seven or eight excruciating hours by Model T—we
passed many sloughs swarming with nesting ducks. On the
homestead itself, dry country far from any slough, it was all
flickertails, prairie dogs, badgers, blackfooted ferrets, coyotes,
gopher snakes, and hawks. That prairie, totally unsuited to be
plowed up, was hawk heaven. I find now, decades later, when
it has all been returned to grass, that ornithologists come from
far-off universities to study ferruginous hawks there. I never
knew their species name, but I knew their look in the sky or on
a fencepost, and several times one fell out of the empty blue to
strike a pullet within a few yards of me.

We plowed our first field, and dammed our coulee, and built
our shack, in the summer of 1915, and thereafter we spent the
summers on the homestead, the winters in town. It was an
uneven division, for in that latitude a wheat crop, from seedtime
to harvest, took only about three months. But either on the
prairie or in town we were only a step from the wild, and we
wavered between the pleasure it was to be part of it and the
misguided conviction that it was in our interest to destroy it.
There are two things that growing up on a belated western
frontier gave me: an acquaintance with the wild and wild creatures, and a delayed guilt for my part in their destruction.

I was a sickly child, but hardly a tame one. Like all the boys
I knew, I had a gun, and used it, from the age of eight or nine.
We shot at anything that moved; we killed everything not
domesticated or protected. In winter we trapped the small
fur-bearers of the river bottom; in summer my brother and I
spent hours of every day trapping, shooting, snaring, poisoning,
or drowning out the gophers that gathered in our wheatfield and
the dependable water of our "rezavoy." We poisoned out the

prairie dogs, and incidentally did in the blackfooted ferrets that lived on them—ferrets that are now the rarest North American mammals. We didn't even know they were ferrets; we called them the big weasels. But we killed them as we killed everything else. Once I speared one with a pitchfork in the chickenhouse and was sickened by its ferocious vitality, dismayed by how hard the wild died. I had the same feeling when I caught a badger in a gopher trap. I would gladly enough have let him loose, but he was too fierce, and lunged at me too savagely, and in the end I had to stone him to death.

Nobody could have been more brainlessly and immorally destructive. And yet there was love there, too. We took delight in knowing intimately the same animals we killed. Our pets were all captives from the wild—burrowing owls, magpies, a coyote pup, a ferret that I caught in a gopher trap and kept in a screened beer case and fed with live gophers. One of the first short stories I ever wrote, "Bugle Song," was a moment from that tranced, murderous summer season when I went from poetry and daydreaming to killing, and back to daydreaming. "Bugle Song" is an idyll counterweighted by death.

Our neighbors were few, and miles away, most of them across the line in Montana. For two weeks at a time we might see no one but ourselves; and when our isolation was broken, it was generally broken by a lonesome Swedish homesteader who came over ostensibly to buy eggs, but more probably to hear the sound of a human voice. We welcomed him. We were as hungry for the sound of a human voice as he was.

I am somewhat skeptical of the fabled western self-reliance, because as I knew it, the West was a place where one depended on neighbors and had to give as well as get. In any trouble while we were on the homestead, I ran, or rode one of the horses, four or five miles to get Tom Larson or Ole Telepo or someone else to help. They came to us the same way. And yet there is *something* to the notion of western independence; there is something about living in big empty space, where people are few and distant, under a great sky that is alternately serene and furious, exposed to sun from four in the morning till nine at night, and to a wind that never seems to rest—there is something about exposure to that big country that not only tells an individual how small he is, but steadily tells him *who* he is. I have never understood identity problems. Any time when I lay awake at night and heard the wind in the screens and saw the moon ride up the sky, or sat reading in the shade of the shack and heard the wind moan and mourn around the corners, or slept out under the wagon and felt it searching among the spokes of the wheels, I knew well enough who, or *what,* I was, even if I didn't matter. As surely as any pullet in the yard, I was a target, and I had better respect what had me in its sights.

I never came out to the homestead in June without anticipation and delight. I never returned to town in early September without a surge of joy—back to safety and shelter, back to the river and the willow breaks, back to friends, games, Sunday school parties, back to school, where I could shine.

It is a common notion that children reared in lonely, isolated places yearn for the color and action and excitement and stimulation of gaudier places. Adolescents, maybe; not children of the age I was, in the place where I lived. Everything I knew was right around me, and it was enough.

We studied geography and history in school, but those subjects never suggested to me that I was deprived. I knew little history, and none of what I knew was much closer than 1066. I knew no architecture, no art, only the crudest of music, but I never missed what I lacked. We did read a lot of poetry in our school, and I got to "speak pieces" at school and at church parties, and I read every book that fell into my hands, but it never occurred to me to make a conscious effort to expand my horizons, nor did it occur to any of my elders to suggest that I do so.

I lived contentedly at the center of my primitive culture, soaked in its folklore, committed to its harsh code of conduct

even when I despaired of living up to it. I was full to the eyes
with my region's physical, sensuous beauty, and submissive to
its brutal weathers, and familiar, in ridicule or respect, with its
drunken cowboys and its ranting newspaper editors and its limp
English barristers incapable of any spoken syllable more complex than "Haw!" I was at home, and I might have lived there
for a long time, perhaps for the rest of my life, and become a
wheat farmer or a local teacher with a literary streak and a taste
for local lore.

My father's luck took care of that. We had a big 1915 crop,
forty bushels to the acre at nearly three dollars a bushel. That
so exploded the optimistic synapses of his brain that in 1916 he
plowed and seeded another sixty acres besides the forty of his
first field. Nineteen sixteen was very wet. Water stood all
summer in the burnouts, the wheat developed rust, the crop
was small and of poor quality. Very well. Next year, then, with
still more acreage. Next year, 1917, we got burned out by hot
winds. Nineteen eighteen, then, with yet more acreage. It was
a gambler's system—double your bets when you lose. In 1918
we got burned out again. Okay, 1919 was coming up. In 1919
it rained hardly at all, the wheat had barely sprouted before it
withered, the fields were dust before mid-July. In 1920 my
father decided what many families had already decided, and we
gave up our effort to be Canadians and moved to Montana.

In *The Big Rock Candy Mountain* there is a chapter, made out
of an earlier short story called "The Colt," which reports the
Mason family's departure from Eastend, and the desolation of
young Bruce Mason, who is of course based on myself, when
they drive past the dump ground on the way out of town and
he sees the skinned body of his crippled colt, the iron braces still
on the front legs, thrown on the dump. He had thought the colt
was going to be cared for at a ranch downriver, and what he saw
on the dump made him pull a blanket over his head and bawl.

The story is an approximation only. That is not quite the way
we left. I pulled a blanket over my head and bawled, all right,

when I saw my crippled colt dead on the dump. But that had happened the year before. When I wrote the story I needed a justification for the boy's distress; but in reality, his distress was all at the realization that he was leaving behind his friends, the river's wild rose bars and cutbank bends, the secret hideouts in the brush, Chimney Coulee's berry patches, the sound of water running under the sagging snowbanks in May, the Chinook winds with their fierce blizzardy sound and their breath as warm as a cow's. In the very thrill of leaving, it struck him—me—all of a sudden *what* he and I were leaving.

I departed from Saskatchewan mourning what we had left behind and scared of what we were heading toward, and one look at my mother told me she was feeling the same way. My father and brother were leaning out of the car, exhilarated by how the fenceposts flew by on the smooth dirt road along the South Bench. They leaned and watched the roadside as if they were afraid Great Falls might flash by at any second, and they might miss it. But I was at heart a nester, like my mother. I loved the place I was losing, the place that years of our lives had worn smooth.

Great Falls, Montana, was not a significant part of my boyhood. It was a transition, a roadside stop, between Eastend and Salt Lake City, the two locations where I learned to feel like a placed and not a displaced person. Nevertheless Great Falls couldn't help enlarging me, sometimes painfully.

On my first day there I made the acquaintance of things that I had read about but never seen: lawns, cement sidewalks, streetcars, streets with names, houses with numbers. I had never known anybody with a street address. Now I had one myself: 448 Fourth Avenue North. And in the house on Fourth Avenue North were other things I had never seen—hardwood floors that were wonderful to skate around on in stocking feet, a bathroom with a tub and running water, a flush toilet. It was incredible to me that only the day before we had lived in a world of privies and washbasins and slop buckets. I grew vastly in my own estimation by what I was now introduced to.

But I hung around the house, unwilling to risk meeting strange kids in the street, and my first day of school was a disaster. In the flurry of our moving in, my mother had not been able to get my brother and me properly outfitted and had to ask us, apologetically, if we minded going in our old clothes for the first day or two. My brother, who was headed for a junior high school, would have gone in his long underwear rather than miss it; and in fact I was almost as eager. I had a fantasy of walking into this new school in my Canadian clothes and being a sensation, a frontiersman, a fellow from wild country. I had an orange sweater with a wide white stripe around the chest, something I had picked out myself from the T. Eaton catalogue, and I wore my elkhide moccasins, the standard footwear in Eastend until snow made the change to shoepacs necessary. On the way to school I practiced stalking, rising on my toes at each step, and I kept a taciturn half-sneer on my face, wanting to look as I imagined Daniel Boone might have looked while tracking a bear.

Unfortunately I was not six feet three but four feet ten. My moccasins drew stares, my sweater laughter. *Hey, f'Gawd's sake, lookit what's comin', a Hampshire shoat. Hey, shoat, how'd you leave things down to the pigpen?* What compounded my outsiderness was that I was two years ahead of myself in school, and at eleven was supposed to enter the eighth grade, where everybody else was at least thirteen or fourteen, and where there was one boy six feet high and in need of a shave.

I came late to Miss Temby's class and stood in the door, and a wave of laughter burst in my face. My ears on fire, I slunk to the seat Miss Temby pointed me to, and when she gave us, that very first day, a review test in geometry to see how much we had remembered over the summer, I remembered nothing, for geometry was a seventh-grade subject and I had skipped the seventh grade. By intuition and guesswork I managed a score of twelve out of a possible hundred.

That day left permanent scars on my self-confidence, though by working my head off I got to the top of Miss Temby's praise list before the year was over. When she assigned us ten lines of Joaquin Miller's "Columbus" to memorize, I memorized the whole poem and recited it, as she exclaimed delightedly, "*without a single mistake!*" She read aloud a couple of themes of mine (about Eastend, naturally), and by her praise may have given me an unnoticed shove toward a literary career.

But Miss Temby was the easy part. My classmates, once they stopped staring and laughing, were too intent on their own pubescent affairs to notice a runt like me, except once, when I split my thumb down to the first joint on a bench saw in shop, and bled all over the place, and bawled, not so much in pain as in outrage that the world could treat me so. And when my mother, learning to drive, knocked a streetcar off its tracks and threw me against the back of the front seat so hard it loosened my ribs and bent my new Eversharp pencil into a pretzel, even the notice in the paper managed to demean me. Listing the injuries, the reporter concluded that "the little boy, Wallace, was more frightened than hurt."

I was too little for school sports, which here were organized. I was too young to be a Boy Scout. I was too little to get a job, as my brother did, tending the furnace of Charlie Russell, down the street, though in the spring I did get to mow the Russell lawn a couple of times. I was too little for anything, and I missed my friends. Psychiatrists nowadays would have explanations for why I reverted for a month or two to baby talk that drove my father wild.

By spring I was beginning to come out of it. I had a friend named Sloppy Thompson; I was able to join the Boy Scouts. We spent our weekends hiking down to the Giant Spring, or Black Eagle Falls, or wading the rocky shallows above the Great Falls trying to catch carp in our bare hands. We hiked up the Missouri and swam a channel and camped on Third Island. We spent some spring Sundays on Sun River. Given time, I would have felt at home there, as I had in Eastend. But by late June of 1921 we were on the road again, heading south through the Little Belt Mountains and the Smith River Valley, through Yellowstone and over Targhee Pass and through the eastern Idaho towns, seeing the world, seeing the West, in a Hudson Supersix with our camp beds and Stoll autotent on the running boards and a big grub box on the rear bumper.

On the road again, which was exciting, and much less of a wrench than our departure from Eastend. But uprooted again, which made me uneasy.

I needn't have worried. Luck was with us. Though we saw a lot of the West in the years following 1921, and had short stays in Hollywood and Reno, we did our wandering from the fixed base of Salt Lake City, or within its boundaries. Between my twelfth and twenty-first years we must have lived in twenty different houses, and we never again became, as we had been in Eastend, a family with an attic and a growing accumulation of memorabilia and worn-out life gear and the artifacts of memory. Nevertheless we all, and my brother and I especially, began very soon to feel at home.

Salt Lake was then a city of little more than a hundred thousand, small enough to know, and I learned it, on foot or by streetcar. The Mormons who built it and lived in it had a strong sense of family and community, something the Stegners and the people they had lived among were notably short of. My brother and I found, near the first house we moved into, a municipal playground (pronounced "muni-sípple"), where he, a good athlete, was welcomed and even I was tolerated. We discovered the Mormon institution known as Mutual, for Mutual Improvement Association, which on Tuesday evenings, in every ward house in Zion, provided everything from Boy Scout meetings and Bible classes to basketball leagues and teenage dances. There may have been a covert proselytizing motive in the welcome that the wards extended to strange gentile kids, but there was a lot of plain warmth and goodwill, too. I have never ceased to be grateful for what they gave us when what they gave mattered a great deal; and though I was never tempted to adopt their beliefs, I could never write about them, when it came to that, except as a friend. Their obsession with their history, too, eventually made me aware of growing up entirely *without* history, and set me on the trail to find or construct some for myself.

What I most wanted, it seems to me now, was to belong to something, and Mormon institutions are made to order for belongers. Once in the Boy Scouts, I went up through the ranks from tenderfoot to eagle like smoke up a chimney. I was a demon activist in school Latin clubs and dramatic societies (I played saucy bellhops and brattish boys). In my first year at East High School I was desolated when they wouldn't let me into the ROTC, which was compulsory for boys, because I didn't weigh a hundred pounds. Attempting to work the angles, I tried out for the rifle team and made it, assuming that then they would have to let me in. Instead, they barred me from competing because I wasn't a member of the ROTC. By overeating and muscling bricks I made it over the hundred-pound mark by the next year, and went through the ranks the way I had gone through the ranks of the Boy Scouts—corporal to sergeant, sergeant to first sergeant, first sergeant to second lieutenant, second lieutenant to first lieutenant. I had my moment of glory when, in Sam Browne belt, leather puttees, shoulder pips, and sword, I led a platoon down Main Street in the Decoration Day parade.

Then in my senior year, between the ages of fifteen and sixteen, I grew six inches. It was like a graduation, more important to me than graduation from high school, and the beginning of the happiest years I ever knew or ever will know.

Suddenly I was big enough to hold my own in sports. Suddenly I had friends who looked on me as an equal and not as a mascot. Suddenly, at the University of Utah, I was playing on the freshman basketball team and a little later on the tennis team. Suddenly I was being rushed by a fraternity, and acquired brothers, and a secret grip, and a book of tong songs. Beatitude.

In the middle of my freshman year I got a job working afternoons and Saturdays in a floor-coverings store, at twenty-five cents an hour, and with financial independence achieved, began to date girls who a year earlier had looked over my head. The success of my transition from have-not to have was measured by my grades: straight A's as a freshman, straight B's as a sophomore. My companions included few intellectuals; most were cardplayers, beer drinkers, and jocks. My long-term addiction to books, which had been intensified by access to the Carnegie Library on State Street, suffered. My literary ambitions, which had been stimulated by the novelist Vardis Fisher, my freshman English instructor, got shelved. I was almost glad that Fisher left after my first year, for he had a caustic tongue and a great contempt for time-wasters. Just the same, I wouldn't have traded my newly achieved life as an insider for an introduction to Clara Bow.

Then in September 1930, more by accident and the efforts of friends than by my own doing, I was offered a teaching assistantship at the State University of Iowa, and was uprooted again, this time alone. I suppose I learned more, and faster, during two years in Iowa City than in any other two-year period of my life, and some of what I learned was about myself. I had always known, not entirely happily, *what* I was. I was a target. Now I began to understand *who* I was. I was a Westerner.

Homesickness is a great teacher. It taught me, during an endless rainy fall, that I came from the arid lands, and liked where I came from. I was used to a dry clarity and sharpness in the air. I was used to horizons that either lifted into jagged ranges or rimmed the geometrical circle of the flat world. I was used to seeing a long way. I was used to earth colors—tan, rusty red, toned white—and the endless green of Iowa offended me. I was used to a sun that came up over mountains and went down behind other mountains. I missed the color and smell of sage-brush, and the sight of bare ground.

The homesickness was not merely for Salt Lake, a city in a valley under the lee of mountains, with the glint of the lake off westward, but for a whole region, a whole lifetime of acclimati-zation and expectation. I had been deprived of Eastend, and Great Falls, and the Missouri River, and the Great Basin desert that we had crossed many times on the way to Los Angeles or Reno or San Francisco. I was missing the red-rock country of the plateaus, where we had had a summer cottage on the Fish Lake Plateau for several years, in the fir-and-aspen-fragrant air of eight thousand feet. I was too far from places where we had gone camping—Bryce and Zion and the Grand Canyon and Capitol Reef and the Granddaddy Lakes wilderness in the Uin-tas. I had left behind the whole West, and I began to realize how lucky I had been to see so much of it. I also began to realize how deeply it had been involved in my making.

Both of the places I had lived in for any length of time since the age of five had been close to wild country. Even Salt Lake City, which had looked as vast as Rome to me, opened west-ward onto empty desert and sterile lake, and eastward led into the Wasatch Mountains through seven major and many minor canyons. In my high school years we used to catch rides on D&RG freights at the mouth of Parley's Canyon and ride up as far as Lamb's Canyon, and from there hike off into the remoter mountains around Holladay Park and other pockets. In Iowa City, during the long intense studious winter, I used to find myself thinking almost hypnotically of the little gouge of Hughes Canyon, between Big and Little Cottonwood, where in the spring there were carpets of dogtooth violets.

I became a booster, talking up my home territory. What was more significant, I began to write my life, and my life was all western. I remember telling Stephen Vincent Benét, when he came lecturing to Iowa City, that I was going to write a three-decker peasant novel about Saskatchewan. I didn't do anything that foolish, but I did, not too many years later, write *The Big Rock Candy Mountain*. And every story that crowded to the typewriter evoked the smells and colors and horizons and air and people of the region where I had most lived.

That is essentially the whole story: I grew up western, and the very first time I moved out of the West I realized what it meant to me. The rest is documentation, detail.

At the end of that first Iowa year, I couldn't wait to get home, which by that time was Reno instead of Salt Lake but was at least in the dry country. The summer gave me the steam to go back to Iowa, which, if the truth were told, was enlarging me faster than the West ever did. The next school year, 1932–33, I enrolled at Berkeley, because my parents had moved to California and my mother was ill. At the Fish Lake cottage the following summer I began the desolate duty of helping her die. When she did die, in November, we buried her in Salt Lake next to my brother, who had died of pneumonia two years earlier, and I went back to Iowa to finish my degree. Before I quite finished it, I was married to Mary Page of Dubuque, and when we took our first real teaching job, we took it at the University of Utah, back where I had come from and yearned to return to.

If contentment were the only basis for choice, we might have chosen to stay there, but I had my father's restless blood in me, and the habit of moving. Accident was sure to blow me out of any rut I found comfortable. Around October 1936 I started writing a short novel based on a story that Mary had told me about some of her grandfather's relatives in a western Iowa town. By December I had sent it in to a contest that was being sponsored by Little, Brown. In January I got word that I had won the $2,500 prize. That was a lot of money in 1937, to people in our circumstances, and it was shortly doubled by a serial magazine sale. Rich, we took off into the wider world.

Part of the summer of 1937 we spent on bicycles in France and England. Coming home broke, we took another teaching job, this time at the University of Wisconsin in Madison. Many years later I would write up those two years, fictionalized to taste, in the novel *Crossing to Safety*. But we did not, like the Morgans of that book, end up with dismissal, polio, and a safety-net job in the publishing business. We ended up teaching at Harvard, in conformity with our pattern of moving from our center out into wider and wider peripheries.

Wider worlds, but with one foot always kept in the center circle. At Harvard, lapping up ideas and enjoying associations of the kind I had always hungered for, I could never forget who I was and where I came from. In Madison I had written a jejune little novel called *On a Darkling Plain,* and had started what would become *The Big Rock Candy Mountain,* both stories trying out fictionally the textures of a Saskatchewan childhood. In Cambridge, out of sheer nostalgia, I wrote the nonfiction book *Mormon Country,* and when that was done, I sat down seriously to what most mattered to me and finished *The Big Rock Candy Mountain.* After that, we took the first opportunity to come back west, living in Santa Barbara while I finished the wartime study of racial and religious minorities called *One Nation,* done in collaboration with *Look* magazine, and then moving to Stanford without ever going back to Cambridge.

By the time we arrived in Palo Alto I was already involved in the biography of Major John Wesley Powell, the quintessential student of the West, and had pretty well committed myself to a lifetime of writing about the country I had grown up in. My childhood was buried in Saskatchewan, my youth and my dead in Salt Lake City, and I was never going back to either of those places to live. Nevertheless I was at home, where I belonged, and I thought I had lived away from home long enough to know where it was and to have some perspective on it.

It is not an unusual life-curve for Westerners—to live in and

be shaped by the bigness, sparseness, space, clarity, and hopefulness of the West, to go away for study and enlargement and the
perspective that distance and dissatisfaction can give, and then
to return to what pleases the sight and enlists the loyalty and
demands the commitment.

LETTER,
MUCH TOO LATE

Mom, listen.

In three months I will be eighty years old, thirty years older than you were when you died, twenty years older than my father was when he died, fifty-seven years older than my brother was when *he* died. I got the genes and the luck. The rest of you have been gone a long time.

Except when I have to tie my shoelaces, I don't feel eighty years old. I, the sickly child, have outlasted you all. But if I don't feel decrepit, neither do I feel wise or confident. Age and experience have not made me a Nestor qualified to tell others about how to live their lives. I feel more like Theodore Dreiser, who confessed that he would depart from life more bewildered than he had arrived in it. Instead of being embittered, or stoical, or calm, or resigned, or any of the standard things that a long life might have made me, I confess that I am often simply lost, as much in need of comfort, understanding, forgiveness, uncritical love—the things you used to give me—as I ever was at five, or ten, or fifteen.

Fifty-five years ago, sitting up with you after midnight while the nurse rested, I watched you take your last breath. A few minutes before you died you half raised your head and said, "Which . . . way?" I understood that: you were at a dark, unmarked crossing. Then a minute later you said, "You're a good . . . boy . . . Wallace," and died.

My name was the last word you spoke, your faith in me and love for me were your last thoughts. I could bear them no better than I could bear your death, and I went blindly out into the November darkness and walked for hours with my mind clenched like a fist.

I knew how far from true your last words were. There had been plenty of times when I had not been a good boy or a thoughtful one. I knew you could no longer see my face, that you spoke from a clouded, drugged dream, that I had already faded to a memory that you clung to even while you waned from life. I knew that it was love speaking, not you, that you had already gone, that your love lasted longer than you yourself did. And I had some dim awareness that as you went away you laid on me an immense and unavoidable obligation. I would never get over trying, however badly or sadly or confusedly, to be what you thought I was.

Obviously you did not die. Death is a convention, a certification to the end of pain, something for the vital-statistics book, not binding upon anyone but the keepers of graveyard records. For as I sit here at the desk, trying to tell you something fifty-five years too late, I have a clear mental image of your pursed lips and your crinkling eyes, and I know that nothing I can say will persuade you that I was ever less than you thought me. Your kind of love, once given, is never lost. You are alive and luminous in my head. Except when I fail to listen, you will speak through me when I face some crisis of feeling or sympathy or consideration for others. You are a curb on my natural impatience and competitiveness and arrogance. When I have been less than myself, you make me ashamed even as you forgive me. You're a good . . . boy . . . Wallace.

In the more than fifty years that I have been writing books and stories, I have tried several times to do you justice, and have never been satisfied with what I did. The character who represents you in *The Big Rock Candy Mountain* and *Recapitulation,* two novels of a semiautobiographical kind, is a sort of passive victim. I am afraid I let your selfish and violent husband, my father, steal the scene from you and push you into the background in the novels as he did in life. Somehow I should have been able to say how strong and resilient you were, what a patient and abiding and bonding force, the softness that proved in the long run stronger than what it seemed to yield to.

But you must understand that you are the hardest sort of human character to make credible on paper. We are skeptical of kindness so unfailing, sympathy so instant and constant, trouble so patiently borne, forgiveness so wholehearted. Writing about you, I felt always on the edge of the unbelievable, as if I were writing a saint's life, or the legend of some Patient Griselda. I felt that I should warp you a little, give you some human failing or selfish motive; for saintly qualities, besides looking sentimental on the page, are a rebuke to those—and they are most of us—who have failed at them. What is more, saintly and long-suffering women tend to infuriate the current partisans of women's liberation, who look upon them as a masculine invention, the too submissive and too much praised victims of male dominance.

Well, you were seldom aggressive, not by the time I knew you, and you were an authentic victim. How truly submissive, that is another matter. Some, I suppose, are born unselfish, some achieve unselfishness, and some have unselfishness thrust upon them. You used to tell me that you were born with a redheaded temper, and had to learn to control it. I think you were also born with a normal complement of dreams and hopes and desires and a great capacity for intellectual and cultural growth, and had to learn to suppress them.

Your life gave you plenty of practice in both controlling and suppressing. You were robbed of your childhood, and as a young, inexperienced woman you made a fatal love choice. But you blamed no one but yourself. You lay in the bed you had made, partly because, as a woman, and without much education, you had few options, and partly because your morality counseled responsibility for what you did, but mostly because love told you your highest obligation was to look after your two boys and the feckless husband who needed you more even than they did. Your reward, all too often, was to be taken for granted.

Just now, thinking about you, I got out *The Big Rock Candy Mountain* and found the passage in which I wrote of your death. I couldn't bear to read it. It broke me down in tears to read the words that I wrote in tears nearly a half century ago. You are at once a lasting presence and an unhealed wound.

I was twenty-four, still a schoolboy, when you died, but I have lived with you more than three times twenty-four years. Self-obsessed, sports crazy or book crazy or girl crazy or otherwise preoccupied, I never got around to telling you during your lifetime how much you meant. Except in those moments when your life bore down on you with particular weight, as when my brother, Cece, died and you turned to me because you had no one else, I don't suppose I realized how much you meant. Now I feel mainly regret, regret that I took you for granted as the others did, regret that you were dead by the time my life began to expand, so that I was unable to take you along and compensate you a little for your first fifty years. Cinderella should end happily, released from the unwholesome house of her servitude.

One of my friends in that later life that you did not live to share was the Irish writer Frank O'Connor, who was born Michael O'Donovan in a shabby cottage in Cork. His father was a drunk; his mother, he firmly believed, was a saint. He put her into many of his short stories, and he wrote her a book of tribute called *An Only Child*. Though he was not much of a Catholic, he expected to meet her in heaven, garbed in glory. From what he told me, she was much like you: she was incomparably herself, and yet she always thought of herself last. I can't believe that he is with her now in heaven, though I wish I could. I can't believe either that eventually, pretty soon in fact, I will meet you there. But what a reunion that would be! It would be worth conversion to assure it—the four of us enjoying whatever it is that immortals enjoy, and enjoying it together. I admired Frank O'Connor for his great gifts; but I loved Michael O'Donovan for the way he felt about his mother, and envied him for the chance he got, as a mature man, to show it. If the man-dominated world, with all its injustices, now and then produces women like his mother and mine, it can't be all bad.

I began this rumination in a dark mood, remembering the anniversary of your death. Already you have cheered me up. I have said that you didn't die, and you didn't. I can still hear you being cheerful on the slightest provocation, or no provocation at all, singing as you work and shedding your cheerfulness on others. So let us remember your life, such a life as many women of your generation shared to some extent, though not always with your special trials and rarely with your stoicism and grace.

I have heard enough about your childhood and youth to know how life went on that Iowa farm and in the town where everybody spoke Norwegian, read Norwegian, did business in Norwegian, heard Norwegian in church. The family Bible that somehow descended to me is in Norwegian, and in Gothic type at that. Next to it on my shelf is the preposterous five-pound book that they gave you on your fifth birthday: *Sandheden i Kristus*, Truths in Christ, a compendium of instructions and meditations geared to the religious year. You would have had to be as old as I am, and as rigid a Lutheran as your father, to tolerate five minutes of it.

Though your father was born in this country, you did not learn English until you started school. You learned it eagerly. Some of our mutual relatives, after five generations in the United States, still speak with an accent, but you never did. You loved reading, and you sang all the time: you knew the words to a thousand songs. When I was in college I was astonished to discover that some songs I had heard you sing as you worked around the house were lyrics from Tennyson's *The Princess*. Maybe you got the words from *McGuffey's Reader*. Where you got the tunes, God knows. You always made the most of what little was offered you, and you kept hold of it.

School was your happy time, with friends, games, parties, the delight of learning. You had it for only six years. When you were twelve, your mother died of tuberculosis and you became an instant adult: housekeeper to your father, mother to your two younger brothers and sister, farmhand when not otherwise employed. All through the years when you should have had the chance to be girlish, even frivolous, you had responsibilities that would have broken down most adults.

Many farm wives had a "hired girl." You did not. You were It, you did it all. At twelve, thirteen, fourteen, you made beds, cleaned, cooked, sewed, mended, for a family of five. You baked the bread, biscuits, cakes, pies, in a cranky coal range. You made the *lefse* and *fattigmand* and prepared the *lutefisk* without which a Norwegian Christmas is not Christmas. You washed all the clothes, and I don't mean you put lightly soiled clothes into a washing machine. I mean you boiled and scrubbed dirty farm clothes with only the copper boiler, tin tub, brass washboard, harsh soap, and hand wringer of the 1890s—one long backbreaking day every week.

At harvest time you often worked in the field most of the morning and then came in to cook dinner for the crew. You were over a hot stove in a suffocating kitchen for hours at a time, canning peas, beans, corn, tomatoes, putting up cucumber and watermelon pickles or piccalilli. When a hog was slaughtered, you swallowed your nausea and caught the blood for the blood pudding your father relished. You pickled pigs' feet and made headcheese. You fried and put down in crocks of their own lard the sausage patties that would last all winter. Morning and evening you helped with the milking. You skimmed the cream and churned the butter in the dasher churn, you hung cheesecloth bags of curd on the clothesline to drip and become cottage cheese. Maybe you got a little help from your brothers and sister, especially as they got older; but they were in school all day, and whined about having homework at night.

I am sure there were times when you bitterly resented your bond-servant life, when you thumped your lazy and evasive brothers, or sent hot glances at your father where he sat reading *Scandinaven* in the parlor, totally unaware of you as you staggered in with a scuttle of coal and set it down loudly by the heater, and opened the heater door and lifted the scuttle and fed the fire and set the scuttle down again and slammed the heater door with a bang. Those were the years when you had unselfishness thrust upon you; you had not yet got through the difficult process of achieving it.

But however you might rebel, there was no shedding your siblings. They were your responsibility and there was no one to relieve you of them. They called you Sis. All your life people called you Sis, because that was what you were, or what you became—big sister, helpful sister, the one upon whom everyone depended, the one they all came to for everything from help with homework to a sliver under the fingernail.

Six years of that, at the end of which your father announced that he was going to marry a school friend of yours, a girl barely older than yourself. I wonder if it was outrage that drove you from his house, or if your anger was not lightened by the perception that here at last was freedom and opportunity. You were eighteen, a tall, strong, direct-eyed girl with a pile of

gorgeous red hair. In the tintypes of the time you look determined. You do not yet have the sad mouth your last photographs show. Maybe the world then seemed all before you, your
imprisonment over.

But nobody had prepared you for opportunity and freedom.
Nobody had taught you to dream big. You couldn't have imagined going to Chicago or New York and winning your way, you
could never have dreamed of becoming an actress or the editor
of a women's magazine. They had only taught you, and most of
that you had learned on your own, to keep house and to look
after others. You were very good at both. So when you were
displaced as your father's housekeeper, you could think of
nothing better to do with your freedom than to go to North
Dakota and keep house for a bachelor uncle.

There you met something else they had not prepared you for,
a man unlike any you had ever seen, a husky, laughing, reckless,
irreverent, storytelling charmer, a ballplayer, a fancy skater, a
trapshooting champion, a pursuer of the main chance, a true
believer in the American dream of something for nothing, a
rolling stone who confidently expected to be eventually covered
with moss. He was marking time between get-rich-quick
schemes by running a "blind pig"—an illegal saloon. He offended every piety your father stood for. Perhaps that was why
you married him, against loud protests from home. Perhaps
your father was as much to blame as anyone for the mistake you
made.

You had a stillborn child. Later you had a living one, my
brother, Cecil. Later still, on a peacemaking visit back to Iowa,
you had me. Then, as you told me once, you discovered how
not to have any more, and didn't. You had enough to be
responsible for with two.

To run through your life would be lugubrious if it were not
you we were talking about. You made it something else by your
total competence, your cheerfulness under most uncheerful
conditions, your resilience after every defeat. "Better luck next

time!'' I have heard you say as we fled from some disaster, and after a minute, with your special mixture of endurance, hope, and irony, ''Well, if it didn't kill us, I guess it must have been good for us.''

Dakota I don't remember. My memories begin in the woods of Washington, where we lived in a tent and ran a lunchroom in the logging town of Redmond. By getting scarlet fever, I had balked my father's dream of going to Alaska and digging up baseball-sized nuggets. Then there was a bad time. You left my father, or he you; nobody ever told me. But Cece and I found ourselves in a Seattle orphans' home, put there while you worked at the Bon Marché. In 1913 you didn't have a chance as a husbandless woman with two children. When you found how miserable we were in that home, you took us out and brought us back to the only safety available, your father's house in Iowa.

I can imagine what that cost you in humiliation. I can imagine the letters that must have passed between you and my father. I can imagine his promises, your concessions. At any rate, in June 1914 we were on our way to join him in the valley of the Whitemud, or Frenchman, River in Saskatchewan. Perhaps it sounded romantic and adventurous to you, perhaps you let yourself listen to his come-all-ye enthusiasm, perhaps you thought that on a real frontier he might be happy and do well. Very probably you hoped that in a raw village five hundred miles from anywhere we could make a new start and be a family, something for which you had both a yearning and a gift. If you went in resignation, this time your resignation was not forced on you. It was a choice. By 1914, at the age of thirty-one, you had finally achieved unselfishness.

Saskatchewan is the richest page in my memory, for that was where I first began to understand some things, and that was where, for a half dozen years, we had what you had always wanted: a house of our own, a united family, and a living, however hard.

I remember good days for the shared pleasure we took in them—family expeditions to pick berries in the Cypress Hills, when we picnicked on the edge of Chimney Coulee and watched great fleets of clouds sail eastward over the prairie. Raising a sandwich to your mouth, you exclaimed, "Oh! Smell your hands!" and we did, inhaling the fragrance of the saskatoons, gooseberries, chokecherries, pin cherries, and highbush cranberries we had been working in. I remember that on our way home from one of those expeditions the democrat wagon tipped over on a steep hillside and spilled us and our overflowing pans and pails of berries out onto the grass. You took one quick look to see if anyone was hurt, and then began to laugh, pointing to the embarrassed and bewildered team standing among the twisted tugs. We sat in the sudden grass and laughed ourselves silly before we got up and scraped together the spilled berries and straightened out the buggy and relieved the team and drove home. Singing, naturally. You never lost an opportunity to sing. You sang, too, among the rich smells in the kitchen as you made those wild berries into pies and jams and sauces and jellies and put a lot of them up in jars and glasses to be stored on the cellar shelves.

Do you remember a day on the homestead when Pa came back from Chinook with a big watermelon, and we cooled it as well as we could in the reservoir and then sat down in the shade of the shack and ate it all? How simple and memorable a good day can be when expectation is low! You made us save the rinds for pickles. Your training had been thorough, you never wasted anything. One of our neighbors, years later, wrote me about how amazed he was to see you, after you had peeled a lot of apples and made pies of them, boil up the peelings and turn them into jelly.

I think you loved that little burg in spite of its limitations. You loved having neighbors, visiting with neighbors, helping neighbors. When it was our turn to host the monthly Sunday school party, you had more fun than the kids, playing crocinole or beanbag like the child you had never been allowed to be. You loved the times when the river froze without wind or snow, and the whole channel was clean, skatable ice, and the town gathered around big night fires, and skaters in red mackinaws and bright scarfs moved like Brueghel figures across the light, and firelight glinted off eyeballs and teeth, and the breath of the community went up in white plumes.

You loved having your children in a steady school, and doing well in it. You read all the books you could lay hands on. When your North Dakota uncle died and left you a thousand dollars you didn't let my father take it, though I am sure he would have found a use for it. Instead, you bought a Sears, Roebuck piano and you set my brother and me to learn to play it under the instruction of the French doctor's wife. Alas, we disappointed you, resisted practice, dawdled and fooled around. Eventually you gave up. But you could no more let that piano sit there unused than you could throw perfectly good apple peelings out to the pig. You learned to play it yourself, painstakingly working things out chord by chord from the sheet music of popular songs. How hungry you were! How you would have responded to the opportunities ignored by so many who have them!

Many good days. Also, increasingly, bad ones. Hard times. While you lived your way deeper into the remote and limited place where my father's enthusiasms had brought you, he felt more and more trapped in what he called "this dirty little dung-heeled sagebrush town." On the homestead where we spent our summers, he had made one good and one average crop out of five. One summer he grew hundreds of bushels of potatoes on rented bottomland near town and stored them in the basement of the hotel, waiting for the right price, and the hotel burned down. That winter he supported us by playing poker. By the summer of 1920 he was raging to get out, do something, find some way of making a real living.

Eventually he got his way, and we abandoned what little you had been able to get together as a life. During the next fourteen years you lived in much greater comfort, and you saw a lot of the western United States. You continued to make a home for your boys and your husband, but it was a cheerless home for you. We lived in a dozen towns and cities, three dozen neighborhoods, half a hundred houses. My brother and I kept some continuity through school and the friends we made there, but your continuity was cut every few months; you lost friends and never saw them again, or got the chance to make new ones, or have a kitchen where women could drop in and have a cup of coffee and a chat. Too much of your time, in Great Falls, Salt Lake, Reno, Los Angeles, Long Beach, you were alone.

You believed in all the beauties and strengths and human associations of place; my father believed only in movement. You believed in a life of giving, he in a life of getting. When Cecil died at the age of twenty-three, you did not have a single woman friend to whom you could talk, not a single family of neighbors or friends to help you bear the loss of half your loving life.

You're a good . . . boy . . . Wallace. That shames me. You had little in your life to judge goodness by. I was not as dense or as selfish as my father, and I got more credit than I deserved. But I was not intelligent enough to comprehend the kind of example you had been setting me, until it was too late to do anything but hold your hand while you died. And here I am, nearly eighty years old, too old to be capable of any significant improvement but not too old for regret.

"All you can do is try," you used to tell me when I was scared of undertaking something. You got me to undertake many things I would not have dared undertake without your encouragement. You also taught me how to take defeat when it came, and it was bound to now and then. You taught me that if it hadn't killed me it was probably good for me.

I can hear you laugh while you say it. Any minute now I will hear you singing.

CROSSING
INTO EDEN

Now and then nature produces a combination of land, water, sky, space, trees, animals, flowers, distances, and weather so perfect it looks like the hatching of a romantic fantasy, or the effort of a nineteenth-century artist to illustrate Hiawatha's childhood by the shores of Gitche Gumee. Every time we go off into the wilderness, we are looking for that perfect primitive Eden. This time, we have found it.

Nothing superlative or enchanting should be easily accessible. We walked no sword edge to get here, but we worked, and had blisters to prove it.

First there were thirty miles of dirt road through a dwarf forest of piñon, juniper, and sage, where the only life was range steers as sparse as the bunch grass they subsisted on, and the principal excitement was holding our breath for a minute at a time to survive the dust every time we met a pickup. Then, at a ranch on a creek where the dwarf forest gave way to scrub oak and yellow pine, we abandoned the wheels and started hiking.

We were to follow the creek up the canyon; the packer would catch up after a few miles.

It began as a stroll through flowers. Then the country stood on end and the creek roared out of a formidable gateway. Hades Canyon, this gulch was called, and it earned its name. It was steep, dusty, full of ankle-breaking stones. The trail, no more than a trace, had us wading the creek every fifty yards. Our boots squished coldly, the sun burned on our necks, the pumice-like dust settled in our sweaty crevices. But we pushed it. We wanted to impress the packer with how far and fast we could walk. He had not caught us by noon. We stopped among boulders to rest and eat lunch. Even if our eyes had not told us that we had climbed out of the Transition life zone into the Canadian, among aspen, balsam fir, and blue spruce, our lungs would have known that we were up around eight thousand feet. The basin that we were heading for was high, around ten thousand. Plenty of *up* still ahead of us. A couple of us were getting blisters from wet socks and boots. We patched ourselves with Band-Aids and went on.

Canyon walls narrowed the sky and cut off the view. Where the creek was not cascades, it was falls. Inside an hour, the balsam and blue spruce were beginning to be crowded out by Engelmann spruce and straight, tall, spiry alpine firs. At least nine thousand feet. This life zone, the Hudsonian, would reach to timberline. We would be camping in it, and were ready to at any time. We estimated that we had come at least ten miles, all practically straight up.

Resting after a steep scramble, we heard hoofs behind us. Here came the pack string. The packer, lounging in the saddle and looking insufferably comfortable and unheated, was not amazed at how far we had come and how fast. He nodded, but did not stop. His animals kicked stones around us and raised a dust. "How much farther?" we called to him, suddenly without pride. He held up four fingers without turning, and we cursed his slouching back.

Four more miles. More than an hour, maybe two if it didn't soon level out. To our relief, it did just that. The walls folded back and away, the creek that had stood on its hind legs all through the canyon lay down and purred, the trail that had been all rolling stones became soft forest duff. Through the tops of the firs we saw snow peaks to the north. That would be the Uinta crest, thirteen thousand feet and more, bounding the northern rim of our high basin.

Our dead legs and blistered feet welcomed the easier walking. No longer compelled by pride to stay ahead of the packer, we made no effort to catch up with him, but dawdled along his trail, sometimes through mature, open, resin-smelling forest, sometimes across meadows so dense with flowers—red, blue, pink, yellow, white—that at every step we crushed a dozen. The sky above those meadows was very dark blue, and wide, with whipped-cream clouds at its edge.

We still followed the creek. Every few hundred yards, hung on that thread of bright water, was a bead lake, part of the leavings of the glacier that had scooped the broad back of this uplift. Some lakes were small, some were eutrophic, on their way to becoming flowery meadows; but at one we stopped, incredulous and rebellious. It was almost perfectly round, a half mile in diameter. Its surface, riffled by a light, changeable wind, was dimpled all over with the circles of rising trout. There was a grassy glade above a crescent of black-sand beach. Good God, we asked each other, where is the fool taking us? What's the matter with *this*?

Ospreys watched us from their dead snags. Envying them their habitat, promising ourselves that if we didn't like where the packer stopped we would make him bring us back here, limping, pooped, and irritable, we reluctantly went on.

Finally we heard a bell and saw the hobbled horses grazing among big, well-spaced trees. The packer, driving picket pins with the butt of an ax and setting up a stained white tent, gave us a cheerful greeting. Beyond him, the trees thinned out to nothing at some kind of edge. Still not sure we didn't want to go back to the black-sand beach, we went to the edge to look.

The land fell away at our feet; the sky opened like a hot air balloon filling, a gust of blue. Twenty feet below us was deep water; spread out before us was an oval lake. We were between curves of blue like a clam between the valves of its shell. Nobody said a word. We watched the breeze move on the water, darkening that blue; we saw how the blue shaded into green under the forested far shore; we felt, as much as saw, how infinite the sky was, with clouds and snow peaks dreaming at its edge, and none of us would have argued with the packer's choice.

This place has everything—every essential, every conceivable extra. It has the level ground, the good grass, the wood, the easy access to water, that make a camp comfortable. It has the shelter and shade, the wide views, the openness and breeziness, that raise comfort to luxuriousness. There are no mosquitoes on that clifftop; there are trees shaped to the back where a man can sit and read; the ground is the coarse granular kind that produces no dust and that, in the remote possibility of rain, would not produce mud either. Every tree has stubs of branches at the proper height for hanging things; there are enough downed logs for benches and cooking tables. And this air, at ten thousand feet, hits the bottom of the lungs like ether.

We do not spend much time on the cliff edge looking over the forested basin and the far rims of the world. In minutes we are tearing off our clothes. Like streakers, following one another, we leap off into the lake. The succession is too fast for warning to have any effect. The screams of the first victims rise to meet the others already coming down. The water is instant paralysis, it freezes even screams. Gasping, we practically walk on the water in our frenzy to escape it and we pick our goose-pimpled, tender-footed way up the cliff into the sun and dry ourselves on our shirts, shuddering. But how marvelous when even a wet shirt goes on and the chilling breeze is balked! How wonderful to warm up, shrink by shudder, on that expansive, world-overlooking cliff! We have shed our skins like spring snakes, we are reborn clean.

Fishing? we wonder. How about all those dimples on the lake surface? Up here the trout will be natives, cutthroats, resident only on this side of the Continental Divide. Should we try to catch one and cut him open and see what hatch is on? We tie on a fly, any old standby we happen to have handy in the fly box or our hatband, and try a cast. *Bam,* one hits it. Another cast. *Bam!* We stand in a line casting from shore, and every cast is a strike and generally a fish. No need to be fancy here. These trout, all twelve to thirteen inches long, have grown so numerous they are in a Malthusian dilemma, in danger of oversubscribing their food supply, or they have never seen anything so delightful as a dry fly. Experimentally, I tie on three flies at once, a black gnat, a silver doctor, and a gray hackle yellow, and cast out to the edge of the cliff shadow. A strike and instantly two more. There I am with a lineful that feels like a twenty-pounder in convulsions. No need to find out what they are feeding on. They are feeding on anything we throw in, and in the next couple of days we find that they are as ravenous at high noon in a dead calm as at dawn or dusk with a riffle. After the second day we fish only for the breakfast frying pan.

It is an experiment with salmon eggs that teaches us how thoroughly the sport of angling depends on difficulty. One of us, finding that trout are attracted even by a finger stirred in the water off a raft, drops a few salmon eggs. They are gone in a flash of silver before they have sunk two feet. Holding his dip net down under, he drops some more eggs. Swish, scoop, he has a foot-long cutthroat. Awed, he unjoints his rod and puts away his gear. Perfection has destroyed sport. This fishing is too good, as the fishing must have been in Eden. Was Adam a fisherman? he asks us. Any record of flycasting in Paradise? No. Fishing is for the sinful, imperfect world. In Paradise, one gives it up. No fun shooting tame hares.

How is it to wake up in Eden? Our sleeping tents are pitched in a half circle facing the cliff and the east, but the weather is so fine that we sleep outside. Night after night we awake at odd hours to see the black sky with big bright stars burning holes in it. We watch the Dipper and Cassiopeia do their slow dance around the Pole Star, and the misshapen boat of the moon sail up and over and down. Finally, we wake to find the east lightening, going pink, the flat clouds in that direction taking fire. Lying snug, we wait until the sun surges up over mountains far to the east. The green-and-brown camp, the white tents, come clear, long shadows stretch, and on the cliff edge, haloed with pure light, the martens have appeared.

There are seven of them, half-grown, apparently left to amuse themselves when their mother takes off before dawn to forage. Their fur is a rich, sleek brown, their throats nearly white; their eyes are black buttons, their whiskers bristle and glisten, their bodies are so slim and undulant that they might be swimming instead of running. In the strong, flat light they appear to leave streams of bubbles behind them as they pounce, wrestle, scoot suddenly into holes, chase each other up trees and out onto limbs. Though their round ears perk in our direction if we move or make a noise, they are more curious than afraid. We have walked within twenty feet of them before they retreat, and they never fully disappear; their button eyes are on us from among roots or behind trees. Within a day or two we have them coming boldly for scraps we throw.

.   .   .

Pine martens, first cousins to Russian sables, shy and rare and coveted and hunted, held to be intolerant of the human presence, share that peaceable kingdom with us for the length of our limited stay, and on Eviction Day, as we walk the trail back toward civilization with our eyes looking back over our shoulders, we see their silhouettes looping and undulating along the cliff edge. Like the Ancient Mariner burdened with his albatross, we bless those happy living things, and some weight drops away, leaving us freer and better than when we came.

Where is this place? somebody asks. How do we get to it?

Ordinarily I would not answer that question. Places as perfect as this should be as secret as they are inaccessible. They cannot stand advertising, because we have a habit of destroying what we love. But in this case there is no problem. I can tell you that the high basin we penetrated was the Granddaddy Lakes Basin in the Uinta Mountains of northeastern Utah, that the lake we camped on was called Wall Lake, and that we reached it with the help of an outfitter whose post office was Hanna, on the Duchesne River. I can let that information out because we visited Eden in 1923, sixty-six years ago. No visitor, however destructive, can touch what lives in my head as bright and dawn-struck as if I had left it just last week.

Not that it has vanished from the map. It has even been protected to some extent, first by being included, in 1931, in the High Uintas Primitive Area, whose rules permitted grazing, prospecting, and mining but prohibited roads and permanent settlements. In 1984 that limited protection, subject always to the administrative whim of the Forest Service, was extended when the whole basin of which the Granddaddy Lakes are a part was incorporated into the 460,000-acre High Uintas wilderness, one of the permanent reserves where, in the language of the 1964 Wilderness Act, "the earth and its community of life are untrammeled by man, where man himself is a visitor who does not remain."

So I could go back, if I chose to and had the legs to hike up

Hades Canyon, or the bottom to ride a mule up, and I would find the lake not too much changed or the weather any different or the morning light less exhilarating. The fishing would certainly be more sporting, and the morality of trout fishing now would prevent my experimenting with salmon eggs or tying three flies on a single leader. The martens would almost certainly be gone, for even as permanent wilderness, the basin receives many more visitors than it used to, and martens will long since have been either illegally shot or trapped, or have retreated deeper, into country that is not only without roads but without trails or frequented camps.

But what pleasure it is to know that there is back country for them to retreat to, that nobody is going to push roads through that wilderness, that no RVs or trail bikes or tote goats will roar through those forests and stink up that clean air. The best thing we have learned from nearly five hundred years of contact with the American wilderness is restraint, the willingness to hold our hand: to visit such places for our souls' good, but leave no tracks.

PART TWO
HABITAT

THOUGHTS IN
A DRY LAND

You have to get over the color green; you have to quit associating beauty with gardens and lawns; you have to get used to an inhuman scale.

The western landscape is of the wildest variety and contains every sort of topography and landform, even most of those familiar from farther east. Bits of East and Middle West are buried here and there in the West, but no physical part of the true West is buried in the East. The West is short-grass plains, alpine mountains, geyser basins, plateaus and mesas and canyons and cliffs, salinas and sinks, sagebrush and Joshua tree and saguaro deserts. If only by reason of their size, the forms of things are different, but there is more than mere size to differentiate them. There is nothing in the East like the granite horns of Grand Teton or Teewinot, nothing like the volcanic neck of Devil's Tower, nothing like the travertine terraces of Mammoth Hot Springs, nothing like the flat crestline and repetitive profile of the Vermilion Cliffs. You know that these differences are themselves regional—that the West, which stretches from around the ninety-eighth meridian to the Pacific, and from the forty-ninth parallel to the Mexican border, is actually half a dozen subregions as different from one another as the Olympic rain forest is from Utah's slickrock country, or Seattle from Santa Fe.

You know also that the western landscape is more than topography and landforms, dirt and rock. It is, most fundamentally, climate—climate which expresses itself not only as landforms but as atmosphere, flora, fauna. And here, despite all the local variety, there is a large, abiding simplicity. Not all the West is arid, yet except at its Pacific edge, aridity surrounds and encompasses it. Landscape includes such facts as this. It includes and is shaped by the way continental masses bend ocean currents, by the way the prevailing winds blow from the West, by the way mountains are pushed up across them to create well-watered coastal or alpine islands, by the way the mountains catch and store the snowpack that makes settled life possible in the dry lowlands, by the way they literally create the dry lowlands by throwing a long rain shadow eastward. Much of the West except the narrow Pacific littoral lies in one or another of those rain shadows, such as the Great Basin and lower Colorado River country, or in the semi-arid steppes of the Montana, Dakota, Nebraska, Wyoming, Colorado, and New Mexico plains.

Aridity, more than anything else, gives the western landscape its character. It is aridity that gives the air its special dry clarity; aridity that puts brilliance in the light and polishes and enlarges the stars; aridity that leads the grasses to evolve as bunches rather than as turf; aridity that exposes the pigmentation of the raw earth and limits, almost eliminates, the color of chlorophyll; aridity that erodes the earth in cliffs and badlands rather than in softened and vegetated slopes, that has shaped the characteristically swift and mobile animals of the dry grasslands and the characteristically nocturnal life of the deserts. The West, Walter Webb said, is "a semi-desert with a desert heart." If I prefer to think of it as two long chains of mountain ranges with deserts or semi-deserts in their rain shadow, that is

not to deny his assertion that the primary unity of the West is
a shortage of water.

The consequences of aridity multiply by a kind of domino
effect. In the attempt to compensate for nature's lacks we have
remade whole sections of the western landscape. The modern
West is as surely Lake Mead and Lake Powell and the Fort Peck
reservoir, the irrigated greenery of the Salt River Valley and the
smog blanket over Phoenix, as it is the high Wind River Range
or the Wasatch or the Grand Canyon. We have acted upon the
western landscape with the force of a geological agent. But
aridity still calls the tune, directs our tinkering, prevents the
healing of our mistakes; and vast unwatered reaches still emphasize the contrast between the desert and the sown.

Aridity has made a lot of difference in us, too, since Americans first ventured up the Missouri into the unknown in the
spring of 1804. Our intentions varied all the way from romantic
adventurousness to schemes of settlement and empire; all the
way from delight in dehumanized nature to a fear of the land
empty of human settlements, monuments, and even, seemingly,
history. Let me call your attention to one book that contains
most of the possible responses. It is called *The Great Lone Land,*
and it is about the Canadian, not the American, West; it was
written by an Irish officer in the British army, William F. Butler.
But the report out of which the book grew was responsible for
the creation of the Royal Northwest Mounted Police, and so had
a big hand in the development of western Canada. Butler was
also an intelligent observer, a romantic, and a man who loved
both wild country and words. He is writing in 1872:

> The old, old maps which the navigators of the sixteenth
> century framed from the discoveries of Cabot and Cartier,
> of Verrazano and Hudson, played strange pranks with
> the geography of the New World. The coastline, with the
> estuaries of large rivers, was tolerably accurate; but the

center of America was represented as a vast inland sea
whose shores stretched far into the Polar North; a sea
through which lay the much-coveted passage to the long-
sought treasures of the old realms of Cathay. Well, the
geographers of that period erred only in the description of
ocean which they placed in the central continent, for an
ocean there is, and an ocean through which men seek the
treasures of Cathay, even in our own times. But the ocean
is one of grass, and the shores are the crests of the mountain ranges, and the dark pine forests of sub-Arctic regions. The great ocean itself does not present more infinite
variety than does this prairie-ocean of which we speak. In
winter, a dazzling surface of purest snow; in early summer, a vast expanse of grass and pale pink roses; in autumn
too often a wild sea of raging fire. No ocean or water in
the world can vie with its gorgeous sunsets; no solitude
can equal the loneliness of a night-shadowed prairie; one
feels the stillness, and hears the silence, the wail of the
prowling wolf makes the voice of solitude audible, the
stars look down through infinite silence upon a silence
almost as intense. One saw here the world as it had taken
shape and form from the hands of the Creator.

History builds slowly, starting from scratch, and understanding of a new country depends upon every sort of report, including some that are unreliable, biased, or motivated by personal
interest—such a report, say, as Lansford Hastings's *The Emi-
grant's Guide to Oregon and California*. Across a century and three
quarters since Lewis and Clark pushed off into the Missouri, we
have had multitudinous reports on the West—Pike and Long;
Catlin and Maximilian of Wied Neuwied; Ashley and Jedediah
Smith and Frémont; Bonneville and the Astorians and Nathaniel
Wyeth; Spalding and Whitman; the random Oregon and California gold rush diarists; the historians of the compact Mormon
migration; the Pacific Railroad Surveys of the 1850s, which for
many areas were the basis of precise knowledge; the Powell,

Hayden, King, and Wheeler surveys and the U.S. Geological Survey that united and continued them. And the dime novels and the Currier and Ives prints; the reports of missionaries and soldiers; the reporters and illustrators for *Leslie's* and *Harper's Weekly;* the painters, from Catlin and Miller and Bodmer to Bierstadt and Moran; the photographers, from Jackson and Hillers and Haynes and Savage onward; the Fenimore Coopers, Mark Twains, Bret Hartes, Dan de Quilles, Horace Greeleys; the Owen Wisters and Frederick Remingtons; the Andy Adamses and Zane Greys and Eugene Manlove Rhodeses.

True or false, observant or blind, impartial or interested, factual or fanciful, it has all gone into the hopper and influenced our understanding and response at least as much as first-hand acquaintance has. But it took a long time. Even learning the basic facts—extents, boundaries, animals, ranges, tribes of men—took a long time. The physical exploration that began with Lewis and Clark was not completed until Almon Thompson led a Powell Survey party into Potato Valley in 1872, and discovered the Escalante River and verified the Henry Mountains, which Powell had seen from a distance on his voyages down the Colorado. The surveying and mapping of great areas of the West was not completed for decades after real exploration had ended; and the trial and error (emphasis on the error) by which we began to be an oasis civilization was forced upon us by country and climate, but against the most mule-headed resistance and unwillingness to understand, accept, and change.

In the actual desert, and especially among the Mormons, where intelligent leadership, community settlement, and the habit of cooperation and obedience were present, agricultural adaptation was swift. But in the marginal zone between humid Midwest and arid West it was easy to be deluded, for the difference of just one inch in rainfall or a slight variation in the seasonal distribution would make the difference between success and failure. And delusion was promoted. The individualism of the frontier, the folklore and habit learned in other regions, the usual politics and boosterism, and land speculation encouraged settlement on terms sure sooner or later to defeat it. Cooperation was one lesson the West enforced, and it was learned hard. Bernard DeVoto once caustically remarked, in connection with the myth of western individualism, that the only real individualists in the West had wound up on one end of a rope whose other end was in the hands of a bunch of cooperators. But a lot of other individualists wound up in the hands of the bank, or trailed back eastward from the dry plains in wagons with signs reading, "In God we trusted, in Kansas we busted," leaving a half-ruined land behind them.

John Wesley Powell submitted his *Report on the Lands of the Arid Region of the United States, with a More Detailed Account of the Lands of Utah,* on April 1, 1878. That early, partly from studying Mormon, Hispano, and Indian irrigation, he understood and accepted both the fact of aridity and the adaptations that men, institutions, and laws would have to go through if we were ever to settle the West instead of simply raiding and ruining it. He comprehended the symbiotic relationship between highlands and lowlands; he understood rivers as common carriers, like railroads, which should not be encumbered by political boundaries. He knew that the Homestead Act and the rectilinear cadastral surveys that worked in well-watered country would not work in the West, and he advocated a change in the land laws that would limit irrigated farms to eighty acres—all a man needed and all he could work—and enlarge stock farms to four full sections, needed by a small farmer's herd in the way of range. He proposed surveys and political divisions not by arbitrary boundaries but by drainage divides, and he and his pupils and associates virtually created the "Wyoming doctrine," which ties water rights to land.

A revolutionary. He might have spared the West the dust bowls of the 1890s, 1930s, and 1950s, as well as the worst consequences of river floods. He might have saved the lives and hopes of all the innocents who put their straddlebugs on dryland homesteads in the Dakotas, Kansas, Nebraska, and Montana. But the boosters and the politicians always proclaimed that rain followed the plow; free land and movement westward were ingrained expectations. Habit, politics, and real estate booster-ism won out over experience and good sense, and that is part of the history of the West, and of western landscape. Even yet the battle, though to some extent won, is not universally under-stood. There are historians who grow so incensed over the "myth" of the Great American Desert, which began with Pike and Long, that they resent any admission of aridity, as well as all "deficiency terminology" in connection with the shortgrass plains.

Ultimately, the settlers of the shortgrass plains learned that water was more important to them than land. They became, by degrees, that oasis civilization and settled down to a relatively thin population because that was what the land would bear.

Karl Frederick Kranzel, in *The Great Plains in Transition,* even suggests that men in the Dakotas and elsewhere had to develop the same mobility that marked the buffalo, antelope, wolves, coyotes, and horse Indians in that country. They go as far for a swim or for shopping as an antelope will go for a drink, and for very similar reasons. They often go hundreds of miles to farm. There is a kind of farmer called a suitcase farmer who spends the winter in some town or city, Grand Forks or Bismarck or Minneapolis, but who in early spring hitches his trailer-home to his pickup and takes off for the West—Dakota, Montana, or Saskatchewan. There he plants his wheat and works his summer fallow, living through the summer in his trailer and driving forty or fifty miles for his supplies and entertainment. In the fall, he harvests and hauls his crop, does his fall plowing, hitches up his trailer again, and returns to the fleshpots of Bismarck. I know one who goes every winter to San Miguel d'Allende. His alter-native would be what the early homesteaders attempted—to make a home out in the desolate plains and live there isolated through the worst winters on the continent. Having lived that life as a boy, I can tell you his mobility, which is as natural as the mobility of the buffalo, is a sensible adaptation.

That is only one sample of how, as we have gone about modifying the western landscape, it has been at work modifying us. And what applies to agricultural and social institutions applies just as surely to our pictorial and literary representations. Perceptions trained in another climate and another landscape have had to be modified. That means we have had to learn to quit depending on perceptual habit. Our first and hardest adaptation was to learn all over again how to see. Our second was to learn to like the new forms and colors and light and scale when we had learned to see them. Our third was to develop new techniques, a new palette, to communicate them. And our fourth, unfortunately out of our control, was to train an audience that would respond to what we wrote or painted.

Years ago I picked up an Iowa aunt of mine in Salt Lake City and drove her down to our cottage on Fish Lake. She was not looking as we drove—she was talking—and she missed the Wasatch, and Mount Nebo, and the Sanpete Valley, and even Sigurd Mountain—the Pahvant—which some people down there call the Big Rock Candy Mountain and which is about as colorful as a peppermint stick. The first thing she really saw, as we turned east at Sigurd, was the towering, level front of the Sevier Plateau above Richfield—level as a rooftree, steep as a cliff, and surging more than a mile straight up above that lush valley. I saw it hit her, and I heard it too, for the talk stopped. I said, "How do you like that, Aunt Min?" for like any Westerner I like to impress Iowans, and the easiest way to do it is with size. She blinked and ruffled up her feathers and assembled herself after the moment of confusion and said, "That's nice. It reminds me of the river bluffs in the county park at Fort Dodge."

She couldn't even see it. She had no experience, no scale, by which to judge an unbroken mountain wall more than a mile high, and her startled mental circuitry could respond with nothing better than the fifty-foot clay banks that her mind had learned to call scenery. She was like the soldiers of Cárdenas, the first white men who ever looked into the Grand Canyon. The river that the Indians had said was half a league wide they judged was about six feet, until they climbed a third of the way down and found that rocks the size of a man grew into things taller than the great tower of Seville, and the six-foot creek, even from four thousand feet above it, was clearly a mighty torrent.

Scale is the first and easiest of the West's lessons. Colors and forms are harder. Easterners are constantly being surprised and somehow offended that California's summer hills are gold, not green. We are creatures shaped by our experiences; we like what we know, more often than we know what we like. To eyes trained on universal chlorophyll, gold or brown hills may look repulsive. Sagebrush is an acquired taste, as are raw earth and alkali flats. The erosional forms of the dry country strike the attention without ringing the bells of appreciation. It is almost pathetic to read the journals of people who came west up the Platte Valley in the 1840s and 1850s and tried to find words for Chimney Rock and Scott's Bluff, and found and clung for dear life to the clichés of castles and silent sentinels.

Listen to Clarence Dutton on the canyon country, whose forms and colors are as far from Hudson River School standards as any in the West:

> The lover of nature, whose perceptions have been trained in the Alps, in Italy, Germany, or New England, in the Appalachians or Cordilleras, in Scotland or Colorado, would enter this strange region with a shock, and dwell there for a time with a sense of oppression, and perhaps with horror. Whatsoever things he had learned to regard as beautiful and noble he would seldom or never see, and whatsoever he might see would appear to him as anything but beautiful and noble. Whatsoever might be

bold and striking would at first seem only grotesque. The colors would be the very ones he had learned to shun as tawdry and bizarre. The tones and shades, modest and tender, subdued yet rich, in which his fancy had always taken special delight, would be the ones which are conspicuously absent. But time would bring a gradual change. Some day he would suddenly become conscious that outlines which at first seemed harsh and trivial have grace and meaning; that forms which seemed grotesque are full of dignity; that magnitudes which had added enormity to coarseness have become replete with strength and even majesty; that colors which had been esteemed unrefined, immodest, and glaring, are as expressive, tender, changeful, and capacious of effects as any others. Great innovations, whether in art or literature, in science or in nature, seldom take the world by storm. They must be understood before they can be estimated, and must be cultivated before they can be understood.

Amen. Dutton describes a process of westernization of the perceptions that has to happen before the West is beautiful to us. You have to get over the color green; you have to quit associating beauty with gardens and lawns; you have to get used to an inhuman scale; you have to understand geological time.

Painters of the West have been hunting a new palette for the western landscape, from Miller and Bodmer to Georgia O'Keeffe, Maynard Dixon, and Millard Sheets. They have been trying to see western landforms with a clear eye ever since the Baron von Egloffstein, illustrating the report of Lieutenant Ives, showed the Grand Canyon with rims like puffs of cloud, exaggerated its narrowness and depth, and showed nothing of what the trained eye sees first—the persistence of the level strata and the persistent profile of the cliffs. Writers have been trying to learn how to see, and have been groping for a vocabulary better than castles and silent sentinels, but often amateurs of a scientific bent, such as Dutton, have had to show them how. And audiences, taught partly by direct contact with the landscape and partly by studying its interpreters, have been slowly acquiring a set of perceptual habits and responses appropriate to western forms and colors. Perception, like art and literature, like history, is an artifact, a human creation, and it is not created overnight.

The Westerner is less a person than a continuing adaptation. The West is less a place than a process. And the western landscape that it has taken us a century and three quarters to learn about, and partially adapt our farming, our social institutions, our laws, and our aesthetic perceptions to, has now become our most valuable natural resource, as subject to raid and ruin as the more concrete resources that have suffered from our rapacity. We are in danger of becoming scenery sellers— and scenery is subject to as much enthusiastic overuse and overdevelopment as grass and water. It can lead us into an ill-considered crowding on the heels of our resources. Landscape, with its basis of aridity, is both our peculiar splendor and our peculiar limitation. Without careful controls and restrictions and planning, tourists can be as destructive as locusts—can destroy everything we have learned to love about the West. I include you and me among the tourists, and I include you and me in my warning to entrepreneurs. We should all be forced to file an environmental impact study before we build so much as a privy or a summer cottage, much less a motel, a freeway, or a resort.

Sometimes I wonder if Lewis and Clark shouldn't have been made to file an environmental impact study before they started west, and Columbus before he ever sailed. They might never have got their permits. But then we wouldn't have been here to learn from our mistakes, either. I really only want to say that we may love a place and still be dangerous to it. We ought to file that environmental impact study before we undertake anything that exploits or alters or endangers the splendid, spacious, varied, magnificent, and terribly fragile earth that supports us.

If we can't find an appropriate government agency with which to file it, we can file it where an Indian would have filed it—with our environmental conscience, our slowly maturing sense that the earth is indeed our mother, worthy of our love and deserving of our care. That may be the last stage of our adaptation to the western landscape, and it may come too late.

LIVING DRY

The West is a region of extraordinary variety within its abiding unity, and of an iron immutability beneath its surface of change. The most splendid part of the American habitat, it is also the most fragile. It has been misinterpreted and mistreated because, coming to it from earlier frontiers where conditions were not unlike those of northern Europe, Anglo-Americans found it different, daunting, exhilarating, dangerous, and unpredictable, and entered it carrying habits that were often inappropriate and expectations that were surely excessive. The dreams they brought to it were recognizable American dreams—a new chance, a little gray home in the West, adventure, danger, bonanza, total freedom from constraint and law and obligation, the Big Rock Candy Mountain, the New Jerusalem. Those dreams had often paid off in parts of America settled earlier, and they paid off for some in the West. For the majority, no. The West has had a way of warping well-carpentered habits, and raising the grain on exposed dreams.

The fact is, it has been as notable for mirages as for the

realization of dreams. Illusion and mirage have been built into it since Coronado came seeking the Seven Cities of Cíbola in 1540. Coronado's failure was an early, spectacular trial run for other and humbler failures. Witness the young men from all over the world who fill graveyards in California's Mother Lode country. There is one I remember: *Nato a Parma 1830, morto a Morfi 1850,* an inscription as significant for its revelation of the youth of many argonauts as for its misspelling of "Murphy's," the camp where this boy died. Witness too the homesteaders who retreated eastward from the dry plains with defeated signs on their covered wagons. Yet we have not even yet fully lost our faith in Cíbola, or the nugget as big as a turnip, or even Kansas.

Anyone pretending to be a guide through wild and fabulous territory should know the territory. I wish I knew it better than I do. I am not Jed Smith. But Jed Smith is not available these days as a guide, and I am. I accept the duty, at least as much for what I myself may learn as for what I may be able to tell others. I can't come to even tentative conclusions about the West without coming to some conclusions about myself.

I have lived in the West, many parts of it, for the best part of seventy-seven years. I have found stories and novels in it, have studied its history and written some of it, have tried to know its landscapes and understand its people, have loved and lamented it, and sometimes rejected its most "western" opinions and prejudices, and pretty consistently despised its most powerful politicians and the general trend of their politics. I have been a lover but not much of a booster. Nevertheless, for better or worse, the West is in my computer, the biggest part of my software.

If there is such a thing as being conditioned by climate and geography, and I think there is, it is the West that has conditioned me. It has the forms and lights and colors that I respond to in nature and in art. If there is a western speech, I speak it; if there is a western character or personality, I am some variant of it; if there is a western culture in the small-*c,* anthropological sense, I have not escaped it. It has to have shaped me. I may even have contributed to it in minor ways, for culture is a pyramid to which each of us brings a stone.

Therefore I ask your indulgence if I sometimes speak in terms of my personal experience, feelings, and values, and put the anecdotal and normative ahead of the statistical, and emphasize personal judgments and trial syntheses rather than the analysis that necessarily preceded them. In doing so, I shall be trying to define myself as well as my native region.

There are other ways of defining the West, but since Major John Wesley Powell's 1878 *Report on the Lands of the Arid Region* it has usually been said that it starts at about the 98th meridian of west longitude and ends at the Pacific Ocean. Neither boundary has the Euclidean perfection of a fixed imaginary line, for on the west the Pacific plate is restless, constantly shoving Los Angeles northward, where it is not wanted, and on the east the boundary between Middle West and West fluctuates a degree or two east or west depending on wet and dry cycles.

Actually it is not the arbitrary 98th meridian that marks the West's beginning, but a perceptible line of real import that roughly coincides with it, reaching southward about a third of the way across the Dakotas, Nebraska, and Kansas, and then swerving more southwestward across Oklahoma and Texas. This is the isohyetal line of twenty inches, beyond which the mean annual rainfall is less than the twenty inches normally necessary for unirrigated crops.

A very little deficiency, even a slight distortion of the season in which the rain falls, makes all the difference. My family homesteaded on the Montana-Saskatchewan border in 1915, and burned out by 1920, after laying the foundation for a little dust bowl by plowing up a lot of buffalo grass. If the rains had been kind, my father would have proved up on that land and become a naturalized Canadian. I estimate that I missed becoming Canadian by no more than an inch or two of rain; but that same deficiency confirmed me as a citizen of the West.

The West is defined, that is, by inadequate rainfall, which means a general deficiency of water. We have water only between the time of its falling as rain or snow and the time when it flows or percolates back into the sea or the deep subsurface reservoirs of the earth. We can't create water or increase the supply. We can only hold back and redistribute what there is. If rainfall is inadequate, then streams will be inadequate, lakes will be few and sometimes saline, underground water will be slow to renew itself when it has been pumped down, the air will be very dry, and surface evaporation from lakes and reservoirs will be extreme. In desert parts of the West it is as much as ten feet a year.

The only exception to western aridity, apart from the mountains that provide the absolutely indispensable snowsheds, is the northwest corner, on the Pacific side of the Cascades. It is a narrow exception: everything east of the mountains, which means two thirds to three quarters of Washington and Oregon, is in the rain shadow.

California, which might seem to be an exception, is not. Though from San Francisco northward the coast gets plenty of rain, that rain, like the lesser rains elsewhere in the state, falls not in the growing season but in winter. From April to November it just about can't rain. In spite of the mild coastal climate and an economy greater than that of all but a handful of nations, California fits Walter Webb's definition of the West as "a semi-desert with a desert heart." It took only the two-year drought of 1976–77, when my part of California got eight inches of rain each year instead of the normal eighteen, to bring the whole state to a panting pause. The five-year drought from 1987 to 1991 has brought it to the point of desperation.

So—the West that we are talking about comprises a dry core of eight public-lands states—Arizona, Colorado, Idaho, Montana, Nevada, New Mexico, Utah, and Wyoming—plus two marginal areas. The first of these is the western part of the Dakotas, Nebraska, Kansas, Oklahoma, and Texas, authentically dry but with only minimal public lands. The second is the West Coast—Washington, Oregon, and California—with extensive arid lands but with well-watered coastal strips and also many rivers. Those marginal areas I do not intend to exclude, but they do complicate statistics. If I cite figures, they will often be for the states of the dry core.

Aridity, and aridity alone, makes the various Wests one. The distinctive western plants and animals, the hard clarity (before power plants and metropolitan traffic altered it) of the western air, the look and location of western towns, the empty spaces that separate them, the way farms and ranches are either densely concentrated where water is plentiful or widely scattered where it is scarce, the pervasive presence of the federal government as landowner and land manager, the even more noticeable federal presence as dam builder and water broker, the snarling states'-rights and antifederal feelings whose burden Bernard DeVoto once characterized in a sentence—"Get out and give us more money"—those are all consequences, and by no means all the consequences, of aridity.

Aridity first brought settlement to a halt at the edge of the dry country and then forced changes in the patterns of settlement. The best guide to those changes is Walter Webb's seminal study, *The Great Plains* (1931). As Webb pointed out, it took a lot of industrial invention to conquer the plains: the Colt revolver, a horseman's weapon, to subdue the horse Indians; barbed wire to control cattle; windmills to fill stock tanks and irrigate little gardens and hayfields; railroads to open otherwise unlivable spaces and bring first buffalo hides and buffalo bones and then cattle and wheat to market; gang machinery to plow, plant, and harvest big fields.

As it altered farming methods, weapons, and tools, so the dry country bent water law and the structure of land ownership. Eastern water law, adopted with little change from English common law, was essentially riparian. The owner of a stream bank, say, a miller, could divert water from the stream to run his mill, but must flow it back when it had done his work for him. But in the arid lands only a little of the water diverted from a stream for any purpose—gold mining, irrigation, municipal or domestic consumption—ever finds its way back. Much is evaporated and lost. Following the practice of Gold Rush miners who diverted streams for their rockers and monitors, all of the dry-core states subscribe to the "Colorado doctrine" of prior appropriation: first come, first served. The three coastal states go by some version of the "California doctrine," which is modified riparian.

Because water is precious, and because either prior appropriation or riparian rights, ruthlessly exercised, could give monopolistic power to an upstream or riparian landowner, both doctrines, over time, have been hedged with safeguards. Not even yet have we fully adapted our water law to western conditions, as was demonstrated when the California Supreme Court in 1983 invoked the "Public Trust" principle to prevent a single user, in this case the Los Angeles Water and Power Authority, from ever again draining a total water supply, in this case the streams that once watered the Owens Valley and fed Mono Lake. The court did not question the validity of Los Angeles' water rights. It said only that those rights could not be exercised at the expense of the public's legitimate interest.

The conditions that modified water use and water law also changed the character of western agriculture. The open-range cattle outfits working north from Texas after the Civil War had only a brief time of uninhibited freedom before they ran into nesters and barbed wire. But the homesteaders who began disputing the plains with cattlemen quickly found that the 160 acres of a dryland homestead were a hand without even openers. Many threw in. Those who stuck either found land on streams or installed windmills; and they moved toward larger acreages and the stock farm, just as the cattlemen eventually moved toward the same adjustment from the other end.

Powell had advocated just such an adjustment in 1878. In country where it took 20, 30, even 50 acres to feed one steer, those 160-acre homesteads were of no use to a stock raiser. But 160 acres of intensively worked irrigated land were more than one family needed or could handle. Furthermore, the rectangular cadastral surveys that had been in use ever since the Northwest Ordinance of 1787 paid no attention to water. Out on the plains, a single quarter or half section might contain all the water within miles, and all the adjacent range was dominated by whoever owned that water.

Powell therefore recommended a new kind of survey defining irrigable homesteads of 80 acres and grazing homesteads of 2,560, four full sections. Every plot should have access to water, and every water right should be tied to land title. Obviously, that program would leave a lot of dry land unsettled.

Unfortunately for homesteaders and the West, Powell's report was buried under dead leaves by Congress. Ten years later, his attempt to close the Public Domain until he could get it surveyed and its irrigable lands identified was defeated by Senator "Big Bill" Stewart of Nevada, the first in a long line of incomparably bad Nevada senators. In 1889 and 1890 the constitutional conventions of Montana, Idaho, and Wyoming territories would not listen when Powell urged them to lay out their political boundaries along drainage divides, so that watershed and timber lands, foothill grazing lands, and valley irrigated lands could be managed intelligently without conflict. The only place where a drainage divide does mark a political boundary is a stretch of the Continental Divide between Idaho and Montana. And to cap this history of old habits stubbornly clung to and hopes out of proportion to possibilities, when Powell addressed the boosters of the Irrigation Congress in Los Angeles in 1893 and warned them that they were laying up a heritage of litigation and failure because there was only enough water to irrigate a fifth of the western lands, the boosters didn't listen either. They booed him.

Powell understood the consequences of aridity, as the boosters did not, and still do not. Westerners who would like to return to the old days of free grab, people of the kind described as having made America great by their initiative and energy in committing mass trespass on the minerals, grass, timber, and water of the Public Domain, complain that no western state is master in its own house. Half its land is not its own: 85 percent of Nevada is not Nevada but the United States; two thirds of Utah and Idaho likewise; nearly half of California, Arizona, and Wyoming—48 percent of the eleven public-lands states.

There are periodic movements, the latest of which was the so-called Sagebrush Rebellion of the 1970s, to get these lands "returned" to the states, which could then dispose of them at bargain-basement rates to favored stockmen, corporations, and entrepreneurs.

The fact is, the states never owned those lands, and gave up all claim to them when they became states. They were always federal lands, acquired by purchase, negotiation, or conquest before any western state existed. The original thirteen colonies created the first Public Domain when they relinquished to the federal government their several claims to what was then the West. The states between the Alleghenies and the Mississippi River were made out of it. All but one of the rest of the contiguous forty-eight were made out of the Louisiana and Florida purchases, the land acquired by the Oregon settlement with Great Britain, and the territory taken from Mexico in the Mexican War or obtained by purchase afterward. All of the western states except Texas, which entered the Union as an independent republic and never had any Public Domain, were created out of federal territory by formal acts of Congress, which then did everything it could to dispose of the public lands within them.

As far as a little beyond the Missouri, the system of disposal worked. Beyond the 98th meridian it did not, except in the spotty way that led Webb to call the West an "oasis civilization." Over time, large areas of forest land and the most spectacular scenery were reserved in the public interest, but much land was not considered worth reserving, and could not be settled or given away. The land laws—the Preemption Act, Homestead Act, Desert Land Act, Carey Act, Timber and Stone Act—produced more failure and fraud than family farms. Not even the Newlands Act of 1902, though it has transformed the West, has put into private hands more than a modest amount of the Public Domain.

Despite all efforts, the West remained substantially federal. In 1930 Herbert Hoover and his secretary of the interior, Ray Lyman Wilbur, tried to give a lot of abused dry land to the states, and the states just laughed. Then in 1934, in the worst Dust Bowl year, the Taylor Grazing Act acknowledged the federal government's reluctant decision to retain—and rescue and manage—the overgrazed, eroded Public Domain. In the 1940s the stockmen's associations tried to steal it, as well as the Forest Service's grazing lands, in a dry rehearsal of the later Sagebrush Rebellion. Bernard DeVoto, in the Easy Chair pages of *Harper's* magazine, almost single-handedly frustrated that grab.

But by the late 1940s people other than stockmen were interested, and more than grass was at stake. During and after World War II the West had revealed treasures of oil, coal, uranium, molybdenum, phosphates, and much else. States whose extractive industries were prevented from unhampered exploitation of these resources again cried foul, demanding "back" the lands they had never owned, cared for, or really wanted, and complaining that the acreages of the Bureau of Land Management, national forests, national parks and monuments, wildlife refuges, military reservations, and dam sites, as well as the arid poor farms where we had filed away our Indian responsibilities, were off the state tax rolls and outside of state control and "locked up" from developers who, given a free hand, would make the West rich and prosperous.

Never mind that grazing fees and coal and oil lease fees and timber sale prices are so low that they amount to a fat subsidy to those who enjoy them. (The flat fee of $1.35 per animal-unit-month set by the Reagan administration as a grazing fee, and still in effect, is about 20 percent of what leasers of private land must pay in most districts. Many timber sales are below cost.) Never mind that half of the money that does come in from fees and leases is given back to the states in lieu of taxes. Never mind that the feds spend the other half, and more, rescuing and rehabilitating the lands whose proper management would bankrupt the states in which they lie. Never mind the federal aid highways, and the federally financed dams, and the write-offs against flood control, and the irrigation water delivered at a few dollars an acre-foot. Take for granted federal assistance, but damn federal control. Your presence as absentee landlord offends us, Uncle. Get out, and give us more money.

There are other objections, too, some of them more legitimate than those of stockmen, lumbermen, and miners greedy for even more than they are getting. There are real difficulties of management when the landscape is checkerboarded with private, state, and federal ownership. And federal space is tempting whenever the nation needs a bombing range, an atomic test site, missile silo locations, or places to dump nuclear waste or store nerve gas. Generally, the West protests that because of its public lands, it gets all the garbage; but sometimes, so odd are we as a species, one or another western state will fight for the garbage, and lobby to become the home of a nuclear dump.

More by oversight than intention, the federal government allowed the states to assert ownership of the water within their boundaries, and that is actually an ownership far more valuable but more complicated than that of land. The feds own the watersheds, the stream and lake beds, the dam sites. Federal bureaus, with the enthusiastic concurrence of western chambers of commerce, have since 1902 done most of the costly impoundment and distribution of water. And federal law, in a pinch, can and does occasionally veto what states and irrigation districts do with that water. It is a good guess that it will have to do so more and more—that unless the states arrive at some relatively uniform set of rules, order will have to be imposed on western water by the federal government.

It will not be easy, and the federal government has created a nasty dilemma for itself by giving its blessing both to the legal fiction of state water ownership and to certain Native American rights to water. As early as 1908, in the so-called Winters doctrine decision, the Supreme Court confirmed the Indians' rights to water originating within or flowing through their reservations. Though those rights have never been quantified or put to use (a beginning has been made by the tribes on the Fort Peck Reservation), Indian tribes all across the West have legitimate but unspecified claims to water already granted by the states to white individuals and corporations. Even without the Indian claims, many western streams—for a prime example, the Colorado—are already oversubscribed. The Colorado River Compact allocated 17.5 million acre-feet annually among the upper basin, lower basin, and Mexico. The actual annual flow since 1930 has averaged about 12 million acre-feet.

Aridity arranged all that complicated natural and human mess, too. In the view of some, it also helped to create a large, spacious, independent, sunburned, self-reliant western character, and a large, open, democratic western society. Of that, despite a wistful desire to believe, I am less than confident.

Nineteenth-century America, overwhelmingly agricultural, assumed that settlement meant agricultural settlement. That assumption underlies—some say it undermines—Frederick

Jackson Turner's famous hypothesis, expressed in his 1893 lecture "The Significance of the Frontier in American History," that both democratic institutions and the American character have been largely shaped by the experience of successive frontiers, with their repeated dream of betterment, their repeated acceptance of primitive hardships, their repeated hope and strenuousness and buoyancy, and their repeated fulfillment as smiling and productive commonwealths of agrarian democrats.

Turner was so intent upon the mass movement toward free land that he paid too little attention to a growing movement toward the industrial cities, and his version of the American character is therefore open to some qualifications. He also paid too little attention to the drastic changes enforced by aridity beyond the 98th meridian, the changes that Powell before him and Webb after him concentrated upon.

The fact is, agriculture at first made little headway in the West, and when it was finally imposed upon the susceptible—and some unsusceptible—spots, it was established pretty much by brute force, and not entirely by agrarian democrats.

Until the Civil War and after, most of the West was not a goal but a barrier. Webb properly remarks that if it had turned out to be country adapted to the slave economy, the South would have fought harder for it, and its history would have been greatly different. He also points out that if the country beyond the Missouri had been wooded and well watered, there would have been no Oregon Trail.

Emigrants bound up the Platte Valley on their way to Oregon, California, or Utah, the first targets of the westward migration, almost universally noted in their journals that a little beyond Grand Island their nostrils dried out and their lips cracked, their wagon wheels began to shrink and wobble, and their estimates of distance began to be ludicrously off the mark. They observed that green had ceased to be the prevailing color of the earth, and had given way to tans, grays, rusty reds, and toned white; that salt often crusted the bottoms of dry lakes (they used some of it, the sodium or potassium bicarbonate that they called saleratus, to leaven their bread); that the grass no longer made a turf, but grew in isolated clumps with bare earth between them; that there was now no timber except on the islands in the Platte; that unfamiliar animals had appeared: horned toads and prairie dogs that seemed to require no water at all, and buffalo, antelope, jackrabbits, and coyotes that could travel long distances for it.

They were at the border of strangeness. Only a few miles into the West, they felt the difference; and as Webb says, the degree of strangeness can be measured by the fact that almost all the new animals they saw they misnamed. The prairie dog is not a dog, the horned toad is not a toad, the jackrabbit is not a rabbit, the buffalo is not a buffalo, and the pronghorn antelope is more goat than antelope. But they could not mistake the aridity. They just didn't know how much their habits would have to change if they wanted to live beyond the 98th meridian. None of them in that generation would have denied aridity to its face, as William Gilpin, the first territorial governor of Colorado, would do a generation later, asserting that it was a simple matter on the plains to *dig* for wood and water, that irrigation was as easy as fencing, which it supplanted, and that the dry plains and the Rockies could handily support a population of two hundred million. That kind of fantasy, like Cyrus Thomas's theory that cultivation increases rainfall, that "rain follows the plow," would have to wait for the boosters.

Two lessons all western travelers had to learn: mobility and sparseness. Mobility was the condition of life beyond the Missouri. Once they acquired the horse, the Plains Indians were as migrant as the buffalo they lived by. The mountain men working the beaver streams were no more fixed than the clouds. And when the change in hat fashions killed the fur trade, and mountain men turned to guiding wagon trains, the whole intention of those trains was to get an early start, as soon as the grass greened up, and then get *through* the West as fast as possible. The Mormons were an exception, a special breed headed for sanctuary in the heart of the desert, a people with a uniquely cohesive social order and a theocratic discipline that made them better able to survive.

But even the Mormons were villages on the march, as mobile as the rest until, like Moses from Pisgah's top, they looked upon Zion. Once there, they quickly made themselves into the West's stablest society. But notice: Now, a hundred and forty years after their hegira, they have managed to put only about 3 percent of Utah's land under cultivation; and because they took seriously the Lord's command to be fruitful and multiply, Zion has been overpopulated, and exporting manpower, for at least half a century. One of the bitterest conflicts in modern Utah is that between the environmentalists, who want to see much of that superlative wilderness preserved roadless and wild, and the stubborn Mormon determination to make it support more saints than it possibly can.

Lieutenant Zebulon Pike, sent out in 1806 to explore the country between the Missouri and Santa Fe, had called the high plains the Great American Desert. In 1819 the expedition of Major Stephen Long corroborated that finding, and for two generations nobody seriously questioned it. The plains were unfit for settlement by a civilized, meaning an agricultural, people, and the farther west you went, the worse things got. So for the emigrants who in 1840 began to take wheels westward up the Platte Valley, the interior West was not a place but a way, a trail to the Promised Land, an adventurous, dangerous rite of passage. In the beginning there were only two *places* on its two-thousand-mile length: Fort Laramie on the North Platte and Fort Hall on the Snake. And those were less settlements than way stations, refreshment-and-recruitment stops different only in style from motel-and-gas-and-lunchroom turnouts on a modern interstate.

Insofar as the West was a civilization at all between the time of Lewis and Clark's explorations and about 1870, it was largely a civilization in motion, driven by dreams. The people who composed and represented it were part of a true Folk-Wandering, credulous, hopeful, hardy, largely uninformed. The dreams are not dead even today, and the habit of mobility has only been reinforced by time.

Ever since Daniel Boone took his first excursion over Cumberland Gap, Americans have been wanderers. When Charles Dickens, in the Mississippi Valley, met a full-sized dwelling house coming down the road at a round trot, he was looking at the American people head-on. With a continent to take over and Manifest Destiny to goad us, we could not have avoided being footloose. The initial act of emigration from Europe, an act of extreme, deliberate disaffiliation, was the beginning of a national habit.

It should not be denied, either, that being footloose has always exhilarated us. It is associated in our minds with escape from history and oppression and law and irksome obligations, with absolute freedom, and the road has always led west. Our folk heroes and our archetypal literary figures accurately reflect that side of us. Leatherstocking, Huckleberry Finn, the narrator of *Moby Dick,* all are orphans and wanderers: any of them could say, "Call me Ishmael." The Lone Ranger has no dwelling place except the saddle. And when teenagers run away in the belief that they are running toward freedom, they more often than not run west. Listen to the Haight-Ashbury dialogues in Joan Didion's *Slouching Towards Bethlehem.* Examine the American character as it is self-described in *Habits of the Heart,* by Robert Bellah and others.

But the rootlessness that expresses energy and a thirst for the new and an aspiration toward freedom and personal fulfillment has just as often been a curse. Migrants deprive themselves of the physical and spiritual bonds that develop within a place and a society. Our migratoriness has hindered us from becoming a people of communities and traditions, especially in the West. It has robbed us of the gods who make places holy. It has cut off individuals and families and communities from memory and the continuum of time. It has left at least some of us with a kind of spiritual pellagra, a deficiency disease, a hungering for the ties of a rich and stable social order. Not only is the American home a launching pad, as Margaret Mead said; the American community, especially in the West, is an overnight camp. American individualism, much celebrated and cherished, has developed without its essential corrective, which is belonging. Freedom, when found, can turn out to be airless and unsustaining. Especially in the West, what we have instead of place is space. Place is more than half memory, shared memory. Rarely do Westerners stay long enough at one stop to share much of anything.

The principal invention of western American culture is the motel, the principal exhibit of that culture the automotive roadside. A principal western industry is tourism, which exploits the mobile and the seasonal. Whatever it might want to be, the West is still primarily a series of brief visitations or a trail to somewhere else; and western literature, from *Roughing It* to *On the Road,* from *The Log of a Cowboy* to *Lonesome Dove,* from *The Big Rock Candy Mountain* to *The Big Sky,* has been largely a literature not of place but of motion.

Trying to capture America in a sentence, Gertrude Stein said, "Conceive a space that is filled with moving." If she had been reared in Boston she might not have seen it so plainly; but she was reared in Oakland. She knew that few Westerners die where they were born, that most live out their lives as a series of uprootings.

. . .

Adaptation is the covenant that all successful organisms sign with the dry country. In *The Land of Little Rain* Mary Austin, writing of the Owens Valley in the rain shadow of the Sierra, remarked that "the manner of the country makes the usage of life there, and the land will not be lived in except in its own fashion. The Shoshones live like their trees, with great spaces between. . . ."

She might have added, though I don't remember that she did, how often Shoshonean place names contain the syllable *pah*: Tonopah, Ivanpah, Pahrump, Paria. In the Shoshonean language, *pah* means water, or water hole. The Pah-Utes are the Water Utes, taking their name from their rarest and most precious resource. They live mainly in Utah and Nevada, the two driest states in the Union, and in those regions water is safety, home, life, *place*. All around those precious watered places is only space, forbidding and unlivable, what one must travel through between places of safety.

Thoroughly adapted, the Pah-Utes (Paiutes) were migratory between fixed points marked by seasonal food supplies and by water. White Americans, once they began to edge into the dry country from east, west, and south, likewise established their settlements on dependable water, and those towns have a special shared quality, a family resemblance.

For the moment, forget the Pacific Coast, furiously bent on becoming Conurbia from Portland to San Diego. Forget the metropolitan sprawl of Denver, Phoenix, Tucson, Albuquerque, Dallas–Fort Worth, and Salt Lake City, growing to the limits of their water and beyond, like bacterial cultures overflowing the edges of their agar dishes and beginning to sicken on their own wastes. If we want characteristic western towns we must look for them, paradoxically, beyond the West's prevailing urbanism, out in the boondocks where the interstates do not reach, mainline planes do not fly, and branch plants do not locate. The towns that are most western have had to strike a balance between mobility and stability, and the law of sparseness has kept them from growing too big. They are the places where the stickers stuck, and perhaps were stuck, the places where adaptation has gone furthest.

Whether they are winter wheat towns like Minot, North Dakota, on the subhumid edge, whose elevators and bulbous silver water towers announce them miles away, or county towns like Roundup, Montana, in ranch country, or intensely green towns like Fallon, Nevada, in irrigated desert valleys, they have a sort of forlorn, proud rightness. They look at once lost and self-sufficient, scruffy and indispensable. A road leads in out of wide emptiness, threads a fringe of service stations, taverns, and a motel or two, widens to a couple of blocks of commercial buildings, some still false-fronted, with glimpses of side streets and green lawns, narrows to another strip of automotive roadside, and disappears into more wide emptiness.

The loneliness and vulnerability of those towns always moves me, for I have lived in them. I know how the world of a child in one of them is bounded by weedy prairie, or the spine of the nearest dry range, or by flats where plugged tin cans lie rusting and the wind has pasted paper and plastic against the sagebrush. I know how precious is the safety of a few known streets and vacant lots and familiar houses. I know how the road in each direction both threatens and beckons. I know that most of the children in such a town will sooner or later take that road, and that only a few will take it back.

In mining country, vulnerability has already gone most or all of the way to death. In those ghosts or near ghosts where the placers have been gutted or the lodes played out, the shafts and drifts and tailings piles, the saloons and stores and hotels and houses, have been left to the lizards and a few survivors who have rejected the command of mobility. The deader the town, the more oppressive the emptiness that surrounds and will soon reclaim it. Unless, of course, the federal government has installed an atomic testing site, or new migrant entrepreneurs have come in to exploit the winter skiing or bring summer-festival culture. Then the ghost will have turned, at least temporarily, into a Searchlight, an Aspen, a Telluride, a Park City—a new way station for new kinds of migrants.

We return to mobility and the space that enforces it. Consider the observations of William Least Heat Moon, touring the blue highways of America. "The true West," he says (and notice that he too finds the true West somewhere outside the cities where 75 percent of Westerners live),

> differs from the East in one great, pervasive, influential, and awesome way: space. The vast openness changes the roads, towns, houses, farms, crops, machinery, politics, economics, and, naturally, ways of thinking. . . . Space west of the line is perceptible and often palpable, especially when it appears empty, and it's that apparent emptiness which makes matter look alone, exiled, and unconnected. . . . But as the space diminishes man and his constructions in a material fashion it also—paradoxically—makes them more noticeable. *Things show up out here.* The terrible distances eat up speed. Even dawn takes nearly an hour just to cross Texas. (*Blue Highways,* p. 136)

Distance, space, affects people as surely as it has bred keen eyesight into pronghorn antelope. And what makes that western space and distance? The same condition that enforces mobility on all adapted creatures, and tolerates only small or temporary concentrations of human or other life.

Aridity.

And what do you do about aridity if you are a nation accustomed to plenty and impatient of restrictions and led westward by pillars of fire and cloud? You may deny it for a while. Then you must either try to engineer it out of existence or adapt to it.

STRIKING
THE ROCK

The summer of 1948 my family and I spent on Struthers Burt's ranch in Jackson Hole. I was just beginning a biography of John Wesley Powell, and beginning to understand some things about the West that I had not understood before. But during that busy and instructive interval my wife and I were also acting as western editors and scouts for a publishing house, and now and then someone came by with a manuscript or the idea for a book. The most memorable of these was a famous architect contemplating his autobiography. One night he showed us slides of some of his houses, including a million-dollar palace in the California desert of which he was very proud. He said it demonstrated that with imagination, technical know-how, modern materials, and enough money, an architect could build anywhere without constraints, imposing his designed vision on any site, in any climate.

In that waterless pale desert spotted with shad scale and creosote bush and backed by barren lion-colored mountains, another sort of architect, say, Frank Lloyd Wright, might have designed something contextual, something low, broad-eaved, thick-walled, something that would mitigate the hot light, something half-underground so that people could retire like the lizards and rattlesnakes from the intolerable daytime temperatures, something made of native stone or adobe or tamped earth in the colors and shapes of the country, something no more visually intrusive than an outcrop.

Not our architect. He had built of cinderblock, in the form of Bauhaus cubes, the only right angles in that desert. He had painted them a dazzling white. Instead of softening the lines between building and site, he had accentuated them, surrounding his sugary cubes with acres of lawn and a tropical oasis of oleanders, hibiscus, and palms—not the native *Washingtonia* palms either, which are a little scraggly, but sugar and royal palms, with a classier, more Santa Barbara look. Water for this estancia, enough water to have sustained a whole tribe of desert Indians, he had brought by private pipeline from the mountains literally miles away.

The patio around the pool—who would live in the desert without a pool?—would have fried the feet of swimmers three hundred days out of the year, and so he had designed canopies that could be extended and retracted by push button, and under the patio's concrete he had laid pipes through which cool water circulated by day. By night, after the desert chill came on, the circulating water was heated. He had created an artificial climate, inside and out.

Studying that luxurious, ingenious, beautiful, sterile incongruity, I told its creator, sincerely, that I thought he could build a comfortable house in hell. That pleased him; he thought so too. What I didn't tell him, what he would not have understood, was that we thought his desert house immoral. It exceeded limits, it offended our sense not of the possible but of the desirable. There was no economic or social reason for anyone's living on a barren flat, however beautiful, where every form of life sought shelter during the unbearable daylight hours.

The only reasons for building there were to let mad dogs and rich men go out in the midday sun, and to let them own and dominate a view they admired. The house didn't fit the country, it challenged it. It asserted America's never-say-never spirit and America's ingenious know-how. It seemed to us an act of arrogance on the part of both owner and architect.

I felt like asking him, What if a superrich Eskimo wanted a luxury house on Point Hope? Would you build it for him? Would you dam the Kobuk and bring megawatts of power across hundreds of miles of tundra, and set up batteries of blower-heaters to melt the snow and thaw the permafrost, and would you erect an international-style house with picture windows through which the Eskimo family could look out across the lawn and strawberry bed and watch polar bears on the pack ice?

He might have taken on such a job, and he was good enough to make it work, too—until the power line blew down or shorted out. Then the Eskimos he had encouraged to forget igloo building and seal-oil lamps would freeze into ice sculptures, monuments to human pride. But of course that is all fantasy. Eskimos, a highly adapted and adaptable people, would have more sense than to challenge their arctic habitat that way. Even if they had unlimited money. Which they don't.

That desert house seemed to me, and still seems to me, a paradigm—hardly a paradigm, more a caricature—of what we have been doing to the West in my lifetime. Instead of adapting, as we began to do, we have tried to make country and climate over to fit our existing habits and desires. Instead of listening to the silence, we have shouted into the void. We have tried to make the arid West into what it was never meant to be and cannot remain, the Garden of the World and the home of multiple millions.

That does not mean either that the West should never have been settled or that water should never be managed. The West—the habitable parts of it—is a splendid habitat for a limited population living within the country's rules of sparseness and mobility. If the unrestrained engineering of western water was original sin, as I believe, it was essentially a sin of scale. Anyone who wants to live in the West has to manage water to some degree.

Ranchers learned early to turn creeks onto their hay land. Homesteaders not on a creek learned to dam a runoff coulee to create a "rezavoy," as we did in Saskatchewan in 1915. Kansas and Oklahoma farmers set windmills to pumping up the underground water. Towns brought their water, by ditch or siphon, from streams up on the watershed. Irrigation, developed first by the Southwestern Indians and the New Mexico Spanish, and reinvented by the Mormons—it was a necessity that came with the territory—was expanded in the 1870s and 1880s by such cooperative communities as Greeley, Colorado, and by small to medium corporate ventures such as the one I wrote about in *Angle of Repose*—the project on the Boise River that after its failure was taken over by the Bureau of Reclamation and called the Arrowrock Dam.

Early water engineers and irrigators bit off what they and the local community could chew. They harnessed the streams that they could manage. Some dreamers did take on larger rivers, as Arthur Foote took on the Boise, and went broke at it. By and large, by 1890, individual, corporate, and cooperative irrigators had gone about as far as they could go with water engineering; their modest works were for local use and under local control. It might have been better if the West had stopped there. Instead, all through the 1890s the unsatisfied boosters called for federal aid to let the West realize its destiny, and in 1902 they got the Newlands Act. This *permitted* the feds to undertake water projects—remember that water was state owned, or at least state regulated—and created the Bureau of Reclamation.

Reclamation projects were to be paid for by fees charged irrigation districts, the period for paying off the interest-free indebtedness being first set at ten years. Later that was upped to twenty, later still to forty. Eventually much of the burden of repayment was shifted from the sale of water to the sale of hydropower, and a lot of the burden eliminated entirely by the practice of river-basin accounting, with write-offs for flood control, job creation, and other public goods. Once it was lured in, the federal government—which meant taxpayers throughout the country, including taxpayers in states that resented western reclamation because they saw themselves asked to pay for something that would compete unfairly with their own farmers—absorbed or wrote off more and more of the costs, accepting the fact that reclamation was a continuing subsidy to western agriculture. Even today, when municipal and industrial demands for water have greatly increased, 80 to 90 percent of the water used in the West is used, often wastefully, on fields, to produce crops generally in surplus elsewhere. After all the billions spent by the Bureau of Reclamation, the total area irrigated by its projects is about the size of Ohio, and the water impounded and distributed by the bureau is about 15 percent of all the water utilized in the West. What has been won is only a beachhead, and a beachhead that is bound to shrink.

One of the things Westerners should ponder, but generally do not, is their relation to and attitude toward the federal presence. The bureaus administering all the empty space that gives Westerners much of their outdoor pleasure and many of their special privileges and a lot of their pride and self-image are frequently resented, resisted, or manipulated by those who benefit economically from them but would like to benefit more, and are generally taken for granted by the general public.

The federal presence should be recognized as what it at least partly is: a reaction against our former profligacy and wastefulness, an effort at adaptation and stewardship in the interest of the environment and the future. In contrast to the principal water agency, the Bureau of Reclamation, which was a creation of the boosters and remains their creature, and whose prime purpose is technological conversion of the arid lands, the land-managing bureaus all have as at least part of their purpose the preservation of the West in a relatively natural, healthy, and sustainable condition.

Yellowstone became the first national park in 1872 because a party of Montana tourists around a campfire voted down a proposal to exploit it for profit, pledged themselves to try to get it protected as a permanent pleasuring-ground for the whole country, and successfully took their case to Washington. The national forests began because the bad example of Michigan scared Congress about the future of the country's forests, and induced it in 1891 to authorize the reservation of public forest lands by presidential proclamation. Benjamin Harrison took large advantage of the opportunity. Later, Grover Cleveland did the same, and so did Theodore Roosevelt. The West, predictably, cried aloud at having that much plunder removed from circulation, and in 1907 western congressmen put a rider on an agricultural appropriations bill that forbade any more presidential reservations without the prior consent of Congress. Roosevelt could have pocket-vetoed it. Instead, he and Chief Forester Gifford Pinchot sat up all night over the maps and surveys of potential reserves, and by morning Roosevelt had signed into existence twenty-one new national forests, sixteen million acres of them. Then he signed the bill that would have stopped him.

It was Theodore Roosevelt, too, who created the first wild-life refuge in 1903, thus beginning a service whose territories, since passage of the Alaska National Interest Lands Conservation Act of 1980, now exceed those of the National Park Service by ten million acres.

As for the biggest land manager of all, the Bureau of Land Management (BLM), it is the inheritor of the old General Land Office, whose job was to dispose of the Public Domain to homesteaders, and its lands are the leftovers once (erroneously) thought to be worthless. Worthless or not, they could not be indefinitely neglected and abused. The health of lands around them depended on their health.

They were assumed as a permanent federal responsibility by the Taylor Grazing Act of 1934, but the Grazing Service then created was a helpless and toothless bureau dominated by local councils packed by local stockmen—foxes set by other foxes to watch the henhouse, in a travesty of democratic local control. The Grazing Service was succeeded by the Bureau of Land Management, which was finally given some teeth by the Federal Land Policy and Management Act of 1976. No sooner did it get the teeth that would have let it do its job than the Sagebrush Rebels offered to knock them out. The Rebels didn't have to. Instead, President Reagan gave them James Watt as secretary of the interior, and James Watt gave them Robert Burford as head of the BLM. The rebels simmered down, their battle won for them by administrative appointment, and BLM remains a toothless bureau.

All of the bureaus walk a line somewhere between preservation and exploitation. The enabling act of the National Park Service in 1916 charged it to provide for the *use without impairment* of the parks. It is an impossible assignment, especially now that more than three hundred million people visit the national parks annually, but the Park Service tries.

The National Forest Service, born out of Pinchot's philosophy of "wise use," began with the primary purpose of halting unwise use, and as late as the 1940s so informed a critic as Bernard DeVoto thought it the very best of the federal bureaus. But it changed its spots during the first Eisenhower administration, under the Mormon patriarch Ezra Taft Benson as secretary of agriculture, and began aggressively to harvest board feet. Other legitimate uses—recreation, watershed and wildlife protection, the gene banking of wild plant and animal species, and especially wilderness preservation—it either neglected or resisted whenever they conflicted with logging.

By now, unhappily, environmental groups tend to see the

Forest Service not as the protector of an invaluable public resource and the true champion of multiple use, but as one of the enemy, allied with the timber interests. The Forest Service, under attack, has reacted with a hostility bred of its conviction that it is unjustly criticized. As a consequence of that continuing confrontation, nearly every master plan prepared in obedience to the National Forest Management Act of 1976 has been challenged and will be fought, in the courts if necessary, by the Wilderness Society, the Sierra Club, the Natural Resources Defense Council, and other organizations. The usual charge: too many timber sales, too often at a loss in money as well as in other legitimate values, and far too much roading—roading being a preliminary to logging and a way of forestalling wilderness designation by spoiling the wilderness in advance.

What is taking place is that Congress has been responding to public pressures to use the national forests for newly perceived social goods; and the National Forest Service, for many years an almost autonomous bureau with a high morale and, from a forester's point of view, high principles, is resisting that imposition of control.

Not even the Fish and Wildlife Service, dedicated to the preservation of wild species and their habitats, escapes criticism, for under pressure from stockmen it has historically waged war on predators, especially coyotes, and the poison baits that it used to distribute destroyed not only coyotes but hawks, eagles, and other wildlife that the agency was created to protect. One result has been a good deal of public suspicion. Even the current device of 1080-poisoned collars for sheep and lambs, designed to affect only an attacking predator, is banned in thirty states.

The protection provided by these several agencies is of course imperfect. Every reserve is an island, and its boundaries are leaky. Nevertheless this is the best protection we have, and not to be disparaged. All Americans, but especially Westerners, whose backyard is at stake, need to ask themselves whose bureaus these should be. Half of the West is in their hands. Do

they exist to provide bargain-basement grass to favored stockmen whose grazing privileges have become all but hereditary,
assumed and bought and sold along with the title to the home
spread? Are they hired exterminators of wildlife? Is it their
function to negotiate loss-leader coal leases with energy con-
glomerates, and to sell timber below cost to Louisiana Pacific?
Or should they be serving the much larger public whose outdoor recreations of backpacking, camping, fishing, hunting,
river running, mountain climbing, hang gliding, and, God help
us, dirt biking are incompatible with clear-cut forests and overgrazed, poison-baited, and strip-mined grasslands? Or is there a
still higher duty—to maintain the health and beauty of the lands
they manage, protecting from everybody, including such destructive segments of the public as dirt bikers and pothunters,
the watersheds and spawning streams, forests and grasslands,
geological and scenic splendors, historical and archaeological
remains, air and water and serene space, that once led me, in
a reckless moment, to call the western public lands part of the
geography of hope?

As I have known them, most of the field representatives of
all the bureaus, including the BLM, do have a sense of responsibility about the resources they oversee, and a frequent frustra-
tion that they are not permitted to oversee them better. But that
sense of duty is not visible in some, and for the past ten years
has been least visible in the political appointees who make or
enunciate policy. Even when policy is intelligently made and
well understood, it sometimes cannot be enforced because of
local opposition. More than one Forest Service ranger or BLM
man who tried to enforce the rules has had to be transferred out
of a district to save him from violence.

There are many books on the Public Domain. One of the new-
est and best is *These American Lands,* by Dyan Zaslowsky and the
Wilderness Society, published in 1986 by Henry Holt and Company. I recommend it not only for its factual accuracy and clarity
but for its isolation of problems and its suggestions of solutions.

Here and now, all I can do is repeat that the land bureaus have a strong, often disregarded, influence on how life is lived in the West. They provide and protect the visible, available, unfenced space that surrounds almost all western cities and towns—surrounds them as water surrounds fish, and is their living element.

The bureaus need, and some would welcome, the kind of public attention that would force them to behave in the long-range public interest. Though I have been involved in controversies with some of them, the last thing I would want to see is their dissolution and a return to the policy of disposal, for that would be the end of the West as I have known and loved it. Neither state ownership nor private ownership—which state ownership would soon become—could offer anywhere near the usually disinterested stewardship that these imperfect and embattled federal bureaus do, while at the same time making western space available to millions. They have been the strongest impediment to the careless ruin of what remains of the Public Domain, and they will be necessary as far ahead as I, at least, can see.

The Bureau of Reclamation is something else. From the beginning, its aim has been not the preservation but the remaking—in effect the mining—of the West.

A principal justification for the Newlands Act was that fabled Jeffersonian yeoman, the small freehold farmer, who was supposed to benefit from the Homestead Act, the Desert Land Act, the Timber and Stone Act, and other land-disposal legislation, but rarely did so west of the 98th meridian. The publicized purpose of federal reclamation was the creation of family farms that would eventually feed the world and build prosperous rural commonwealths in deserts formerly fit for nothing but horned toads and rattlesnakes. To ensure that these small farmers would not be done out of their rights by large landowners and water users, Congress wrote into the act a clause limiting the use of water under Reclamation Bureau dams to the amount that would serve a family farm of 160 acres.

Behind the pragmatic, manifest-destinarian purpose of pushing western settlement was another motive: the hard determination to dominate nature that historian Lynn White, in the essay "Historical Roots of Our Ecologic Crisis," identified as part of our Judeo-Christian heritage. Nobody implemented that impulse more uncomplicatedly than the Mormons, a chosen people who believed the Lord when He told them to make the desert blossom as the rose. Nobody expressed it more bluntly than a Mormon hierarch, John Widtsoe, in the middle of the irrigation campaigns: "The destiny of man is to possess the whole earth; the destiny of the earth is to be subject to man. There can be no full conquest of the earth, and no real satisfaction to humanity, if large portions of the earth remain beyond his highest control" (*Success on Irrigation Projects*, p. 138).

That doctrine offends me to the bottom of my not-very-Christian soul. It is related to the spirit that builds castles of incongruous luxury in the desert. It is the same spirit that between 1930 and the present has so dammed, diverted, used, and reused the Colorado River that its saline waters now never reach the Gulf of California, but die in the sand miles from the sea; that has set the Columbia, a far mightier river, to tamely turning turbines; that has reduced the Missouri, the greatest river on the continent, to a string of ponds; that has recklessly pumped down the water table of every western valley and threatens to dry up even so prolific a source as the Ogalalla Aquifer; that has made the Salt River Valley of Arizona and the Imperial, Coachella, and great Central valleys of California into gardens of fabulous but deceptive richness; that has promoted a new rush to the West fated, like the beaver and grass and gold rushes, to recede after doing great environmental damage.

The Garden of the World has been a glittering dream, and many find its fulfillment exhilarating. I do not. I have already said that I think of the main-stem dams that made it possible as original sin, but there is neither a serpent nor a guilty first couple in the story. In Adam's fall we sinnéd all. Our very virtues as a pioneering people, the very genius of our industrial civilization, drove us to act as we did. God and Manifest Destiny spoke with one voice urging us to "conquer" or "win" the West; and there was no voice of comparable authority to remind us of Mary Austin's quiet but profound truth, that "the manner of the country makes the usage of life there, and the land will not be lived in except in its own fashion."

Obviously, reclamation is not the panacea it once seemed. Plenty of people in 1986 are opposed to more dams, and there is plenty of evidence against the long-range viability and the social and environmental desirability of large-scale irrigation agriculture. Nevertheless, millions of Americans continue to think of the water engineering in the West as one of our proudest achievements, a technology that we should export to backward Third World nations to help them become as we are. We go on praising apples as if eating them were an injunction of the Ten Commandments.

For its first thirty years, the Bureau of Reclamation struggled, plagued by money problems and unable to perform as its boosters had promised. It got a black eye for being involved, in shady ways, with William Mulholland's steal of the Owens Valley's water for the benefit of Los Angeles. The early dams it completed sometimes served not an acre of public land. It did increase homestead filings substantially, but not all those homesteads ended up in the hands of Jeffersonian yeomen: according to a 1922 survey, it had created few family farms; the 160-acre limitation was never enforced; three quarters of the farmers in some reclamation districts were tenants.

Drought, the Great Depression, and the New Deal's effort to make public works jobs gave the bureau new life. It got quick appropriations for the building of the Boulder (Hoover) Dam, already authorized, and it took over from the state of California construction of the enormous complex of dams and ditches called the Central Valley Project, designed to harness all the rivers flowing westward out of the Sierra. It grew like a mushroom, like an exhalation. By the 1940s the bureau, which only a few years before had been hanging on by a shoestring, had built or was building the four greatest dams ever built on earth up to that time—Hoover, Shasta, Bonneville, and Grand Coulee—and was already the greatest force in the West. It had discovered where power was, and allied itself with it: with the growers and landowners, private and corporate, whose interests it served, and with the political delegations, often elected out of this same group, who carried the effort in Washington for more and more pork-barrel projects. In matters of western water there are no political parties. You cannot tell Barry Goldwater from Moe Udall, or Orrin Hatch from Richard Lamm.

Nevertheless there was growing opposition to dams from nature lovers, from economists and cost counters, and from political representatives of areas that resented paying these costs in subsidy of their agricultural competition. Uniting behind the clause in the National Park Service Act that enjoined "use without impairment," environmental groups in 1955 blocked two dams in Dinosaur National Monument and stopped the whole Upper Colorado River Storage Project in its tracks. Later, in the 1960s, they also blocked a dam in Marble Canyon, on the Colorado, and another in Grand Canyon National Monument, at the foot of the Grand Canyon.

In the process they accumulated substantial evidence, economic, political, and environmental, against dams, the bureau that built them, and the principles that guided that bureau. President Jimmy Carter had a lot of public sympathy when he tried to stop nine water-project boondoggles, most of them in the West, in 1977. Though the hornet's nest he stirred up taught him something about western water politics, observers noted that no new water projects were authorized by Congress until the very last days of the 99th Congress, in October 1986. Pork was out of fashion.

The great days of dam building are clearly over, for the best dam sites are used up, most of the rivers are "tamed," costs have risen exponentially, and public support of reclamation has given way to widespread and searching criticism. It is not a bad time to assess what the big era of water engineering has done to the West.

The voices of reappraisal are already a chorus. Four books in particular, all published in recent years, have examined western water developments and practices in detail. They are Philip Fradkin's *A River No More,* about the killing of the Colorado; William A. Kahrl's *Water and Power,* on the rape of the Owens Valley by Los Angeles; Donald Worster's *Rivers of Empire,* a dismaying survey of our irrigation society in the light of Karl Wittvogel's studies of the ancient hydraulic civilizations of Mesopotamia and China; and Marc Reisner's *Cadillac Desert,* a history that pays particular unfriendly attention to the Bureau of Reclamation and its most empire-building director, Floyd Dominy.

None of those books is calculated to please agribusiness or the politicians and bureaucrats who have served it. Their consensus is that reclamation dams and their little brother the centrifugal pump have made an impressive omelet but have broken many eggs, some of them golden, and are in the process of killing the goose that laid them.

Begin with some environmental consequences of "taming" rivers, if only because the first substantial opposition to dams was environmental.

First, dams do literally kill rivers, which means they kill not only living water and natural scenery but a whole congeries of values associated with them. The scenery they kill is often of the grandest, for most main-stem dams are in splendid canyons, which they drown. San Francisco drowned the Hetch Hetchy Valley, which many thought as beautiful as Yosemite itself, to ensure its future water supply. Los Angeles turned the Owens Valley into a desert by draining off its natural water supplies. The Bureau of Reclamation drowned Glen Canyon, the most serene and lovely rock funhouse in the West, to provide peaking power for Los Angeles and the Las Vegas Strip.

The lakes formed behind dams are sometimes cited as great additions to public recreation, and Floyd Dominy even published a book to prove that the Glen Canyon Dam had beautified Glen Canyon by drowning it. But drawdown reservoirs rarely live up to their billing. Nothing grows in the zone between low-water mark and high-water mark, and except when brimming full, any drawdown reservoir, even Glen Canyon, which escapes the worst effects because its walls are vertical, is not unlike a dirty bathtub with a ring of mud and mineral stain around it.

A dammed river is not only stoppered like a bathtub, but it is turned on and off like a tap, creating a fluctuation of flow that destroys the riverine and riparian wildlife and creates problems for recreational boatmen, who have to adjust to times when the river is mainly boulders and times when it rises thirty feet and washes their tied boats off the beaches. And since dams prohibit the really high flows of the spring runoff, boulders, gravel, and detritus pile up into the channel at the mouths of side gulches and never get washed away.

Fishing, too, suffers, and not merely today's fishing but the future of fishing. Despite their fish ladders, the dams on the Columbia seriously reduced the spawning runs of salmon and steelhead, and they also trapped and killed so many smolts on their way downriver that eventually the federal government had to regulate the river's flow. The reduction of fishing is felt not only by the offshore fishing fleets and by Indian tribes with traditional or treaty fishing rights, but by sports fishermen all the way upstream to the Salmon River Mountains in Idaho.

If impaired rafting and fishing and sight-seeing seem a trivial price to pay for all the economic benefits supposedly brought by dams, reflect that rafting and fishing and sight-seeing are not trivial economic activities. The national parks, which are mainly in the public-lands states, saw over three hundred million visitors in 1984. The national forests saw even more. A generation ago, only five thousand people in all the United States had ever rafted a river; by 1985, thirty-five million had. Every western river from the Rogue and the Owyhee to the Yampa, Green, San Juan, and Colorado is booked solid through the running season. As the country at large grows more stressful as a dwelling place, the quiet, remoteness, and solitude of a week on a wild river become more and more precious to more and more people. It is a good question whether we may not need that silence, space, and solitude for the healing of our raw spirits more than we need surplus cotton and alfalfa, produced for private profit at great public expense.

The objections to reclamation go beyond the obvious fact that reservoirs in desert country lose a substantial amount of their impounded water through surface evaporation; and the equally obvious fact that all such reservoirs eventually silt up and become mud flats ending in concrete waterfalls; and the further fact that an occasional dam, because of faulty siting or construction, will go out, as the Teton Dam went out in 1976, bringing disaster to people, towns, and fields below. They go beyond the fact that underground water, recklessly pumped, is quickly depleted, and that some of it will be renewed only in geological time, and that the management of underground water and that of surface water are necessarily linked. The ultimate objection is that irrigation agriculture itself, in deserts where surface evaporation is extreme, has a limited though unpredictable life. Marc Reisner predicts that in the next half century as much irrigated land will go out of production as the Bureau of Reclamation has "reclaimed" in its whole history.

Over time, salts brought to the surface by constant flooding and evaporation poison the soil: the ultimate, natural end of an irrigated field in arid country is an alkali flat. That was the end of fields in every historic irrigation civilization except Egypt, where, until the Aswan Dam, the annual Nile flood leached away salts and renewed the soil with fresh silt.

Leaching can sometimes be managed if you have enough sweet water and a place to put the runoff. But there is rarely water enough—the water is already 125 percent allocated and 100 percent used—and what water is available is often itself saline from having run through other fields upstream and having brought their salts back to the river. Colorado River water near the headwaters at Grand Lake is 200 parts per million (ppm) salt. Below the Wellton-Mohawk District on the Gila it is 6,300 ppm salt. The 1.5 million acre-feet that we are pledged to deliver to Mexico is so saline that we are having to build a desalinization plant to sweeten it before we send it across the border.

Furthermore, even if you have enough water for occasional leaching, you have to have somewhere to drain off the waste water, which is likely not only to be saline, but to be contaminated with fertilizers, pesticides, and poisonous trace minerals such as selenium. Kesterson Reservoir, in the Central Valley near Los Banos, is a recent notorious instance, whose two-headed, three-legged, or merely dead waterfowl publicized the dangers of draining waste water off into a slough. If it is drained off into a river, or out to sea, the results are not usually so dramatic. But the inedible fish of the New River draining into the Salton Sea, and the periodically polluted beaches of Monterey Bay near the mouth of the Salinas River, demonstrate that agricultural runoff is poison anywhere.

The West's irrigated bounty is not forever, not on the scale or at the rate we have been gathering it in. The part of it that is dependent on wells is even more precarious than that dependent on dams. In California's San Joaquin Valley, streams and dams supply only 60 percent of the demand for water; the rest is pumped from wells—hundreds and thousands of wells. Pumping exceeds replenishment by a half trillion gallons a year. In places the water table has been pumped down three hundred feet; in places the ground itself has sunk thirty feet or more. But with those facts known, and an end clearly in sight, nobody is willing to stop, and there is as yet no state regulation of groundwater pumping.

In Arizona the situation is if anything worse. Ninety percent of Arizona's irrigation depends on pumping. And in Nebraska and Kansas and Oklahoma, old Dust Bowl country, they prepare for the next dust bowl, which is as inevitable as sunrise though a little harder to time, by pumping away the groundwater through center-pivot sprinklers.

Add to the facts about irrigation the fact of the oversubscribing of rivers. The optimists say that when more water is needed, the engineers will find a way—"augmentation" from the Columbia or elsewhere for the Colorado's overdrawn reservoirs, or the implementation of cosmic schemes such as NAWAPA (North American Water and Power Alliance), which would dam all the Canadian rivers up against the east face of the Rockies, and from that Mediterranean-sized reservoir supply water to every needy district from Minneapolis to Yuma. I think that there are geological as well as political difficulties in the way of water redistribution on that scale. The solution of western problems does not lie in more grandiose engineering.

Throw into the fact barrel, finally, a 1983 report from the Council on Environmental Quality concluding that desertification—the process of converting a viable arid-lands ecology into a lifeless waste—proceeds faster in the western United States than in Africa. Some of that desertification is the result of overgrazing, but the salinization of fields does its bit. When the hydraulic society falls back from its outermost frontiers, it will have done its part in the creation of new deserts.

The hydraulic society. I borrow the term from Donald Worster, who borrowed it from Karl Wittvogel. Wittvogel's studies convinced him that every hydraulic society is by necessity an autocracy. Power, he thought, inevitably comes to reside in the elite that understands and exercises control over water. He quotes C. S. Lewis: "What we call man's power over nature turns out to be a power exercised by some men over other men with nature as its instrument" (*The Abolition of Man,* p. 35); and André Gorz: "The total domination of nature inevitably entails a domination of people by the techniques of domination" (*Ecology as Politics,* p. 20). Those quotations suggest a very different approach from the human domination advocated by such as John Widtsoe.

The hydraulic society involves the maximum domination of nature. And the American West, Worster insists, is the greatest hydraulic society the world ever saw, far surpassing in its techniques of domination the societies on the Indus, the Tigris-Euphrates, or the Yellow River. The West, which Walter Webb and Bernard DeVoto both feared might remain a colonial dependency of the East, has instead become an empire and gotten the East to pay most of the bills.

The case as Worster puts it is probably overstated. There are, one hopes, more democratic islands than he allows for, more areas outside the domination of the water managers and users. Few parts of the West are totally controlled by what Worster sees as a hydraulic elite. Nevertheless, no one is likely to mistake the agribusiness West, with most of its power concentrated in the Iron Triangle of growers, politicians, and bureaucratic experts and its work done by a permanent underclass of dispossessed, mainly alien migrants, for the agrarian democracy that the Newlands Act was supposed to create.

John Wesley Powell understood that a degree of land monopoly could easily come about in the West through control of water. A thorough Populist, he advocated cooperative rather than federal waterworks, and he probably never conceived of anything on the imperial scale later realized by the Bureau of Reclamation. But if he were alive today he would have to agree at least partway with Worster: water experts ambitious to build and expand their bureau and perhaps honestly convinced of the worth of what they are doing have allied themselves with landowners and politicians, and by making land monopoly through water control immensely profitable for their backers, they have made it inevitable.

How profitable? Worster cites figures from one of the most recent of the mammoth projects, the Westlands, that brought water to the western side of the San Joaquin Valley. Including interest over forty years, the cost to the taxpayers was $3 billion. Water is delivered to the beneficiaries, mostly large landholders, at $7.50 an acre-foot—far below actual cost, barely enough to pay operation and maintenance costs. According to a study conducted by economists Philip LaVeen and George Goldman, the subsidy amounted to $2,200 an acre, $352,000 per quarter section—and very few quarter-section family farmers were among the beneficiaries. Large landholders obliged by the 160-acre limitation to dispose of their excess lands disposed of them to family members and cronies, paper farmers, according to a pattern by now well established among water users.

So much for the Jeffersonian yeoman and the agrarian democracy. As for another problem that Powell foresaw, the difficulty that a family would have in handling even 160 acres of intensively farmed irrigated land, both the corporate and the family farmers solve it the same way: with migrant labor, much of it illegally recruited below the Rio Grande. It is anybody's guess what will happen now that Congress has passed the Immigration Reform and Control Act, but up to the present the border has been a sieve, carefully kept open from this side. On a recent rafting trip through the Big Bend canyons of the Rio Grande, my son twice surprised sheepdog functionaries herding Mexican hopefuls to safety in America.

Those hopefuls are visible not merely in California and Texas, but pretty much throughout the West. Visiting Rigby, Idaho, up in the farming country below the washed-out Teton Dam, I found a shantytown where the universal language was Spanish. Wherever there are jobs to do, especially laborious or dirty jobs—picking crops, killing turkeys—there have been aliens brought in to do them. Like drug running, the importation of illegals has resulted from a strong, continuing American demand, most of it from the factories in the fields of the hydraulic society. One has to wonder if penalties for such importations will inhibit growers any more than the 160-acre limitation historically did.

Marc Reisner, in *Cadillac Desert,* is less concerned with the social consequences than with the costs and environmental losses and the plain absurdities of our long battle with aridity.

> Only a government that disposes of a billion dollars every few hours would still be selling water in deserts for less than a penny a ton. And only an agency as antediluvian as the Bureau of Reclamation, hiding in a government as elephantine as ours, could successfully camouflage the enormous losses the taxpayer has to bear for its generosity. (P. 500)

Charles P. Berkey of Columbia University, a hydrologist, wrote in 1946,

The United States has virtually set up an empire on impounded and re-distributed water. The nation is encourag-
ing development, on a scale never before attempted, of
lands that are almost worthless except for the water that
can be delivered to them by the works of man. There is
building up, through settlement and new population, a
line of industries foreign to the normal resources of the
region. . . . One can claim (and it is true) that much has
been added to the world; but the longer-range view in this
field, as in many others, is threatened by apparently incur-
able ailments and this one of slowly choking to death with
silt is the most stubborn of all. There are no permanent
cures. (Letter quoted in Raphael Kazmann, *Modern Hydrology,* p. 124)

Kazmann himself agrees:

The reservoir construction program, objectively considered, is really a program for the continued and endless
expenditure of ever-increasing sums of public money to
combat the effects of geologic forces, as these forces strive
to reach positions of relative equilibrium in the region of
rivers and the flow of water. It may be that future research
in the field of modern hydrology will be primarily to find
a method of extricating ourselves from this unequal struggle with minimum loss to the nation. (*Modern Hydrology,*
p. 125)

And Donald Worster pronounces the benediction: ''The
next stage after empire is decline.'' The West, aware of its own
history, might phrase it differently: The next stage after boom
is bust. Again.

What should one make of facts as depressing as these? What do
such facts do to the self-gratifying image of the West as the

home of freedom, independence, largeness, spaciousness, and of the Westerner as total self-reliance on a white stallion? I confess they make this Westerner yearn for the old days on the Milk and the Missouri when those rivers ran free, and we were trying to learn how to live with the country, and the country seemed both hard and simple, and the world and I were young, when irrigation had not yet grown beyond its legitimate bounds and the West provided for its thin population a hard living but a wonderful life.

Sad to say, they make me admit, when I face them, that the West is no more the Eden that I once thought it than the Garden of the World that the boosters and engineers tried to make it; and that neither nostalgia nor boosterism can any longer make a case for it as the geography of hope.

VARIATIONS ON A THEME BY CRÈVECOEUR

There are many kinds of wildernesses, Aldo Leopold wrote in *A Sand County Almanac,* and each kind forces on people a different set of adaptations and creates a different pattern of life, custom, and belief. These patterns we call cultures.

By that criterion, the West should have a different cultural look from other American regions, and within the regional culture there should be discernible a half dozen subcultures stemming from our adaptations to shortgrass plains, alpine mountains, slickrock canyons, volcanic scablands, and both high and low deserts.

But cultural differentiation takes a long time, and happens most completely in isolation and to homogeneous peoples, as it happened to the Paiutes. The West has had neither time nor isolation nor homogeneity of race and occupation. Change, both homegrown and imported, has overtaken time, time and again. We have to adapt not only to our changed physical environment but to our own adaptations, and sometimes we have to backtrack from our own mistakes.

Cultures evolving within heterogeneous populations do not grow steadily from definable quality to definable quality. Not only is their development complicated by class, caste, and social mobility, but they undergo simultaneous processes of erosion and deposition. They start from something, not from nothing. Habits and attitudes that have come to us embedded in our inherited culture, especially our inherited language, come incorporated in everything from nursery rhymes to laws and prayers, and they often have the durability of flint pebbles in puddingstone. No matter how completely their old matrix is dissolved, they remain intact, and are deposited almost unchanged in the strata of the new culture.

The population that for the eleven public-lands states and territories was four million in 1900 was forty-five million in 1984, with at least a couple of million more, and perhaps twice that many, who weren't counted and didn't want to be. Many of those forty-five or forty-seven or forty-nine million came yesterday, since the end of World War II. They have not adapted, in the cultural sense, very completely. Some of them are living anonymously in the Spanish-speaking barrios of San Diego, El Paso, Los Angeles, San Jose, where the Immigration Service can't find them. Some are experimenting with quick-change life-styles in the cultural confusion of western cities. Some are reading *Sunset Magazine* to find out what they should try to become. Some think they already know, from the movies and TV.

Being a Westerner is not simple. If you live, say, in Los Angeles, you live in the second-largest city in the nation, urban as far as the eye can see in every direction except west. There is, or was in 1980—the chances would be somewhat greater now—a 6.6 percent chance that you are Asian, a 16.7 percent chance that you are black, and a 27 percent chance that you are Hispanic. You have only a 48 percent chance of being a non-Hispanic white.

This means that instead of being suitable for casting in the cowboy and pioneer roles familiar from the mythic and movie West, you may be one of those "Chinks" or "Spics" or "Greasers" for whom the legendary West had a violent contempt. You'd like to be a hero, and you may adopt the costume and attitudes you admire, but your color or language or the slant of your eyes tells you that you are one of the kind once scheduled to be a villain or a victim, and your current status as second-class citizen confirms that view. You're part of a subculture envious of or hostile to the dominant one.

This ethnic and cultural confusion exists not only in Los Angeles but in varying proportions in every western city and many western towns. Much of the adaptation that is going on is adaptation to an uncertain reality or to a reality whose past and present do not match. The western culture and western character with which it is easiest to identify exist largely in the West of make-believe, where they can be kept simple.

As invaders, we were rarely, or only temporarily, dependent on the materials, foods, or ideas of the regions we pioneered. The champagne and oysters that cheered midnight suppers during San Francisco's Gold Rush period were not local, nor was the taste that demanded them. The dominant white culture was always aware of its origins; it brought its origins with it across the plains or around the Horn, and it kept in touch with them.

The Spanish of New Mexico, who also brought their origins with them, are in other ways an exception. Settled at the end of the sixteenth century, before Jamestown and Quebec and well before the Massachusetts Bay Colony, New Mexico existed in isolation, dependent largely on itself, until the newer Americans forcibly took it over in 1846; and during those two and a half centuries it had a high Indian culture close at hand to teach it how to live with the country. Culturally, the Spanish Southwest is an island, adapted in its own ways, in many ways alien.

By contrast, the Anglo-American West, barely breached until

the middle of the nineteenth century, was opened during a time of rapid communication. It was linked with the world by ship, rail, and telegraph before the end of the 1860s, and the isolation of even its brief, explosive outposts, its Alder Gulches and Cripple Creeks, was anything but total. Excited travelers reported the West in words to match its mountains; it was viewed in Currier and Ives prints drawn by enthusiasts who had never been there except in imagination. The outside never got over its heightened and romantic notion of the West. The West never got over its heightened and romantic notion of itself.

The pronounced differences that some people see between the West and other parts of America need to be examined. Except as they involve Spanish or Indian cultures, they could be mainly illusory, the result of the tendency to see the West in its mythic enlargement rather than as it is, and of the corollary tendency to take our cues from myths in the effort to enhance our lives. Life does sometimes copy art. Not only drugstore cowboys and street-corner Kit Carsons succumb. Plenty of authentic ranch hands have read pulp Westerns in the shade of the bunkhouse and got up walking, talking, and thinking like Buck Duane or Hopalong Cassidy.

No matter what kind of wilderness it developed in, every part of the real West was a melting-pot mixture of people from everywhere, operating under the standard American drives of restlessness, aggressiveness, and great expectations, and with the standard American freedom that often crossed the line into violence. It was supposed to be a democracy, and at least in the sense that it was often every man for himself, it was. Though some of its phases—the fur trade, the gold rushes, the open-range cattle industry—lasted hardly longer than the blink of an eye, other phases—logging, irrigation farming, the stock farm with cattle or sheep—have lasted by now for a century or more, and have formed the basis for a number of relatively stable communities with some of the attributes of place, some identity as subcultures of the prevailing postfrontier culture of America. If Turner's thesis is applicable beyond the 98th meridian, then the West ought to be, with minor local variations, America only more so.

Actually it is and it isn't. It would take fast footwork to dance the society based on big reclamation projects into a democracy. Even the cattle kingdom from which we derive our most individualistic and independent folk hero was never a democracy as the Middle West, say, was a democracy. The real-life cattle baron was and is about as democratic as a feudal baron. The cowboy in practice was and is an overworked, underpaid hireling, almost as homeless and dispossessed as a modern crop worker, and his fabled independence was and is chiefly the privilege of quitting his job in order to go looking for another just as bad. Some went outside the law. There is a discrepancy between the real conditions of the West, which even among outlaws enforced cooperation and group effort, and the folklore of the West, which celebrated the dissidence of dissent, the most outrageous independence.

The dynamics of contemporary adaptation work ambiguously. The best imitators of frontier individualism these days are probably Silicon Valley and conglomerate executives, whose entrepreneurial attributes are not greatly different from those of an old-time cattle baron. Little people must salve with daydreams and fantasy the wounds of living. Some may imagine themselves becoming captains of industry, garage inventors whose inventions grow into Fortune 500 companies overnight; but I think that more of them are likely to cuddle up to a culture hero independent of the system and even opposed to it—a culture hero given them by Owen Wister, an eastern snob who saw in the common cowherd the lineaments of Lancelot. Chivalry, or the daydream of it, is at least as common among daydreamers as among entrepreneurs.

. . .

Physically, the West could only be itself. Its scale, its colors, its landforms, its plants and animals, tell a traveler what country he is in, and a native that he is at home. Even western cities owe most of their distinctiveness to their physical setting. Albuquerque with its mud-colored houses spreading like clay banks along the valley of the Rio Grande could only be New Mexico. Denver's ringworm suburbs on the apron of the Front Range could only be boom-time Colorado. Salt Lake City bracing back against the Wasatch and looking out toward the dead sea and the barren ranges could only be the Great Basin.

But is anything except their setting distinctive? The people in them live on streets named Main and State, Elm and Poplar, First and Second, like Americans elsewhere. They eat the same Wheaties and Wonder Bread and Big Macs, watch the same ball games and soaps and sitcoms on TV, work at the same industrial or service jobs, suffer from the same domestic crises and industrial blights, join the same health clubs and neighborhood protective associations, and in general behave and misbehave much as they would in Omaha or Chicago or East Orange. The homogenizing media have certainly been at work on them, perhaps with more effect than the arid spaciousness of the region itself, and while making them more like everybody else have also given them misleading clues about who they are.

"Who is the American, this new man?" Crèvecoeur asked rhetorically in his *Letters from an American Farmer* more than two hundred years ago, and went on to idealize him as the American farmer—industrious, optimistic, upwardly mobile, family-oriented, socially responsible, a new man given new hope in the new world, a lover of both hearth and earth, a builder of communities. He defined him in the terms of a new freedom, emancipated from feudalism, oppression, and poverty, but with no wish to escape society or its responsibilities. Quite the contrary.

Crèvecoeur also sketched, with distaste, another kind of American, a kind he thought would fade away with the raw frontier that had created him. This kind lived alone or with a slattern woman and a litter of kids out in the woods. He had no fixed abode, tilled no ground or tilled it only fitfully, lived by killing, was footloose, uncouth, antisocial, impatient of responsibility and law. The eating of wild meat, Crèvecoeur said, made him ferocious and gloomy. Too much freedom promoted in him a coarse selfishness and a readiness to violence.

The pioneer farmer as Crèvecoeur conceived him has a place in western history, and as the Jeffersonian yeoman he had a prominent place in the mistaken effort that oversettled the West, first by homestead and later by reclamation. Traces of him are to be found in western literature, art, and myth. Sculptors have liked his sturdy figure plodding beside the covered wagon on which ride his poke-bonneted wife and his barefoot children. He strides through a lot of WPA murals. The Mormons, farmers in the beginning, idealize him. He has achieved more than life size in such novels of the migration as *The Covered Wagon* and *The Way West*.

But those, as I have already suggested, are novels more of motion than of place, and the emigrants in them are simply farmer-pioneers on their way to new farms. They have not adapted to the West in the slightest degree. They belong where the soil is deep, where the Homestead Act worked, where settlers planted potato peelings in their fireguards and adjourned to build a combination school–church–social hall almost before they had roofs on their shanties. The pioneer farmer is a midwestern, not a western, figure. He is a pedestrian, and in the West, horseman's country even for people who never got on a horse in their lives, pedestrians suffer from the horseman's contempt that seems as old as the Scythians. The farmer's very virtues as responsible husband, father, and home builder are against him as a figure of the imagination. To the fantasizing mind he is dull, the ancestor of the clodhopper, the hayseed, and the hick. I have heard Wyoming ranch hands jeer their relatives from Idaho, not because the relatives were Mormons—so were the ranch hands—but because they were farmers, potato diggers.

It was Crèvecoeur's wild man, the borderer emancipated into total freedom, first in eastern forests and then in the plains and mountains of the West, who really fired our imaginations, and still does. We have sanitized him somewhat, but our principal folk hero, in all his shapes, good and bad, is essentially antisocial.

In real life, as Boone, Bridger, Jed Smith, Kit Carson, he appeals to us as having lived a life of heroic courage, skill, and self-reliance. Some of his manifestations, such as Wild Bill Hickok and Buffalo Bill Cody, are tainted with outlawry or showmanship, but they remain more than life-size. Even psychopathic killers such as Billy the Kid and Tom Horn throw a long shadow, and some outlaws, such as Butch Cassidy and Harry Longabaugh, have all the engaging imitability of Robin Hood. What charms us in them is partly their daring, skill, and invulnerability, partly their chivalry; but not to be overlooked is their impatience with all restraint, their freedom from the social responsibility that Crèvecoeur admired in his citizen-farmer, and that on occasion bows the shoulders of every man born.

Why should I stand up for civilization? Thoreau asked a lecture audience. Any burgher or churchwarden would stand up for that. Thoreau chose instead to stand up for wildness and the savage heart.

We all know that impulse. When youths run away from home, they don't run away to become farmers. They run away to become romantic isolates, lone riders who slit their eyes against steely distance and loosen the carbine in its scabbard when they see law, or obligation, or even company, approaching.

Lawlessness, like wildness, is attractive, and we conceive the last remaining home of both to be the West. In a folklore predominantly masculine and macho, even women take on the look. Calamity Jane is more familiar to us than Dame Shirley, though Dame Shirley had it all over Jane in brains, and could have matched her in courage, and lived in mining camps every bit as rough as the cow towns and camps that Calamity Jane frequented. But then, Jane grew up in the shortgrass West, Dame Shirley in Massachusetts.

The attraction of lawlessness did not die with the frontier, either. Look at the survivalist Claude Dallas, who a few years ago killed two Idaho game wardens when they caught him poaching—shot them and then finished them off with a bullet in the back of the head. In that act of unchivalrous violence Dallas was expressing more than an unwillingness to pay a little fine. For months, until he was captured early in 1987, he hid out in the deserts of Idaho and Nevada, protected by people all over the area. Why did they protect him? Because his belated frontiersman style, his total self-reliance and physical competence, his repudiation of any control, appealed to them more than murder repelled them or law enlisted their support.

All this may seem remote from the life of the average Westerner, who lives in a city and is more immediately concerned with taxes, schools, his job, drugs, the World Series, or even disarmament, than with archetypal figures out of folklore. But it is not so remote as it seems. Habits persist. The hoodlums who come to San Francisco to beat up gays are vigilantes, enforcing their prejudices with violence, just as surely as were the miners who used to hunt down Indians and hang Chinese in the Mother Lode, or the ranchers who rode out to exterminate the nesters in Wyoming's Johnson County War.

Habits persist. The hard, aggressive, single-minded energy

that according to politicians made America great is demonstrated every day in resource raids and leveraged takeovers by entrepreneurs; and along with that competitive individualism and ruthlessness goes a rejection of any controlling past or tradition. What matters is here, now, the seizable opportunity. "We don't need any history," said one Silicon Valley executive when the Santa Clara County Historical Society tried to bring the electronics industry together with the few remaining farmers to discuss what was happening to the valley that only a decade or two ago was the fruit bowl of the world. "What we need is more attention to our computers and the moves of the competition."

We are not so far from our models, real and fictional, as we think. As on a wild river, the water passes, the waves remain. A high degree of mobility, a degree of ruthlessness, a large component of both self-sufficiency and self-righteousness, mark the historical pioneer, the lone-riding folk hero, and the modern businessman intent on opening new industrial frontiers and getting his own in the process. The same qualities inform the extreme individualists who believe that they belong to nothing except what they choose to belong to, those who try on lifestyles as some try on clothes, whose only communal association is with what Robert Bellah calls "life-style enclaves," casual and temporary groupings of the like-minded. One reason why it is so difficult to isolate any definitely western culture is that so many Westerners, like other Americans only more so, shy away from commitment. Mobility of every sort—physical, familial, social, corporate, occupational, religious, sexual—confirms and reinforces the illusion of independence.

Back to the freedom-loving loner, whom we might call Leatherstocking's descendant, as Henry Nash Smith taught us to, if all that tribe were not childless as well as orphaned. In the West this figure acquired an irresistible costume—the boots, spurs, chaps, and sombrero bequeathed to him by Mexican vaqueros, plus the copper-riveted canvas pants invented for California miners by a peddler named Levi Strauss—but he remained estranged from real time, real place, and any real society or occupation. In fact, it is often organized society, in the shape of a crooked sheriff and his cronies, that this loner confronts and confounds.

The notion of civilization's corruption, the notion that the conscience of an antisocial savage is less calloused than the conscience of society, is of course a bequest from Jean-Jacques Rousseau. The chivalry of the antisocial one, his protectiveness of the weak and oppressed, especially those whom James Fenimore Cooper customarily referred to as "females," is from Cooper, with reinforcement from two later romantics, Frederic Remington and Owen Wister, collaborators in the creation of the knight-errant in chaps.

The hero of Wister's 1902 novel *The Virginian* is gentle-seeming, easygoing, humorous, but when the wicked force him into action he is the very gun of God, better at violence than the wicked are. He is a daydream of glory made flesh. But note that the Virginian not only defeats Trampas in a gunfight as formalized as a fourteenth-century joust, the first of a thousand literary and movie walk-downs, but he also joins the vigilantes and in the name of law and order acts as jury, judge, and hangman for his friend Shorty, who has gone bad and become a rustler.

The Virginian feels sorry about Shorty, but he never questions that the stealing of a few mavericks should be punished by death, any more than Wister questioned the motives of his Wyoming rancher host who led the Johnson County vigilantes against the homesteaders they despised and called rustlers. This culture hero is himself law. Law is whatever he and his companions (and employers) believe (which means law is his and their self-interest). Whatever action he takes is law enforcement. Compare Larry McMurtry's two former Texas Rangers in *Lonesome Dove*. They kill more people than all the outlaws in that book put together do, but their killings are *right*. Their lawlessness is justified by the lack of any competing socialized law, and by a supreme confidence in themselves, as if every judgment of theirs could be checked back to Coke and Blackstone, if not to Leviticus.

Critics have noted that in *The Virginian* (and for that matter in most of its successors, though not in *Lonesome Dove*) there are no scenes involving cattle. There is no manure, no punching of postholes or stringing of barbed wire, none of the branding, castrating, dehorning, dipping, and horseshoeing that real cowboys, hired men on horseback, spend their laborious and unromantic lives at. The physical universe is simplified like the moral one. Time is stopped.

The Virginian is the standard American orphan, dislocated from family, church, and place of origin, with an uncertain past identified only by his nickname. With his knightly sense of honor and his capacity to outviolence the violent, he remains an irresistible model for romantic adolescents of any age, and he transfers readily from the cowboy setting to more modern ones. It is only a step from his "When you call me that, smile" to the remark made famous by a recent mayor of Carmel and by the fortieth president of the United States: "Go ahead, make my day."

There are thousands more federal employees in the West than there are cowboys—more bookkeepers, aircraft and electronics workers, auto mechanics, printers, fry cooks. There may be more writers. Nevertheless, when most Americans east of the Missouri—most people in the world—hear the word "West" they think "cowboy." Recently a documentary filmmaker asked me to be a consultant on a film that would finally reveal the true West, without romanticizing or adornment. It was to be done by chronicling the life of a single real-life individual. Guess who he was. A cowboy, and a rodeo cowboy at that—a man who had run away from his home in Indiana at the age of seventeen, worked for a year on a Texas ranch, found the work hard, made his way onto the rodeo circuit, and finally retired with a lot of his vertebrae out of line to an Oklahoma town, where he made silver-mounted saddles and bridles suitable for the Sheriff's Posse in a Frontier Days parade and spun yarns for the wide-eyed local young.

Apart from the fantasy involved, which is absolutely authentic, that show business life is about as typically western as a bullfighter's is typically Spanish. The critics will probably praise the film for its realism.

I spend this much time on a mythic figure who has irritated me all my life because I would obviously like to bury him. But I know I can't. He is a faster gun than I am. He is too attractive to the daydreaming imagination. It gets me nowhere to object to the self-righteous, limited, violent code that governs him, or to disparage the novels of Louis L'Amour because they were mass-produced with interchangeable parts. Mr. L'Amour sells in the millions, and at times has readers in the White House.

But what one can say, and be sure of, is that even while the cowboy myth romanticizes and falsifies western life, it says something true about western, and hence about American, character.

Western culture and character, hard to define in the first place because they are only half-formed and constantly changing, are further clouded by the mythic stereotype. Why hasn't the stereotype faded away as real cowboys became less and less typical of western life? Because we can't or won't do without it, obviously. But also there is the visible, pervasive fact of western space, which acts as a preservative. Space, itself the product of incorrigible aridity and hence more or less permanent, continues to suggest unrestricted freedom, unlimited opportunity for testings and heroisms, a continuing need for self-reliance and physical competence. The untrammeled individualist persists partly as a residue of the real and romantic frontiers, but also partly because runaways from more restricted regions keep reimporting him. The stereotype continues to affect romantic Westerners and non-Westerners in romantic ways, but if I am right it also affects real Westerners in real ways.

In the West it is impossible to be unconscious of or indifferent to space. At every city's edge it confronts us as federal lands kept open by aridity and the custodial bureaus; out in the boondocks it engulfs us. And it does contribute to individualism, if only because in that much emptiness people have the dignity of rareness and must do much of what they do without help, and because self-reliance becomes a social imperative, part of a code. Witness the crudely violent code that governed a young Westerner like Norman Maclean, as he reported it in the stories of *A River Runs Through It*. Witness the way in which space haunts the poetry of such western poets as William Stafford, Richard Hugo, Gary Snyder. Witness the lonely, halfattached childhood of a writer such as Ivan Doig. I feel the childhood reported in his *This House of Sky* because it is so much like my own.

Even in the cities, even among the dispossessed migrants of the factories in the fields, space exerts a diluted influence as illusion and reprieve. Westerners live outdoors more than people elsewhere because outdoors is mainly what they've got. For clerks and students, factory workers and mechanics, the outdoors is freedom, just as surely as it is for the folkloric and mythic figures. They don't have to own the outdoors, or get permission, or cut fences, in order to use it. It is public land, partly theirs, and that space is a continuing influence on their minds and senses. It encourages a fatal carelessness and destructiveness because it seems so limitless and because what is everybody's is nobody's responsibility. It also encourages, in some, an impassioned protectiveness: the battlegrounds of the environmental movement lie in the western public lands. Finally, it promotes certain needs, tastes, attitudes, skills. It is those tastes, attitudes, and skills, as well as the prevailing destructiveness and its corrective, love of the land, that relate real Westerners to the myth.

David Rains Wallace, in *The Wilder Shore,* has traced the effect of the California landscape—the several California landscapes from the Pacific shore to the inner deserts—on California writers. From Dana to Didion, the influence has been varied and powerful. It is there in John Muir ecstatically riding a storm in the top of a two-hundred-foot sugar pine; in Mary Austin quietly absorbing wisdom from a Paiute basketmaker; in Jack London's Nietzschean supermen pitting themselves not only against society but against the universe; in Frank Norris's atavistic McTeague, shackled to a corpse that he drags through the 130-degree heat of Death Valley; and in Robinson Jeffers on his stone platform between the stars and the sea, falling in love outward toward space. It is also there in the work of western photographers, notably Ansel Adams, whose grand, manless images are full of the awe men feel in the face of majestic nature. Awe is common in that California tradition. Humility is not.

Similar studies could be made, and undoubtedly will be, of the literature of other parts of the West, and of special groups of writers such as Native Americans who are mainly western. The country lives, still holy, in Scott Momaday's *Way to Rainy Mountain.* It is there like a half-forgotten promise in Leslie Marmon Silko's *Ceremony,* and like a homeland lost to invaders in James Welch's *Winter in the Blood* and Louise Erdrich's *Love Medicine.* It is a dominating presence, as I have already said, in the work of Northwest writers.

Western writing turns out, not surprisingly, to be largely about things that happen outdoors. It often involves characters who show a family resemblance of energetic individualism, great physical competence, stoicism, determination, recklessness, endurance, toughness, rebelliousness, resistance to control. It has, that is, residual qualities of the heroic, as the country in which it takes place has residual qualities of the wilderness frontier.

Those characteristics are not the self-conscious creation of regional patriotism, or the result of imitation of older by younger, or greater by lesser, writers. They are inescapable; western life and space generate them; they are what the faithful mirror shows. When I wrote *The Big Rock Candy Mountain* I was ignorant of almost everything except what I myself had lived, and I had no context for that. By the time I wrote *Wolf Willow,* a dozen years later, and dealt with some of the same experience from another stance, I began to realize that my Bo Mason was a character with relatives throughout western fiction. I could see in him resemblance to Ole Rölvaag's Per Hansa, to Mari San-doz's Old Jules, to A. B. Guthrie's Boone Caudill, even to the hard-jawed and invulnerable heroes of the myth. But I had not been copying other writers. I had been trying to paint a portrait of my father, and it happened that my father, an observed and particular individual, was also a type—a very western type.

Nothing suggests the separateness of western experience so clearly as the response to it of critics nourished in the Europe-oriented, politicized, sophisticated, and antiheroic tradition of between-the-wars and postwar New York. Edmund Wilson, commenting on Hollywood writers, thought of them as wreathed in sunshine and bougainvillea, "spelling cat for the unlettered"; or as sentimental toughs, the boys in the back room; or as Easterners of talent (Scott Fitzgerald was his prime example) lost to significant achievement and drowning in the La Brea tar pits.

Leslie Fiedler, an exponent of the *Partisan Review* subculture, came west to teach in Missoula in the 1950s and discovered "the Montana face"—strong, grave, silent, bland, untroubled by thought, the face of a man playing a role invented for him two centuries earlier and a continent-and-ocean away by a French romantic philosopher.

Bernard Malamud, making a similar pilgrimage to teach at

Oregon State University in Corvallis, found the life of that little college town intolerable, and retreated from it to write it up in the novel *A New Life*. His Gogolian antihero S. Levin, an intellectual, heir to a thousand years of caution, deviousness, spiritual subtlety, and airless city living, was never at home in Corvallis. The faculty he was thrown among were suspiciously open, overfriendly, overhearty, outdoorish. Instead of a commerce in abstract ideas, Levin found among his colleagues a devotion to fly-fishing that simply bewildered him. Grown men!

If he had waited to write his novel until Norman Maclean had written the stories of *A River Runs Through It*, Malamud would have discovered that fly-fishing is not simply an art but a religion, a code of conduct and a language, a way of telling the real from the phony. And if Ivan Doig had written before Leslie Fiedler shook up Missoula by the ears, Fiedler would have had another view of the Montana face. It looks different, depending on whether you encounter it as a bizarre cultural artifact on a Montana railroad platform, or whether you see it as young Ivan Doig saw the face of his dependable, skilled, likable, rootless sheepherder father. Whether, that is, you see it from outside the culture or from inside.

In spite of the testimony of Fiedler and Malamud, if I were advising a documentary filmmaker where he might get the most quintessential West in a fifty-six-minute can, I would steer him away from broken-down rodeo riders, away from the towns of the energy boom, away from the cities, and send him to just such a little city as Missoula or Corvallis, some settlement that has managed against difficulty to make itself into a place and is likely to remain one. It wouldn't hurt at all if this little city had a university in it to keep it in touch with its cultural origins and conscious of its changing cultural present. It would do no harm if an occasional Leslie Fiedler came through to stir up its provincialism and set it to some self-questioning. It wouldn't hurt if some native-born writer, some Doig or Hugo or Maclean or Welch or Kittredge or Raymond Carver, was around to serve as culture hero——the individual who transcends his culture without abandoning it, who leaves for a while in search of opportunity and enlargement but never forgets where he left his heart.

It is in places like these, and through individuals like these, that the West will realize itself, if it ever does: these towns and cities still close to the earth, intimate and interdependent in their shared community, shared optimism, and shared memory. These are the seedbeds of an emergent western culture. They are likely to be there when the agribusiness fields have turned to alkali flats and the dams have silted up, when the waves of overpopulation that have been destroying the West have receded, leaving the stickers to get on with the business of adaptation.

A CAPSULE
HISTORY OF
CONSERVATION

Values, both those that we approve and those that we don't, have roots as deep as creosote rings, and live as long, and grow as slowly. Every action is an idea before it is an action, and perhaps a feeling before it is an idea, and every idea rests upon other ideas that have preceded it in time. The modern environmental movement, though it has shifted its emphasis from preservation of precious resources to the control of pollution caused by our industrial and agricultural practices, declares our dependence on the earth and our responsibility to it, and thus derives pretty directly from the nineteenth-century travelers, philosophers, artists, writers, divines, natural historians, and what *Time* has called "upper-class bird-watchers" whose purpose was to know it, celebrate it, and savor its beauty and rightness.

Yes, there was an environmental movement before Earth Day, a long, slow revolution in values of which contemporary environmentalism is a consequence and a continuation. We are still in transition from the notion of man as master of the earth to the notion of man as a part of it.

Our sanction to be a weed species living at the expense of every other species and of the earth itself can be found in the injunction God gave to newly created Adam and Eve in Genesis 1:28: "Be fruitful, and multiply, and replenish the earth, and subdue it." Whether or not God meant it in quite that way, and whether or not men translated Him correctly, many used these words as justification to make the earth serve human purposes alone. But what we are working toward, what with luck we may eventually attain to, is an outlook that was frequently and sometimes eloquently expressed by the first inhabitants of this continent. The Indians stressed the web of life, the interconnectedness of land and man and creature. Chief Luther Standing Bear of the Oglala Sioux put it this way: "Only to the white man was nature a wilderness and only to him was the land 'infested' with 'wild' animals and 'savage' people. To us it was tame. Earth was bountiful and we were surrounded with the blessings of the Great Mystery."

The New World was such a blinding opportunity to Europeans, and lay there so temptingly, like an unlocked treasure house with the watchman sleeping, that nobody thought of limits, nobody thought of preservation, until generations of living in America and "breaking" its wilderness had taught us to know it, and knowing it had taught us to love it, and loving it had taught us to question what we were doing to it. All of that is the background of the environmental movement.

It took us two hundred years from Jamestown and Plymouth Rock to Americanize our perceptions, loyalties, vocabulary, and palette so that we could begin to see America clearly, and take pride in it. New ideas from Europe, especially the interest in nature that came with the Romantic movement, helped that pride along. But what made America the natural garden of those ideas, what most metamorphosed Europeans into something new, was what Europe had long lost and what America was made of: wilderness.

The seventeenth-century settlers did not look on wilderness

with the eyes of a 1990 Sierra Club backpacker. Our wilderness is safe, theirs was not. Our wilderness is islands in a tamed continent, theirs was one vast wild space, totally unknown, prowled by God-knew-what wild beasts and wild men. In New England they also feared it as the trysting place of witches and devils. Even without devils, the struggle to survive fully occupied the first generation or two, and survival meant, in man's version of God's word, "subduing" the wild earth. Nobody questioned the value of that effort. Civilization was a good; wilderness was what had to be subdued to create the human habitations that looked like progress and triumph even when they were only huts in a stump field.

To the boosters, America was always "prosperous" farms, "smiling" villages, "bustling" towns. But life on the frontier was more often crude and brutal and deprived. Crèvecoeur painted a rosy picture of the established farm and the self-reliant industrious farmer; but he had to admit that out on the edge, beyond the settlements, were those surly, verminous men who lived in dirt-floored cabins with slattern wives and broods of dirty children, sustaining themselves by constant killing of animals and growing ever gloomier and more antisocial by the eating of wild meat. Crèvecoeur thought that as settlement caught up with them they would gradually grow out of their barbarous stage and join the ranks of the happy, prosperous, and civilized.

Maybe some of them did. Maybe some just went farther west when the settlements caught up. No matter which they did, the frontiersman was being built by the popular imagination into an idealized archetypal figure, divorced from Europe, divorced from history, homegrown, a demigod in buckskin. His real-life prototype was Daniel Boone. His larger-than-life fictional version was James Fenimore Cooper's Natty Bumppo, "Leatherstocking," who appeared in the novel *The Pioneers* in 1823 and whose story continued in other novels into the 1840s.

Leatherstocking is everything that any American boy ever

dreamed of being. Far from handsome (looks went with the effete and civilized), he is nevertheless fearless, self-reliant, omnicompetent, a keen tracker and a dead shot, a mortal enemy and the most loyal of friends. He is also the soul of chivalry, protecting and saving Cooper's "females" when they go implausibly astray in the wild woods. An orphan, untutored, Natty has kept the innocence of the natural man. From his brief contact with the Moravians, or from the woods themselves, he has imbibed a noble magnanimity, a sensitivity to beauty, and a deep if unorthodox piety. Homeless in the civilized sense, he has made the wilderness his home, and no witches, devils, or fears assail him there: he feels the presence of God in every leaf. There is not a trace in him of the overcivilized fastidiousness that in the eighteenth century could lead the French novelist Mme. de Staël to draw the curtains of her carriage so as not to see the unkempt scenery of the Alps. Natty glories in the scenery of his woods and mountains, the wilder the better.

But what makes the Leatherstocking Tales significant in this context is that Cooper reveals an ambivalence that will become more common as the nineteenth century careens on, and that is basic to much later environmental thinking. Civilization, on whose side Cooper felt obliged to be, was at war with the wilderness, which he loved. The carriers of civilization in Cooper's novels, the settlers, are often as uncouth and repulsive as they were to Crèvecoeur, and they destroy the beauty and liberty and bounty of the woods.

The same townsmen who throw Natty Bumppo into jail for shooting a deer out of season fire into a passing flock of passenger pigeons with every weapon in town, even cannon, and strew the earth with mutilated flesh and feathers. Wilderness man cannot live with settlement man. Like Daniel Boone when he felt too many people nearby, Natty goes on west, and Cooper's sympathy, as well as the reader's, goes with him. The destructive practices of settlement, which Cooper was among the first to lament ("What will the axemen do, when they have cut their way from sea to sea?"), are only a step behind.

Emerson, like Natty Bumppo, saw God in every manifestation of nature, but he was hardly a forerunner of environmental thinking. He declared America's intellectual independence of Europe, and he cheered the rocky, gritty American character that he saw forming on the frontiers, but he was too much enamored of American self-reliance and energy to fear any consequences; and though he professed a liking for the wild, it was for the wild of the Hudson River School paintings, in which wilderness is the backdrop for a foreground of homely husbandry—a farmer's cottage, a fisherman, a herd wading a stream, a rude mill. The Philosophers' Camp in the Adirondacks, where he and fellow spirits gathered to take walks and hone the art of conversation, was wild enough. It was otherwise with his somewhat prickly protégé, Thoreau.

For Thoreau, wildness was a passion. "In wildness is the preservation of the world," he wrote, and meant it. Repudiating his countrymen's concerns—progress, betterment, accumulation—and their predatory habits in the wild, he made his most characteristic gesture by building a shack on Walden Pond and living in it in spartan circumstances for two years. One cannot imagine him as a hunter; he thought every creature was better alive than dead. He loved and studied, not always accurately but devotedly, the creatures of the woods and rivers and ponds around Concord, Massachusetts. From a rustic American base, he strove to look to the edges of the known world, and beyond. Though his life could have been illustrated by the half-tamed, half-wild landscapes of the Hudson River painters, his imagination could not. It demanded the utterly wild, free scenes of a Bierstadt or a Moran.

Thoreau never personally sought the wilderness. His only

excursions into really wild country were his expeditions into the northern woods. As he said, he had traveled extensively in Concord. Nevertheless Thoreau was at one with Emerson in turning his back on the Old World. Even in an afternoon ramble, he said, the needle always settled west. He must walk toward Oregon, not Europe.

In Thoreau there is virtually every idea that later became gospel to the environmental movement, but it is there only as idea, not as action or call to action—unless withdrawal is action. He was not much of a believer in government, and he was the total opposite of a joiner. American as he was, wilderness-lover as he was, he was not a conservationist or environmentalist in our sense. Nevertheless, as the painter George Catlin had anticipated the national park idea by suggesting a wild prairie reservation, so Thoreau anticipated the more modest urban-open-space idea by suggesting that every community should have its patch of woods where people could refresh themselves. His notion of nature as having healing powers has now the force of revealed truth. And the form of Thoreau's essays—rumination hung upon the framework of an outdoor excursion—has influenced virtually every nature writer since, from Burroughs and Muir to Wendell Berry, Edward Abbey, and Barry Lopez.

Unlike Emerson, Thoreau was not one to search for God or the Oversoul in every natural object, but one senses that he was feeling his way toward an identification with nature not too far from that of the Indians. Yet Thoreau did not articulate the concept of the web, the connectedness of all life. The man who did that was George Perkins Marsh.

Marsh was an extraordinary polymath, an architect, linguist, politician, diplomat, and the first man to work backward, with the aid of history and science and observation, to the point of view that primitives know simply by participation. He was an authority on the Icelandic sagas and on Norse explorations. He served as congressman from Vermont and in this capacity was one of the main proponents of using James Smithson's bequest to create the institution that bears his name. He was minister to Turkey, and for twenty-one years minister plenipotentiary to Italy. All of those real distinctions are now forgotten. What remains is a single book, first published in 1864 as *Man and Nature,* and reissued in revised form in 1874 as *The Earth as Modified by Human Action.* It was the rudest kick in the face that American initiative, optimism, and carelessness had yet received.

Growing up in cutover Vermont, Marsh had observed what deforestation did to streams, fish, birds, animals, the land; and serving for many years in the Mediterranean basin and the Fertile Crescent, he had studied man-made deserts, the barren mountains of Greece, the ruins of once-great civilizations. He saw calamity coming to America and wrote his book "to point out the dangers of imprudence and the necessity of caution in all operations which, on a large scale, interfere with the spontaneous arrangements of the organic or the inorganic world."

Deforestation meant far more than a future shortage of lumber; it meant potentially irrevocable damage to what we now call the ecosystem. "Man," Marsh wrote, "is everywhere a disturbing agent. Wherever he plants his foot, the harmonies of nature are turned to discords." The process was the more dangerous because its results were not always immediately apparent. In the last year of a destructive civil war that made any expenditure of resources seem justifiable, and on the brink of the rampant exploitation that would follow, Marsh spoke out against every ingrained American faith, including the faith in an inexhaustible continent. "It is certain that a desolation, like that which has overwhelmed many once beautiful and fertile regions of Europe, awaits an important part of the territory of the United States . . . unless prompt measures are taken to check the action of destructive causes already in operation."

The destructive causes were indeed in operation. Having

skinned New England, the loggers were now skinning the Midwest at appalling speed. Within a single lifetime they deforested an area the size of Europe. The pineries of Minnesota and Wisconsin were going down the Mississippi as huge lumber rafts. By 1897 the sawmills of Michigan would have processed 160 billion board feet of white pine and left no more than 6 billion standing in the whole state.

It was like a feeding frenzy of sharks. There has been nothing like it since, except the current destruction of the Amazon rain forest. Predictably, Marsh's warnings went unheeded except by a concerned few, upper-class bird-watchers probably, the kind who are generally well ahead of the mass public in these matters. Concerned about the destruction of the forests before reading Marsh, they were doubly concerned afterward, and in 1875 a group of them formed the American Forestry Association with the hope of influencing public opinion and perhaps legislation. Sixteen long years later, when the Michigan pineries were obviously nearing the end of their road, the public indignation that had inspired the formation of the AFA got a rider added to the General Revision Act, authorizing the president to establish "forest reserves on the Public Domain." Benjamin Harrison, and after him Grover Cleveland, and after him Theodore Roosevelt, took advantage of the law, and among them they put forty-three million acres of forests, mainly in the West, out of the reach of the loggers. Then in 1907 angry Northwestern congressmen pushed through a bill rescinding the president's power to create forest reserves. With the help of his chief forester, Gifford Pinchot, Roosevelt named twenty-one new forests totaling sixteen million acres, and *then* signed the bill that would have stopped him.

The tracing of ideas is a guessing game. We can't tell who first had an idea; we can only tell who first had it influentially, who formulated it in a striking way and left it in some form, poem or equation or picture, that others could stumble upon with the shock of recognition. The radical ideas that have been changing our attitudes toward our habitat have been around forever. Only if they begin to win substantial public approval and give visible effects do they achieve a plain and even predictable curve of development. But once they reach that stage, they are as easy to trace as a gopher in a spring lawn.

Nearly every aspect of environmentalism since the founding of the AFA has demonstrated the same pattern: a charismatic and influential individual who discerns a problem and formulates a public concern; a group that forms itself around him or around his ideas and exerts educational pressure on the public and political pressure on Congress; legislation that creates some new kind of reserve—national park, national forest, national monument, national wildlife sanctuary, or wilderness area; and finally, an increasingly specific body of regulatory law for the protection of what has been set aside.

Virtually all conservation activity up to the mid-twentieth century was concerned with saving something precious in our national heritage. Thus, as Marsh, and later and more narrowly Gifford Pinchot, galvanized the impulse to protect what remained of our forests, so George Bird Grinnell, a hunting companion and boyhood friend of Theodore Roosevelt's, devoted his time and his magazine, *Forest and Stream,* to the protection of wildlife. He carried on an impassioned campaign against market hunters, poachers, and women who wore feathers on their hats; and he and the Audubon societies (he founded the first one in 1886) can be credited not only with the Park Protection Act of 1894, forbidding hunting within the national parks, but also with the first wildlife sanctuary, Pelican Island, which Roosevelt established in 1903. Wildlife protection came lamely and late—the passenger pigeon, Carolina parakeet, and other species were gone, the buffalo and antelope were down to remnants, mainly in Yellowstone—but it did come, and those who made it come, by publicity and persistence, were an unlikely combination of bleeding hearts and gunners.

The creation of the first national park happened before this pattern of volunteer organizations working upon politicians had been perfected. It came about in 1872 because a party of Montana tourists had been so struck by the wonders of Yellowstone that they carried to Washington the demand that it be set aside as a public playground. F. V. Hayden's U.S. Geological and Geographical Survey of the Territories helped by laying before a dazzled Congress the paintings of Thomas Moran and Henry W. Elliott, and the photographs of William Henry Jackson, its expedition artists. Later it published, with fifteen Moran chromoliths, a book that might have served as a model for the Sierra Club's coffee-table books, perhaps the earliest scenic art book with a political purpose.

That national park resulted from a spontaneous overflow of public enthusiasm. The following ones owed a great deal to a single man, John Muir, and to the organization he founded, the Sierra Club. Yosemite, Sequoia, and General Grant national parks (the last ultimately fused with Sequoia) were largely Muir's doing, as was the Petrified Forest. As John of the Mountains, the grizzled genius of Yosemite, he had entertained the great, among them Emerson and Theodore Roosevelt, on sublime hikes and long campfire talks, and because he knew the Sierra better than anyone else, and was even more persuasive as a talker than as a writer, he got himself listened to. In 1892, two years after the Sierra parks were created, he formed the Sierra Club to look after their interests and enjoy their beauty. In 1905 he and the club finally persuaded California to cede back to the federal government Yosemite Valley itself, which had badly deteriorated under state control, so that it could become the heart of the park it belonged in.

. . .

No story of the national park system would be complete without some mention of the Antiquities Act of 1906, passed because of the depredations of pothunters in archaeological sites in the Southwest. It authorized the president to set aside by proclamation sites that were especially precious or threatened. By 1916 there were twenty such national monuments, many of them scheduled to become national parks by later congressional action. A quarter of all our present national parks owe their first reservation to the Antiquities Act.

By 1916 there were thirteen national parks, crown jewels without an adequately stated purpose or an adequate keeper. Those that were managed at all were managed by the Army. But in that year the National Park Act gave these reserves their stated purpose, public enjoyment, public use *without impairment,* and created the National Park Service to carry it out.

Muir had a hand in the National Park Act, too, but only posthumously and as a result of his greatest failure. For years he and the Sierra Club had fought San Francisco's effort to dam the Hetch Hetchy Valley, which lay within Yosemite National Park and which Muir thought second in beauty only to Yosemite Valley itself. The effort enlisted public and newspaper support throughout the country. It also revealed a mortal split between conservationists of Pinchot's variety, who believed in "wise use" of resources, and preservationists like Muir, who believed that some natural things were too sacred to be exploited for profit, water, power, or any other purpose.

In 1913, Congress voted to approve the dam. Within a year, Muir was dead. But the feelings stirred up by the struggle did not subside, and perhaps there was even some guilt felt by people who had fought on the winning side. Three years after it voted for the Hetch Hetchy dam, Congress passed the National Park Act, with its guarantee that parks should indeed be what Muir and the Sierra Club had insisted they were: sacrosanct, to be enjoyed but not impaired.

That "use without impairment" clause was there when next

the Sierra Club and its allies, this time under the leadership of
David Brower, found themselves in a battle with dam builders.
In the 1950s, as part of the Colorado River Storage Project, the
Bureau of Reclamation proposed to build a dam within Dinosaur
National Monument in northeastern Utah. The case against the
dam was not as strong as that against Hetch Hetchy, for Dinosaur was only a national monument, not a national park, and
there had been damsite withholdings. Nevertheless, Dinosaur
was part of the national park system, and that system was to be
managed for use without impairment; nobody could deny that
to drown a canyon under four hundred feet of water would
impair it. Ultimately it was the "use without impairment"
clause that gave the conservation forces total victory. The Colorado River Storage Project was stalled unless that dam was
removed from it, and it was.

Historians have concluded that the Dinosaur controversy
marked the coming-of-age of conservation, the first time the
diverse single-interest organizations joined together for
strength, and proved they had a lot of it. But Dinosaur is not
understandable without Hetch Hetchy. The tactics, the publicity
campaigns, the political skirmishing, were similar in these in-
stances. The difference between defeat in the first instance and
victory in the second is that Muir did not have the National Park
Act and the "use without impairment" clause to fight from,
while Brower and his alliance did. And the precedent has been
instructive in later struggles. Other laws, notably the Endan-
gered Species Act, have similarly been used as barricades, and
the snail darter, desert pupfish, and spotted owl have been
enlisted on the side of the environment.

If the national park idea is, as Lord Bryce suggested, the best
idea America ever had, wilderness preservation is the highest
refinement of that idea. Parks are designed for careful human
use—they could be justified by a Pinchot. But wildernesses are

something else. Preservation of wilderness implies agreement with Marsh's observation that wherever man plants his foot, nature's harmonies are turned to discords. As the culminating aspect of the preservation sentiment, the wilderness movement differs from the park and forest and wildlife movements in its repudiation of most kinds of human use. What it wants is the continuation of that healthy, natural web of life that Chief Standing Bear and others revered; and if there are human uses implicit in this long-range continuation—watershed protection, protection of genetic variety, the preservation of natural laboratories by which the deteriorating man-managed world can be judged and perhaps saved—the *sentiment* for wilderness, our creature-love for the natural world, is probably as important. Like the other forms of land preservation, wilderness areas are doomed to be islands surrounded by what constantly threatens to invade and damage them, but that is what we get for learning slowly.

The wilderness movement has had its prophets, early and late; of the late ones, Aldo Leopold seems to me the greatest. It has developed its organization, the Wilderness Society, one of the most effective of the environmental groups. It has had its landmark legislation, the Wilderness Act of 1964, which authorized hands-off protection for areas carved out of the national forest, national park, and Bureau of Land Management lands.

One thing wilderness has not lacked is enemies, for its nonutilitarian reserves are said to "lock up" resources and frustrate our fabled American initiative. Not only resource interests but also some destructive recreational groups and both the U.S. Forest Service and the BLM have dragged their heels in the process of wilderness designation. Some people learn late, some never do.

Ironically, wilderness preservation was born in that most utilitarian of organizations, Pinchot's Forest Service. It cropped up here and there like an ineradicable weed. In 1919 Arthur Carhart, a Forest Service architect in Denver, talked his employers out of civilizing Trappers Lake, in Colorado, with summer cottages. He later did the same thing in the boundary-waters area of northern Minnesota. In 1924 Aldo Leopold, from the Albuquerque office of the Forest Service, got nine hundred roadless square miles of the Gila National Forest set aside as a primitive area. (He defined a "wilderness" as something big enough to absorb a two-week pack trip.) In a 1930 issue of *Scientific Monthly,* Robert Marshall, a plant physiologist working in Wyoming's Wind River Range, issued a ringing manifesto calling for identification and rescue of whatever wilderness areas remained. In 1934, after a conference in Knoxville, Tennessee, Marshall, Benton MacKaye, and several other foresters determined that an organization should be formed to promote wilderness, and the following January, with Leopold and Robert Sterling Yard among the charter members, they formed it.

Their purpose was to replace the unreliable administrative designations of wilderness with wildernesses that were established by law, and hence impregnable.

Much of the program, as it developed, was the work of Marshall. The philosophical justifications, the statement of first principles, appeared in 1949 in Aldo Leopold's posthumous *A Sand County Almanac.*

In the forty-one years since its publication, the *Almanac* has become a kind of holy book in environmental circles. It is a superb distillation of what many Americans had been groping toward for more than a century. Leopold loved land, all kinds, but the wilder the better, and over his lifetime of experience with land and its creatures he had come to look upon land as a community, not a commodity. Blessed with a poet's gift of words, trained in forestry, he brought as much sensitivity as Thoreau did to his study of nature, and more science. His book comes to its climax in the essay "The Land Ethic," in which he argues for the kind of responsibility in our land relations that civilized people are supposed to show in their human relations.

Without denying the human need to use natural resources—cut trees, plow prairies, shoot game, whatever—he wanted a portion of the land left wild, for ultimately all human endeavor has to come back to the wilderness for its justification and its new beginnings. He said he would hate to be young again without wild country to grow up in. And he was no lover of public recreation as usually practiced. Recreation could be as dangerous as logging or any extractive use. "Recreational development," he wrote, "is a job not of building roads into lovely country, but of building receptivity into the still unlovely human mind." Knowing how persistent the unloveliness of the human mind could be, he did not expect his land ethic to arrive soon. He perfectly understood that what he described would have its flowering far off, the product of a long, slow, and almost total revolution of American values.

Fifteen years after the publication of *A Sand County Almanac,* and after the extraordinary effort of many people, politicians as well as environmentalists, and especially of Howard Zahniser, executive director of the Wilderness Society, Congress passed the Wilderness Act. Tired of fighting brushfire wars after the Dinosaur struggle, Zahniser had drafted a bill in 1956. During the next eight years he revised it sixty-six times. When, after innumerable hearings and thousands of pages of testimony, it was finally passed, it still contained Zahniser's definition of wilderness as "an area where the earth and its community of life are untrammeled by man, where man himself is a visitor who does not remain."

The passage of the Wilderness Act, and its immediate designation of 9.1 million acres of wilderness in national park, national forest, and wildlife refuge land, marked the climax of preservationist environmentalism. The wilderness designation process, clogged with controversy and sullen with turf battles among the bureaus, and shrilly resisted by resource interests, would go on—still goes on. But a corner had already been turned. Rachel Carson's *Silent Spring,* in 1962, had already made it plain that pollution, not preservation, was to be the principal concern of the future.

And so this is the long road the nation traveled to get to Earth Day, 1970, and beyond. Those who led us down it, the countless individuals and scores of organizations who resisted the lunchbucket and "American initiative" arguments of resource exploiters, did not leave us a bad legacy. Considering the mood in which the continent was settled, and the amount we had to learn, we can be grateful that those battles do not have to be fought, at least not on the same fields, again. We can be just as certain that others will have to be. Environmentalism or conservation or preservation, or whatever it should be called, is not a fact, and never has been. It is a job.

PART THREE
WITNESSES

COMING OF AGE: THE END OF THE BEGINNING

It is exhilarating to me, sixty years after I graduated from a western university and forty-five years after I made the decision to come back West to live and work, to see the country beyond the 100th meridian finally taking its place as a respected and self-respecting part of the literary world.

I used to yearn for the day when the West would have not only writers—it has had those from the very beginning—but all the infrastructure of the literary life: a book-publishing industry, a range of literary and critical magazines, good bookstores, a reviewing corps independent of eastern and foreign opinion, support organizations such as PEN, an alert reading public, and all the rest.

Now it has them. Such publishing ventures as the North Point Press in Berkeley demonstrated that it is possible for makers of books outside of New York, Boston, and a few other eastern cities to publish books for a national audience, escaping the "regional" label that has traditionally been their curse. The independent bookstores of the West—The Chinook Bookshop in Colorado Springs, Powell's in Portland, Elliott Bay in Seattle, the Country Book Shelf in Bozeman, Zion's Bookstore in Salt Lake City, the Tattered Cover in Denver, The Black Oak Bookstore in Berkeley, Kepler's in Menlo Park, The Printers Inc in Palo Alto, and dozens like them—are as well stocked and well staffed and well patronized as bookstores anywhere. Western reviewers, though by no means limited to regional matters, at least understand them as familiar day-by-day realities. PEN has now established a western base. As for the reading public, it probably has more cultural hunger and fewer cultural blahs than its eastern counterparts.

As a writer from the West, I discovered long ago how it felt to be misinterpreted. Even well-intentioned people who came to praise often saw in me, or expected from me, things that I was not prepared to deliver, and misread things I *was* prepared to deliver. Now and then I used to put on my armor and break a lance against the windmill of the cowboy myth that dominated not only much western writing but almost all outside judgment of western writing. We rode under the shadow of the big hat, but as they used to say of Ronald Reagan, we were big hat, no cows. Nothing could convince them in New York or Massachusetts that there was anything of literary interest in the West except cowboys.

Now even the cowboys annually gather in Elko, Nevada, to read their poems to one another. Some of those, maybe most, are real cowboys such as I knew when I was young—hired men on horseback with hands so callused they would hardly close. Some are more literary.

Real cowboys have more brutality and less chivalry in them than the literary kind. Some of them have been subverted by literary propaganda and believe their own myth. Others, I am sure, are trying to do what any writer is trying to do: render the texture and tensions of their own lives, their own occupation, their own place. Their trouble is that if they write with honesty about exploitation, insecurity, hard work, injuries, and cows, none of which make even a walk-on appearance in *The Virginian* and most of the horse opera it has spawned, they will find a smaller and less enthusiastic audience than if they had written about crooked sheriffs and six-guns.

Not being greatly sympathetic with literary cowboys, I have myself written only two cowboy stories in a long life. Both of them are grim little dramas of work, weather, and cows, with no six-guns, no sheriffs, no dance-hall girls, no walk-downs, not even a saloon. One of them, "Genesis," is probably as good a story as I ever wrote; but its audience was considerably smaller than that for Hopalong Cassidy.

I felt from the beginning that there was a great deal about the West in which I had grown up that was not getting into literature, or not finding responsive readers if it did. Like most of my fellows in the 1930s and 1940s, I was to some extent a regional patriot. People in unfashionable or provincial places are made to feel a sort of colonial complex, and one response to that feeling of inferiority is an indignant assertion of equality and maybe even superiority.

But indignation and local puffery are not the ways to achieve stature. You achieve stature only by being good enough to deserve it, by forcing even the contemptuous and indifferent to pay attention, and to acknowledge that human relations and human emotions are of inexhaustible interest wherever they occur. My anguish is potentially as valid as that of Oedipus; my love may be as tragic and romantic as Tristan's; my bond with the earth may have as lasting significance as Wordsworth's; my work, even if it is with cows, may have as much dignity as honest work anywhere.

Though it has had notable writers since Gold Rush days, the West has never until very recently developed the support structures of the literary life. Neither has it ever produced a group of writers homogeneous enough to be called a school. Why should it have been asked to? It is too various for that. How do you find a unity among the Pacific Northwest woods, the Great

Basin deserts, the Rocky Mountains, the high plains, the Mormon plateau country, the Hispanic-and-Indian Southwest, the conurbation of the California littoral? What kind of school can you discern in writers as various as Ivan Doig, Frank Waters, Scott Momaday, Edward Abbey, Thomas McGuane, Larry McMurtry, Joan Didion, and Maxine Hong Kingston?

California, it should be said, is a separate problem, hardly a part of the West at all. As one anthologist recently put it, it is west of the West. But there are a few common characteristics in western writing and western life, and California shares most of them. For one thing, the whole West, including much of California, is arid country, as I've been reiterating ad nauseam for fifty years, and aridity enforces space, which in turn enforces mobility. In an oasis civilization, especially one that has been periodically raided for its extractable resources, you don't find the degree of settled community life that you would find in New England, the Midwest, or the South.

Space does something to the vision. It makes the country itself, for lack of human settlements and other enhancements to the illusion of human importance, into something formidable, alluring, and threatening, and it tends to make human beings as migratory as antelope. Literature reflects this necessity. I noted this once before, in the University of Michigan lectures that are included here. Look at any book that is western in its feel—*Roughing It, The Grapes of Wrath, The Big Sky, The Big Rock Candy Mountain, On the Road, The Way to Rainy Mountain*—and you will find that it is a book not about place but about motion, not about fulfillment but about desire. There is always a seeking, generally unsatisfied.

The country is a very prominent actor in most western writing. It is big and impressive, it is mainly empty, it is unforgiving, it is fragile. Mobility puts us directly in touch with it, without much human interference. And that characteristic is as apparent in California writing as in the writing of any other part of the West.

The California writers whom David Rains Wallace discusses in *The Wilder Shore* are instructive. The whole burden of that book is how important the physical landscape is in the work of almost all California writers of real quality: Jack London, Frank Norris, John Steinbeck, Mary Austin, Joan Didion, many more. The single fact of our preoccupation with landscape is enough to make us unintelligible to or beneath the notice of critical opinion schooled in one or another variety of abstract expressionism. Try writing *The Big Sky* about New Jersey.

Western literature differs from much other American literature in the fact that so much of it happens outdoors. It also differs in that the influence of Europe's ideas, Europe's fashions, and Europe's history is much fainter. Whether a writer comes from Denver or Palm Springs, Missoula or Santa Fe, San Francisco or Los Angeles or Salt Lake City, his book is almost sure to be remote, in spirit as well as in miles, from Europe. Susan Sontag says that she has always taken her cues from Europe. I know of no western writer who could say that. Long ago, Ralph Waldo Emerson declared that we had listened too long to the courtly voice of Europe, and by the time we reached the western half of North America his advice was beginning to be taken. That fact, too, makes books true to the western experience and the western mind-set opaque to critics whose instruction has come from across the Atlantic.

Western literature, especially that written in the inland West, is close to the outdoors and big space, close to the aggressive American Dream, close, too, to the native inhabitants of the continent, who survive in greater numbers and with more societal and cultural integrity west of the 100th meridian. Descendants of Pocahontas or King Philip or Billy Bowlegs or Tecumseh would speak to us now from a long, muted, defeated distance; but Scott Momaday, James Welch, Linda Hogan, Leslie Marmon Silko, Louise Erdrich, and other western Indians speak from the present, from the very battlefields of cultures.

And there are other voices in western literature that do not speak with authority to the East because they stir no recent memories and open no recent wounds.

Nearly 130 years ago, William Gilpin, the first territorial governor of Colorado, made a Fourth of July speech to the Fenian Society on the bank of Cherry Creek, where Denver now stands. Most of his speech was an egregious and misleading boosting of western opportunities, but one thing he said was prophetic. "Asia," he said, "is found, and has become our neighbor."

And fifty years or so ago, the historian Garrett Mattingly remarked to Bernard DeVoto that all American history is history in transition from an Atlantic to a Pacific phase. If they were alive today, Gilpin and Mattingly could congratulate themselves as prophets. In the last generation or two, even our wars have gone Asian, along with much of our trade, some of our religious searching, and a lot of our apprehension.

Since the West leans toward the Pacific Basin, writers west of the continental divide, when they are engaging the universe instead of the local scene, inevitably reflect a different and larger universe—different history, different emphases and expectations, a different ethnic mix, a different culture.

It has been hard for the rest of the country to realize that the West incorporates not only cowboy-and-Indian fantasies but also the Hispanic Southwest, whose beginnings antedate Plymouth Rock by eighty years. The Grand Canyon was discovered by whites before the Mississippi was. And the Far East has been coming east to meet us and fuse with us for a long time now. Maxine Hong Kingston's *Tripmaster Monkey* is not conceivable as a book written about any place but the San Francisco Bay area. In his cockeyed 1960s way, Wittman Ah Sing, a fifth-generation Chinese-American, is as American a character as Huckleberry Finn, and he could have happened only where he happened.

New regions do grow up and acquire their mature voices, and we should never be shamefaced about writing from our own base. I am not talking about method. A lot of experimentation goes on in the matter of method; in the end, we find and use what we like and what we can handle and what fits our material. It is that material, the depth and breadth of our understanding of whatever piece of human trouble is under our microscope, that really matters, and it may take a generation or two to develop writers who can swing what they know, and even longer to train an audience that will appreciate them.

The only life we know well, the one on which we are the ultimate authority, is our own. The only experience to which we can bear witness is that which we have personally endured or observed. That is why Ken Kesey's advice in a *New York Times Magazine* article, "Write what you don't know," strikes me as obfuscating nonsense. That is the way to produce unknowing and unfeeling books, the way to send with a dead key, the way to convince ourselves and perhaps others that antic motions in a void, a meaningless mugging and hoofing, are what literature is supposed to be. I think, on the contrary, that at its best it is a bolt of lightning from me to you, a flash of recognition and feeling within the context of a shared culture.

The West doesn't need to wish for good writers. It has them. It could use a little more confidence in itself, and one way to generate that is to breed up some critics capable, by experience or intuition, of evaluating western literature in the terms of western life. So far, I can't think of a nationally influential critic who reads western writing in the spirit of those who wrote it, and judges them according to their intentions.

Such critics will come. I can remember when every new book by William Faulkner—and these included all five of his greatest—was greeted with incredulous laughter and ribald contempt by the smart reviewers in New York. But as Faulkner himself might have said, they mought of kilt him but they didn't whup him. All it took to establish his quality as a writer fit to speak to the world was the books themselves, a little time for his peculiar variety of genius to sink in, some applause from abroad, especially France, and one perceptive and authoritative critic, Malcolm Cowley.

While we await the day for that critic to arrive, we can settle back and enjoy without apology the books that western writers are bringing us.

ON
STEINBECK'S
STORY
"FLIGHT"

There have been a few writers, such as Chekhov and Frank O'Connor, who have operated without perceptible constraint within the short story form. Their characters take on life the moment they arrive on the page, their narrative never seems to struggle for room to run in, their meanings state themselves economically as epiphanies and nuances, their humanity shines between the lines like a steady light from within. They create their worlds, and illuminate them, in miniature.

John Steinbeck was not one of those natural miniaturists. When he did write a true short story, and he wrote a few splendid ones, he did so only by exercising the strict self-discipline that some critics say he didn't possess. But quite often things that began as short stories refused to stay within bounds. Sometimes they became something longer and more complex, sometimes they developed linkages with other stories and became something less independent.

In *The Pastures of Heaven,* every story strains to include a whole lifetime, sometimes more than one lifetime, of struggle and change. As Steinbeck himself remarked in a letter to his friend Ted Miller, "They are not short stories at all, but tiny novels." Though linked by place, by common characters, and by the pervasive, malignant influence of the Munroes, they are discrete life histories, or family histories. "You see," Steinbeck said in another letter, "each family will be a separate narrative with its own climax and end, and they will be joined by locality, by the same characters entering into each and by this nameless sense and power of evil."

In *Tortilla Flat,* many of whose episodes were begun as short stories, linkage took over more completely than in *The Pastures of Heaven,* and what resulted was not a collection of related tales but a loose novel. The stories about Danny, Pilón, and the rest of the Round Table of Monterey *paisanos* did not want to be discrete. They yearned like certain groupy biological species to operate not separately, or only separately, but in union—to become collectively a larger, more complex, and different animal. Call it a literary demonstration of the Steinbeck-Ricketts theory of the phalanx.

Something similar happened to "The Gift," "The Promise," "The Great Mountains," and "The Leader of the People," stories written separately that later demanded to be put together as *The Red Pony,* almost a short novel.

If the stories in *The Pastures of Heaven* are little novels, and those in *Tortilla Flat* are chapters, and those in *The Red Pony* are something in between, like the sonnets of a cycle, then it is only in the rest of *The Long Valley* that we may look for Steinbeck's real short stories. That is indeed where they are, all of them.

The Long Valley was not published until 1938, riding the popularity of *Tortilla Flat, Of Mice and Men,* and *In Dubious Battle.* But by that time Steinbeck had not written a short story for four years. After June 1934, when he wrote "The Vigilante," "The Snake," and "Breakfast," he wrote nothing more of any significance in that form, devoting himself to the longer writings that commanded a large public. That should surprise no one. It was novels, if we may count *Tortilla Flat* as one, that brought him both money and notice. Short stories had brought him little of either.

Consider the composition and publication of the sixteen stories that make up *The Long Valley*. They were all written (along with *Tortilla Flat*) between the fall of 1933 and the summer of 1934, many of them during the months when Steinbeck was living in the family house in Salinas and helping his mother die. His table was set up outside her room; he wrote in the odd half hours between pills and bedpans, and it is little wonder that he wrote short.

What is surprising is that his stories impressed practically no one, as they should have even in those deep-Depression months. Ted Miller, and later Mavis McIntosh and Elizabeth Otis, hawked them from editorial office to editorial office with a demoralizing lack of success. "You ask why you never see my stuff in *Esquire*," Steinbeck wrote Louis Paul in February 1936. "I guess they were never interested. I have a good many stories in New York but no one wants them. I wrote nine short stories in one sitting recently. I thought some of them were pretty good, too, but that's as far as it got. *The North American Review* used to print some at thirty dollars a crack."

He seems to have been wrong about the price—it was forty-five or fifty dollars, according to his biographer Jackson Benson—but it was true that for a long time only *The North American Review* showed any interest. Between November 1933 and March 1935 it published "The Gift," "The Great Mountains," "The Murder," "The Raid," and "The White Quail," to a maximum audience of a few thousand readers and at a maximum reward to the author of $250. Steinbeck gave "The Snake" to a little magazine called *The Monterey Beacon* in exchange for six months of free rides on a saddle horse. *Argosy* of London published "The Leader of the People" in August 1936, and *The Pacific Weekly* ran "Breakfast" in November of that year. Spurred by the success of *Tortilla Flat* and the advance notice of

In Dubious Battle, Esquire bought "The Vigilante" for its October 1936 issue and "Johnny Bear" for the issue of September 1937. *Harper's* came aboard in 1937, publishing "The Promise" in August and "The Chrysanthemums" in October, and the *Atlantic Monthly* cleared the cupboard of "The Harness" in June 1938, more than four years after it was written. "St. Katy the Virgin" had been published as a Christmas booklet in 1936. "Flight," first called "Manhunt," remained unsold even through the building excitement of Steinbeck's early novels, and never did see publication in a magazine.

Under the circumstances, it is no wonder Steinbeck never came back to writing short stories. Sometime in 1936, when Ted Miller sent him in one batch all the rejection letters he had collected while acting as Steinbeck's agent, the bruised author had indicated how close the experience came to discouraging him utterly: "Thanks for the rejections. They still give me the shivers and always will. Each one was a little doom. Had a personal fight with each one. And it's such a short time ago and it may be again."

In 1938, suddenly famous and already deep into the writing of *The Grapes of Wrath,* he bundled together his stories, including the rejected "Flight," published them as *The Long Valley,* and put the short story behind him.

So much for publication history. But it should be noticed that there was a good practical reason why "Flight" never saw magazine publication. It was long, nearly nine thousand words, twice as long as "The Snake" and more than half again as long as "The Chrysanthemums." It approached that nebulous thing, the novelette or novella—middle-length fiction—and middle-length fiction labors under a disadvantage. At anything from eight thousand to thirty thousand words, it is too small to be a book and too large to fit comfortably into the editorial space of a general magazine. Even in flush times editors view it askance. In times like the mid-1930s they could rarely indulge themselves even with middle-length fiction that they greatly admired.

There is no way of knowing whether any editors admired "Flight," not unless those rejection letters still exist. If they do, I have not seen them. But I do know that the length of "Flight" is not simply sprawl. Neither is it a result of trying to get within the most compact space a whole life history. This is not one of those "little novels," like the stories in *The Pastures of Heaven*. It is a true short story, focused on a few critical hours during which a boy is changed into a man and bears the consequences. It is long because the material demands some length, for this story is, at least from one point of view, an ordeal, and ordeals cannot be done in shorthand. They must be excruciating, and to be excruciating they must have duration—not indefinite duration, which would make them unbearable to read, but just the right duration, which lets us participate and suffer without having to shut our eyes or our minds or the book.

It would be convenient for critics if "Flight" could be shown to have been influenced by Hemingway's "The Snows of Kilimanjaro" and "The Short Happy Life of Francis Macomber"— both published in 1936, both well beyond the usual short story length, both dealing with ordeals of a kind, and at least one of them, "Macomber," chronicling the passage of an individual from ineffective boyhood to manhood in the macho sense. One critic, perhaps yielding to temptation, has said that in "Flight" Steinbeck "grafted Hemingway onto Dreiser." I do not understand the Dreiser connection—I cannot even *smell* Dreiser in this story—and I don't know what Hemingway, unless the stylistic Hemingway, the critic had in mind. If he had "Macomber" in mind, he forgot that "Flight" was written at least two years before "Macomber" was published and could not have been influenced by it. Neither could the reverse have happened, unless Hemingway had his spies greedily reading the unsalable manuscripts in the office of McIntosh and Otis.

The fact is, no writer grafts anybody onto anybody. Steinbeck may have read both Hemingway and Dreiser, he may have liked one or both or neither, he may have been stimulated in some fashion by one or both. But I am sure that when he sat down at his table outside the door of his dying mother, with his senses alert for emergencies and his mind bent on seizing a stolen scrap of time, he was feeling his way into a situation totally *his*. His total experience was on the line, including his reading experience. A writer at that crucial point is a synthesizer, a blender, and everything he has ever heard or seen or read or known is potentially there, available for the creation of his story. It all melts and fuses. No writer as good as Steinbeck ever sat down to a story thinking about whom he would copy, or how he would appropriate what from whom.

A critic, by contrast, is not a synthesizer but an analyzer. He picks apart, he lifts a few cells onto a slide and puts a coverglass over them, he runs tests of the chemical components of spittle and sperm and heartsblood. His is a useful function and, done well, may greatly clarify the reading of a story—may even give a reader the illusion of understanding both the product and the process. But it is more reliable on the product than the process. Some Heisenberg principle frustrates critics who try to analyze how stories are written. Whatever they can analyze has to be dead before it can be dissected. As Hippolyte Taine's theory of "the race, the place, and the time" was said to explain everything but genius, so most critical analysis explains everything but the mystery of literary creation.

It is said that Gertrude Stein gave up the study of medicine because she didn't like the dissection of cadavers, and it is true that she spent her literary life trying to synthesize words— words used plastically—into some new sort of creation. But her skeptical critics always saw her poised over the marble slab with the dead body of language, oozing formaldehyde, under her scalpel. They said she was re-creating from disassembled parts, not creating. The entire problem of criticism, which is happily not the problem of this essay, is how to keep the body alive while it is being studied.

So I would not feel comfortable trying to discuss "Flight" in terms of who or what influenced it. Steinbeck's lifelong acquaintance with Californios influenced it, his reading influenced it, his discussions with Ed Ricketts and his study of marine biology influenced it. We know that he read Malory with devotion all his life, that he planned *Tortilla Flat* as the chronicle of a sort of raffish Table Round, that he went to his death struggling with a modernization of the Arthurian cycle. We know that he bossed Hispanic work gangs in the Spreckels sugar factory and had many friends among Californios and Mexican-Americans. So of course there are elements of the code of chivalry in Pepé. They would be there even if Steinbeck had never read Malory, for a variant of that code survives in the *machismo* of Spanish-American youth. Of course there is the echo of the medieval trial by ordeal. Of course there is much that Steinbeck learned from his study of biology and his friendship with Ed Ricketts—a biological view of human beings which assumes the naturalness of biological death and, like Nature, takes the species to be more important than the specimen. There is even, in the dark watchers, a hint of Steinbeck's faith in omens, a touch of the mystical fatalism so persistent in his writing, especially when he is writing about men in close relationship with the earth.

Finally, there is of course a transcendent sense of place. Steinbeck knew the Santa Lucia Mountains, from the stacks and skerries of the shore through the mist forests of the westward-draining canyons up through the high chamisal country to the baking ridges and waterless valleys of the rain shadow. The story takes Pepé from the narrow humanized belt of the coast benches, through the somber darkness of redwood and fern, and finally out of protective cover into exposure and waterlessness. In the record of that flight there is not a false note: the country is shown to us as it is. It could never have been the same story without that impeccable realization of place.

Critics have noted these and other ingredients in "Flight," including the increasing swarm of animal images as Pepé struggles deeper into the mountains, and the increasing barrenness and starkness of the mountains as his flight becomes more desperate. The ingredients are all there, and must be noticed, for they are the literal instruments of both truth and suspense. But let us not take them apart, and let us not imagine that when we have become aware of them we have "explained" the story, or laid bare the mystery of its composition.

I think very few stories are made by the conscious selection and arrangement of such touches. These had to be intrinsic to the fused experience Steinbeck was imagining, details that come up off the page and are recognized as right the moment they are written. They are as much a part of the forming conception, the discovered form and meaning, as Pepé himself. If a story "begins in delight and ends in wisdom," as Robert Frost said a poem does, then a reader is better advised to note such details in passing, as part of the flow, and understand them only afterward. They first make Pepé's ordeal compelling to us, and afterward they distance us from his private tragedy, make us one with the dark watchers on the ridges. The story is lived from within and understood from without. Steinbeck always tried to become the character he was writing about, and the change of title from "Manhunt," which suggests an exterior view, to "Flight," which expresses how it feels from within, demonstrates that tendency. Nevertheless, our final view of Pepé is from outside and above. Manhood comes to Pepé as terror, struggle, wounds, and death, and we are allowed to share his panic and his pain. But whatever *wisdom* the story suggests about manhood comes to us as spectators, almost as dispassionate as if we had assumed the terrible aloofness of the bare mountains.

Manhood is the theme of this story, and it is stated and restated early. "I am a man," Pepé keeps insisting, in his innocence and his aspiration to assume his father's place. But even armed with his father's knife, which will turn out to have a stern potential, he is still a boy playing games. His mother, though she thinks him fine and brave, knows better than he what being a man may entail, and she protects him with scorn, calling him "big lazy," and "toy-baby," and "peanut," and "foolish chicken." But she sends him to Monterey because there is no one else to send, and because she is already resigned to the knowledge that "a boy gets to be a man when a man is called for."

The irony that the ordeal leading to manhood also leads to danger and death is as true for Pepé as for Francis Macomber. A secondary irony here is that what begins with the assumption of the father's role—investiture with the father's hat, coat, horse, and weapons—ends with every scrap of that borrowed manhood stripped away. The investiture is begun with his trip to Monterey; it is completed after his return, when he is loaded down with jerky, water, his father's gun, and is mounted on a fresh horse. But even in that moment when he has most succeeded his father, he has already begun to lose. His father's knife is in the breast of a quarrelsome stranger in Monterey. "Yes, thou art a man now, my poor little Pepé," his mother says, and to the other children, "Pepé is a man now. He has a man's thing to do."

There is an interesting moment here, and I confess it delights me, for it tends to confound a too-systematic reading of something which should retain some of the contradictions of real life. At the moment when his mother admits he is a man, Pepé's mouth changes, but the change, instead of making him look like his dead father, makes him look "very much like Mama." Does this mean he is still a boy, despite what he has done and despite her words, or does it mean that the manhood toward which he has yearned is as much an attribute of his grimly competent mother as of the father he reveres? In either case, I accept it—it is the way things often are. And the moment he has kicked his horse up the trail, this woman, who remained fierce and concentrated when he looked to her for softness, turns to wailing. She has consigned him to manhood not by her words but by her knowledge that he is doomed.

The mountains at first are solitary but not forbidding. There is cover, coolness, the stream. Fear comes first with the man riding down the trail, and Pepé jacks a shell into the chamber of his father's gun and leaves the gun at half cock. Later the country gets rougher, and very dry, and without cover. Exposure brings greater fear, and along with fear a glimpse of the first of the dark watchers his mother has warned him about. Local superstition? Omen? Reflection of Pepé's emotional state? Death symbol, like the hyenas and the policemen on bicycles in "The Snows of Kilimanjaro"? If superstition, they fit Pepé's society and tradition. If reflection of his state of mind, they are grimly apt. If omen, they throw a shadow on his flight. If death symbol, they let Steinbeck suggest with great economy and force the fate that awaits Pepé. In any case they are not a mere mechanical literary device; they are something that rises from the action like smoke from a campfire.

The country grows still more desolate. Another dark watcher—or is it a pursuer? Pepé misses his knife, the most intimate reminder of his father. The wildness of the mountains is accentuated by the sight and sound of animals—doves, quail, a wildcat, later owls and a coyote—voices of wildness, unhuman but not antihuman. It is just here, in fact, that the desperate figure of Pepé, with whom we have totally identified, begins to recede from us, begins to be a speck riding through a dispassionate and impersonal wilderness, begins to be an object and not a subject. It was probably not planned that way—more likely discovered in the doing—but it is right.

Now begins the divestiture of everything that he acquired in the first stage of his manhood. He loses his father's hat. In the first rifle fire from the pursuers, he loses his horse. Wounded, he crawls on the earth like a hurt animal. As he crawls and scrambles to escape, the encounters with animals multiply—buzzards, a small brown bird, an eagle, a dove, a rattlesnake, lizards. We may read these encounters either as brute detail, the precise life-forms he would be likely to encounter in that wilderness of the Santa Lucias, or we may (the critics generally do) read them as little reiterative emphatic devices meant to show us Pepé stripped more and more completely down to his animal base, remote from family or society or human help. The mountains by now are bare stone, without a hint of softness or shelter. He has a face-to-face encounter with a mountain lion, shyest of wild creatures. Wounded, crawling through scrub and broken rocks, he goes on.

And now he loses his rifle. The pursuers have him cornered. Trying to lance his infected wound, he misses his knife again—the first, the major loss. Squeezing and scraping the wound, he whines like a dog. Eventually, as Thucydides said of the Spartans at Thermopylae, having done what man could, he endures what man must. He stands up to meet it.

But it was surely Steinbeck's intention, whether premeditated or discovered in the act of writing, that it should not be his father's son, but Pepé himself, who stands up to take his manhood and his death. Everything in the story leads to that, every detail corroborates the transformation from a boy imitating his elders to a man, helpless and without support, being nevertheless a man, doing, as Pepé's mother said, a man's thing.

Having gone this far in taking Steinbeck's story apart, we should now do him and it the justice of putting it back together again. Having played critic, we should put ourselves back into the hands of the storyteller, and open the book and read the story through once more, letting its flow carry us and its suspense grip us and its details convince us of its rightness and validity. Reading, we have to be able to accept these mountains into which Pepé flees as both the Ventana wilderness of the Santa Lucias and the mountains of repudiation and no-help, almost as allegorical as the Slough of Despond or the Valley of the Shadow of Death. It is one of the triumphs of the story that they are authentically and simultaneously both. And we should be able to recognize in Pepé not only a callow, pointy-headed Californio youth from the Big Sur coast trying to live up to the foolish and romantic ideal of manhood common to his kind, but one of the incarnations of Everyman pursuing the ideals that, foolish or not, and however harshly tested, in the end give him stature and dignity.

GEORGE R.
STEWART AND
THE AMERICAN
LAND

Of George Stewart's twenty-eight books, I find that I have seventeen on my shelves. Some of them I have read only once. Eight of them I have just reread, to remind myself of George's historical and fictional methods. Three or four of them I read all the time, and refer to, and quote, and steal from, and couldn't get along without.

This morning, exactly a year after his death on August 22, 1980, I am tempted to think of him as a writer who during his life received less attention than was due to him; and that temptation, born of friendship and the respect I had for him, is not entirely without justification. He was a much more important writer than the general public knew.

His interests were essentially regional, and his books reflected his interests, and so his readers and his reputation tended to be regional also. He hit only a few of the jackpots by which writers become famous or notorious. His private life was serene and his habits scholarly, so that he made no copy for the gossip columnists. He would not have known how to behave if he had been lionized. His approach, whether to history or to fiction, was the reverse of sensational. He was thorough, objective, judicious, all qualities that are likely to get a man ignored in the book-news media. Personally and artistically, his impulse was to efface himself. And he never in his life wrote a book that capitalized on a fad or tendency. His books were totally his own. He never went for an audience; he let it come to him.

Nevertheless, it would be doing him and his reputation a disservice to call him an ignored or overlooked writer. He had his modest share of the rewards and notice by which serious readers and critics and colleagues, the durable audience, pay their respects to substance and worth.

In 1938 the Commonwealth Club of California awarded him its Gold Medal for *East of the Giants,* a novel that is a paradigm of California history from Mexican colonialism to American statehood. In 1936 it had given him its Silver Medal for *Ordeal by Hunger,* the story of the Donner-Reed party. Properly, the medals should have been reversed, for *Ordeal by Hunger* is the more enduring book, but never mind. The point is that the Commonwealth Club, which gives recognition to California writers, recognized him twice, and early, as a California writer of stature.

Stewart's greatest popular success came with the novels *Storm* (1941) and *Fire* (1948), both Book-of-the-Month Club choices and both best-sellers. Twenty years after *Fire* an altogether different sort of book, the study of waste-disposal problems entitled *Not So Rich as You Think,* received the Sidney Hillman Award, though it was enough ahead of its time (a common weakness of Stewart books) so that it did not become a major document in the environmental movement. In 1972 the California Historical Society presented him with its Henry R. Wagner Award in recognition of his long and distinguished career as an interpreter of California history. Walkers along the sea on Thornton State Beach, south of the San Francisco city limit, will find a trail dedicated to him. And in the latter years of his life he was honored by the United States Board of Geographical Names, the Association of American Geographers, and the American Names Society for his work on place-names.

All of which is to say that for nearly fifty years he has been a name, a presence, a quietly distinguished part of San Francisco's distinguished literary tradition. If they heard less of him in New York, and if he was never elected to either the American Academy of Arts and Sciences or to the American Academy and Institute of Arts and Letters, why, that was their error and their loss. Equivalent achievement, if he had lived on the East Coast, would have ensured his election thirty years ago.

For there is no way around those several books, adequately recognized or not, which many of us find indispensable. *Ordeal by Hunger* is *the* history of the Donner party, which closed in tragedy the first act of the American occupation of California, and it is not likely to be replaced by any future study. *The California Trail*, though it was written to order as one of a series, is the best single-volume history of the overland migration to California, and is likely to remain so. And *Names on the Land*, a unique book, is the only study we have of how we went about putting our marks on the unnamed continent, and in doing so both added ourselves to the continent and added the continent to ourselves. It can be read as a gloss on Robert Frost's poem "The Gift Outright," with its theme of a people "possessing what we still were unpossessed by," and how we learned to give ourselves "to the land vaguely realizing westward."

George Stewart testified that of all of his many books he liked *Names on the Land* best. As usual, his judgment was sound. That book best expressed his interest in history, his curiosity about the web of organizational structures by which we not only create our institutions but leave tracks and names behind, the sociological and psychological and verbal impulses that permeate and direct such a massive and unpremeditated act as the investment of a continent. Habit, fashion, accident, ritual, poetry, humor, all played a part in the naming, and the naming process—as Stewart saw when no one else did—subsumed our history as a people. Nobody ever wrote such a book as *Names on the Land* before; nobody has written one since.

Besides those three that I could not do without, there are many other books of solid worth and astonishing originality. For those who have missed him, here is the record:

> Seven novels: *East of the Giants, Doctor's Oral, Storm, Fire, Earth Abides, Sheep Rock,* and *The Years of the City.*
>
> Four biographical works: *Bret Harte, Argonaut and Exile; John Phoenix, Esq.; Take Your Bible in One Hand: The Life of William Henry Thomes;* and the Plutarchian *Good Lives.*
>
> Four histories: *Ordeal by Hunger, The California Trail, Committee of Vigilance,* and *Pickett's Charge.*
>
> Four books on names and naming: *Names on the Land; American Given Names; American Placenames, A Concise and Selective Dictionary;* and *Names on the Globe.*
>
> One book, more or less unclassifiable, that I shall call historical anthropology: *Man, An Autobiography.*
>
> A study of waste disposal: *Not So Rich as You Think.*
>
> A study of the loyalty-oath controversy on the Berkeley campus in the 1950s: *The Year of the Oath,* done in collaboration with others.
>
> Three books that can be loosely labeled "description and history": *U.S. 40: Cross Section of the United States of America; N.A. 1,* a two-volume guide to the North-South Continental Highway; and *American Ways of Life,* made up of lectures Stewart gave in Athens during a year as a Fulbright lecturer.
>
> A handful of lesser books, spin-offs of Stewart's lifetime interest in western history and western writers.

It is a formidable lifework, no part of it trivial or hasty, the best of it solid, lively, eminently readable, eminently dependable, and at least one book unique. Almost all of it is focused on California, most especially the Bay Area. Of the seven novels, only *The Years of the City* has a non-California locale. Of the histories and biographies, only *Pickett's Charge* and *Good Lives* concern themselves with non-Californian people and events. Even *Names on the Land,* though, like the two highway-guide books, it ranges across the whole continent, has a strong list to westward, partly because the American people flowed that way, partly, one is sure, because George Stewart's own inclination was westward.

He was a Californian by adoption, as are millions of others, but of long standing. Born in Sewickley, Pennsylvania, in 1895, he was brought to Southern California in 1907, at the age of twelve. Except for his years as an undergraduate at Princeton and as a graduate student at Columbia, he was a California resident the rest of his life. Azusa and Pasadena shaped his boyhood, and a single year as a graduate student at Berkeley in 1919–20 shaped his career, for it put him under the tutelage of Chauncey Wells, who taught him to love literature and writing, and Herbert Bolton, who introduced him to California history.

Something, perhaps the conviction of his Vassar-graduate mother that the East could teach him more than Berkeley could, sent George after one year to Columbia, where he received his Ph.D. in 1922. His dissertation was—of all things—on "Modern Metrical Techniques as Illustrated by the Ballad Meter," an inoculation that clearly did not take. A year as an instructor at the University of Michigan, during which he became engaged to Theodosia Burton, the daughter of the university's president, gave him his teaching apprenticeship. When the job at Berkeley for which he had been aiming opened up, he took it, and a year later brought his young wife west on the first of many cross-country trips, and they settled where he belonged. They never left.

The first writing project he involved himself in, a comprehensive study of the Gold Rush period, very quickly proved too big even for young ambition. It finally reduced itself to Stewart's first book, the biography of Bret Harte, which, fragment or not, is still the authoritative biography. But having been cut back, the Gold Rush theme began to grow again. It was never really abandoned, only divided into manageable portions, and much of what Stewart wrote later was part of it or an extension of it. The Donner party book, the California Trail book, the history of the Committee of Vigilance, the biographies of Harte, John Phoenix, William Henry Thomes, and (in *Good Lives*) of John Bidwell, are all related to it. So, in part, is *East of the Giants*. So are most of the editions of early diaries that Stewart prepared, with introductions, for the Bancroft Library, the California Historical Society, the Book Club of California, and other organizations. In addition, much of that part of his work which is fictional, not historical, is set in the corridor between Donner Pass and San Francisco. Donner Pass, George used to say, was *his* pass. He invented it.

In a career as coherent and as disciplined as this, it is hard to tell cause from effect. Did California history interest George Stewart because it demonstrated the strains and lesions, the violences and disintegrations, the difficult improvisations, of a society in the process of being transplanted, mixed, and reconstituted? Or did he acquire his interest in the processes of social organization and accommodation through his long study of the California frontier? It hardly matters which way we read it, but it is of the highest importance that we do not overlook those social processes, whether disintegrative or integrative, for they are central to book after book, both historical and fictional.

Thus (a word it is impossible to avoid in speaking of George Stewart, for being a man of precise and logical habits he himself found the word "thus" inescapable) the novel *East of the Giants* traces, through the lives of Juan Godoy, Judith Hingham, and David Melton, the formation of a California civilization. The Spanish and American traditions struggle and partly mix, the Indians are suppressed, the dynamics of the Gold Rush modify and end lives and change ways of living, one kind of life declines and another shapes itself to replace it. The emphasis is less on individuals than on forces; what matters at least as much as the fates of Juan, Judith, and David is the emergence of a new society.

Thus *Storm,* and after it *Fire,* celebrated the anonymous and overlooked but indispensable agencies that a later California has evolved to deal with the strokes of nature, acts of God, that threaten its orderly procedures. Any challenge to man's domination of nature and nature's forces and nature's creatures brings out the human counterforces. (One feels that if George were alive now he would be tempted to write a novel about our mobilization against the Medfly.) Disrupt the anthill and the formic specialty forces swarm out to deal with the intrusion. Stewart had a great respect for the skill and organization of those forces, whether he expressed them as Weather Bureau people in *Storm* or Forest Service people in *Fire,* or as telephone linemen, bulldozer skinners, switchboard operators, or any other element of the complex web our society has woven and on which, in both critical and routine situations, it helplessly depends. The people in these two novels, especially, have little identity apart from their jobs and their social organization, but civilization, Stewart more than suggests, would be utterly impossible without their skills and the structures that put them to work.

Thus *Sheep Rock* shows people conditioned by the city adapting their lives and feelings to a harsh land and climate and a fragile ecology, modifying their imported habits in order to live and come into harmony with this environment that accepts them only on sufferance. Twenty years before the seventies made it fashionable, Stewart was writing an "environmental" novel about return to the land and speculating on what such a return would do to human beings both socially and psychologically.

Thus *The Years of the City* chronicles the founding, flourishing, decline, and fall of a Greek colonial city, such a city as Paestum or Sybaris, planted on the frontier of the Italian boot, where the gibberish of the barbarian natives is full of sounds like *ibus* and *orum*. Different though it seems from the bulk of Stewart's work, it is actually a logical extension of it; it simply moves the frontier and its problems twenty-five hundred years closer to the dawn of civilization. Stewart was led into it by his year on a Fulbright lectureship in Greece—carrying, as he said with amusement, culture back to Athens.

Thus, as *The Years of the City* tells the story of a rise and a fall, *Earth Abides* tells of a fall and a rise, or at least the first steps of a rise. Science fiction of a kind, it imaginatively examines the consequences of a worldwide pestilence that wipes out all, except a few pockets of the immune. Characteristically, it is the East Bay from which we witness the end of the world. In the beginning, and for some years after, Isherwood Williams and the handful of other survivors who gather around him are able to scavenge a good and easy living simply by breaking into the stores and using the buildings, equipment, and power left behind by the suddenly stopped high-energy civilization. Ish himself, an educated and thoughtful man, has the enduring hope of being able to reconstitute that civilization: the symbol of his hope is the great University of California library, intact and silent, which holds the seeds of everything the survivors need to know. But as the years pass, supplies and know-how dwindle, fires and earthquakes destroy buildings and streets, animals go wild and become dangerous, gasoline, guns, ammunition, canned foods, and all the other leftovers are no longer available, the automatic hydroelectric power plant stops and all stoves and refrigerators with it. Item by item the old civilization is relinquished. They sink always deeper into simple tribal ways, live by hunting and gathering, dress in skins, reinvent the bow and arrow, evolve superstitions and myths. In the minds of children who never knew it, the past barely exists as a large vague Before. They cannot be made to hold still for education, they never learn to read and write. Indescribably long and dim, the future stretches ahead, awaiting the once-in-a-century lucky accident or man of genius who will move it a millimeter closer to a new cycle of development and accretion, add one small increment to a new racial memory, new arts, new sciences, religions, technologies.

Earth Abides is a fascinating book, as compelling in its development as *Robinson Crusoe.* It is very shrewd in its knowledge of how long, slow, and painful is the development of civilization; how dependent upon perception, invention, luck, cooperation, organization, memory, communication; how vulnerable. Stewart sought scientific advice from colleagues at Berkeley while writing the novel, but one feels that his study of the California frontier had suggested to him most of what he needed to know. As a historian of civilization he had a fair idea of how law and justice might evolve, and how harsh they might be when sheer survival made them necessary. He probably already had in his mind the history of the San Francisco Committee of Vigilance, of which he would later write. In imagining how, forced back to primitive tribal circumstances, people would react to shortage, hardship, threat, competition, he had the whole history of the American frontier for a model. He had already written one version of it in *East of the Giants,* and would shortly write another in *Sheep Rock.* And in his second book, in 1936, he had traced a social disintegration all the way to bestiality and cannibalism.

All those books, diverse in subject, are closely related in theme. Whether they are about storms or forest fires in the Sierra or about a poet being spiritually acclimatized in the Black Rock Desert or about the fate of a Greek city in the sixth century B.C., they reflect the same informed, retentive, curious, speculative mind. The theme never strays far from an examination of the bonds that hold human beings together in families, tribes, cities, or civilizations—how they are forged, how they hold, how they break, how they may be renewed.

. . .

In almost every way—in subject, in method, in attitude—George Stewart was about as far as he could get from the rebellious and dissatisfied stance that in the twentieth century we have come to associate with writers. Changes in society did not fill him with despair or indignation—he expected them, his cyclic view of history incorporated them. He was not agitated about such clichés as "post-Christian man," or "post-industrial man." As he indicated in *Man: An Autobiography,* on the long curve of human development such deviations don't even show. He took the long view, with a vengeance, and he was remarkably free of both Chicken-Littleism and personal spite against the universe.

"Poet and precisionist," his friend Joseph Henry Jackson called him. Precisionist he was, but if poet, then a very apollonian poet, more an old chief than a young warrior, more on the side of wisdom, restraint, negotiation, and compromise than of intransigence and direct action. His defect, or advantage, was that he had studied history. He would have agreed with Frost that there are no new ways to be new. He would have appraised each of the latest revolutionary discoveries in the light of the long slow ages. And he had a constitutional inability to be emotional, partisan, or rabid. His impulse was precisely the other way: to be judicious, to examine evidence, to hold his fire, to be wary of taking either offense or sides.

That impulse reveals itself in nearly all his works but is most evident in the works of history that touch on topics the historians have chosen to quarrel about. In fact, whenever he came across such a topic, Stewart had an inclination to get all the witnesses together, read all the papers, and see if he couldn't straighten out the quarreling factions.

Take, as an example, the cannibalism of the Donner party, and in particular the character of the German Keseberg, whom the conventional historians have made a scapegoat and a ghoul.

Of all the members of the party, he is the least easy to love. He fell further into bestiality, he survived longer, he partook of more man-meat. He was reported to have remarked about Tamsen Donner that she was the best he ever ate; he was suspected of killing a child who was put into his filthy bed in that filthy hut on Donner Lake.

But Stewart, pondering the disintegration of human beings under the harshest conditions, noting how sociability and comradeship gave way to suspicion and quarrelsomeness, and quarrelsomeness to murder, and murder to heightened suspicion and hostility, and how shrinking supplies led first to hoarding and then to heartlessness and then to cannibalism and then to the toasting of the hearts of dear relatives over the fire—noting moreover how nearly every member of the party who survived, survived by eating the dead to some extent—is willing to give Keseberg the benefit of the doubt. He understands the effects of starvation, hardship, solitude; he knows how a man under those circumstances could be crazed and irrational; he believes that many men, in the same circumstances, would show no better than Keseberg did. In that dreadful tragedy he chooses to find no scapegoat, though he finds several heroes.

Or take the Committee of Vigilance, often described by the historians as outlawry in the name of law. Without condoning or softening the harshness of those hangings, Stewart never forgets the provocations, the arrogance of the lawless Sydney Ducks, the venality of some parts of the apparatus of justice. As evidence of the curious impersonality in the Committee and its lack of a lust for power, he notes the fact that with the city more or less in its hands, the Committee of Vigilance voluntarily disbanded. Stewart does not exactly condone vigilantism; he simply reports the facts of the history of this example.

As he did in *Pickett's Charge,* the only historical work by Stewart that deals with events outside the bounds of California. Pickett's Charge was the climax of the climax, the key episode in the key battle of the Civil War. As a battle in which the omniscience of General Robert E. Lee came into serious question, Gettysburg—and especially Pickett's Charge—has been interpreted and reinterpreted by historians north and south. Stewart wrote his book, characteristically, to try to clear the air.

He did it in his customary fashion, from the evidence, impartially and at times skeptically reviewed. He is neither protecting nor attacking reputations, he is only looking at the interpretations put on events by people who *may* have been protecting or attacking. But no one reading his meticulous gun-by-gun, regiment-by-regiment, yard-by-yard report of the charge is likely to come out denying that Lee made a mistake, that with this last great Napoleonic assault he proved Napoleonic tactics outmoded, that some of the outfits, both Union and Confederate, that were accused of panicking did indeed panic (though with provocation), and that others similarly charged have been wronged by history. In short, if anyone wants to know about Pickett's Charge at Gettysburg, and how to interpret it, this is the history book to look into.

There is another kind of history to be examined in George Stewart's work—not the kind that conducts a judicious review to eliminate partisanship and weigh evidence and separate facts from prejudice and determine what truly happened in some given situation, but the kind that takes note of what was never noticed before, or was noticed so partially that its importance was never made clear. We come to that in *Names on the Land.*

"Once," Stewart begins, "from eastern ocean to western ocean, the land stretched away without names. Nameless headlands split the surf; nameless lakes reflected nameless mountains; and nameless rivers flowed through nameless valleys into nameless bays." Like many of the ideas that he hammered into books, that one is a commonplace—the sort of commonplace we never think to examine, also the sort of commonplace that, looked at steadily, begins to glow with strangeness and wonder.

After millennia of occupation by Indian tribes, after the surges of European exploration and imperial wars, after the rise of the mongrel American republic which took over most of what the empires had quarreled over, that blankness was filled.

> The names lay thickly over the land, and the Americans spoke them, great and little, easily and carelessly—Virginia, Susquehanna, Rio Grande, Deadman Creek, Sugarloaf Hill, Detroit, Wall Street—not thinking how they had come to be. Yet the names had grown out of the life, and the life-blood, of all those who had gone before. . . . In older countries the story of the naming was lost in the ancient darkness. But in the land between the two oceans much of the record could still be read—who gave the names and when, and even why one name was given rather than another.

In Europe, not only the origins but the meanings of many place-names have been lost. In a continent as new as North America, both are still traceable, or at least guessable. Place-name societies, place-name books and magazines and monographs, have been forwarding that work for a long time. But not until Stewart did anyone look at the subject curiously and steadily enough to see the historical and psychological, the sociological and ethnic, patterns of naming, and to clarify our history by clarifying those patterns. *Names on the Land* is not a book of place-names—Stewart did that later in the dictionary of American place-names he produced for the Oxford Press—but a book on the ways in which names are given. A book, that is, about people and cultures, and the changes that have happened to them since Spanish ships made landfall in the Indies, a book about the ways in which cultures agglomerate and spread, and swallow other cultures or are swallowed by them or fuse with them, a book about the ways in which a not-too-promising primate has marked the world with his footprints.

The ways are most various. Thus (Stewart's keyword again), Juan Ponce de León named Florida from the double fact that it seemed a flowery land and that he reached it only six days after the Easter of Flowers. Plain observation and an imported religious tradition fused to make a name that future generations accepted without question. Europeans of whatever nation had a strong impulse to impose upon the new continent names they had known in the old, either names of kings and queens and great men whose backing they had or desired, or names of counties and towns where their affections were rooted. Thus all the Bostons and Pomfrets and Portsmouths and Plymouths in New England, thus New England itself (and New Spain, New Galicia, New France, New York, New Amsterdam, and in a secondary ebbing sequence, New Mexico, New Harmony).

Catholic invaders planted innumerable Old World saints in the New World; Catholic and Protestant alike borrowed from (and bowdlerized) Indian names. Heroes of sorts left their names (Houston, all the Washingtons, all the Lincolns, all the MacArthur boulevards and Kennedy airports). Tribes of natives were acknowledged—Massachusetts, Manhattan—and chiefs who were roughly handled in life were made immortal in the place-names of the society that overcame them—Pontiac, Seattle, Chicago.

What Stewart understood was that nothing is comprehended, much less possessed, until it has been given a name, either casually, as in Bear Creek (the creek where someone saw or shot or was attacked by a bear), or formally, as in El Pueblo de Nuestra Señora la Reina de los Angeles de la Porciuncula. Coming at different times, from different branches of European culture, we brought different languages, different habits, different preoccupations, to our naming practices, and we heard the native tongues in different ways and translated native names differently. Moreover, mapmakers back in Europe often created or perpetuated error, simply because they did not understand or could not read the maps and descriptions from which they worked. Champlain's Frenchmen discovered and named a little river flowing into Lake Champlain, calling it La Mouette, the Seagull. But a mapmaker misread it, seeing *ls* where *ts* should be, and made it into the meaningless word Lamoille. Though the headwaters of one branch of the Lamoille flow out of a pond on a Vermont farm I have owned since 1938, I confess it did not occur to me to wonder what the river's name meant until *Names on the Land* informed me that it meant nothing.

A thing that fascinated Stewart, and will fascinate anyone who submits to his book, is the variety of origin, and hence of naming practice, that Europeans brought to this country, and the ways in which America worked on those names, naturalizing and changing them. What determines whether a new town named for its founder shall be Louisburg or Louisville or Louis-town or Louiston? Why does Pittsburgh have a terminal *h* and Harrisburg none? Those fashions—and they *were* fashions, dictated by the temporary dominance of Scottish, French, German, or English populations—are duplicated in our own time by the often-emetic fashions current among subdividers, who think a town called Hills or Ranch or Cove will sell better than one tagged with the once-classy *-ville*.

And not only place-names but generic nomenclature, common nouns designating common geographical features, underwent change. What in New England became known as a *brook* was in Pennsylvania known as a *run*, in New York as a *kill*, in the Southeast as a *branch*, out West as a *creek*. Somehow we developed a way of changing a word like "mountain" depending on whether it came before or after. What makes us say Sourwood *Mountain*, but *Mount* Washington? Our American ears.

When James Fenimore Cooper, in *The American Democrat*, castigated his compatriots for saying *kewcumber* instead of the proper and elegant *cowcumber* he was not keeping up with his own country. Inexorably the new continent with its new conditions, climates, diets, freedoms, worked on language as on

everything else. What in Europe had been called an *elk* acquired
the Algonquian name *moose*. What in England had been a *stag* or
red deer became an *elk*. The English word *master* became progres-
sively more unpopular until it all but died out, and was replaced
by the Dutch word *boss*. What had been a *porch* showed signs of
becoming a *stoop*, and down south a *gallery*, and in New Mexico
a *portal*. European *ripples* became American *riffles*, with a subtly
altered meaning.

As with the language at large, so with the specific function of
language known as place-names. Much is revealed about our
background by whether we call a shallow stagnant lake a *pond*
or a *slough* or a *swamp*, whether we call a shallow dry water-
course a *swale* or a *gully*, a *wash* or a *coulee*. Every region has its
native terms; every ethnic group that ever came to America has
contributed nomenclature. Every historic conflict or movement
of people, every change of climate and habitat, as when settlements moved from the forests through the oak openings out into
the open grasslands, has enforced the borrowing of local native
nomenclature or the invention or adaptation of imported terms.

Which is to say, our history, or tradition, the story of our
five-hundred-year love/hate struggle with the North American
continent, is there in the names we have put on the land. "Bury
my heart at Wounded Knee," says a poem by Stephen Vincent
Benét. Yes. Or at Spuyten Duyvil, or on the banks of the
Picketwire, or on Año Nuevo Island, or in the Wah Wah
Mountains, or wherever American energy has intruded and
American feet have trod. *Names on the Land* will suggest plenty
of choices.

For *Names on the Land,* even more than other books by George
R. Stewart, is provocative in the best sense. It makes a reader
look at things he has taken for granted, it stretches the mind
with analogies and possibilities, it is made luminous by the
learning brought to bear upon a single aspect of our incomparably complex heritage. It is never guilty of losing sight of the
forest while concentrating on the trees. Though he was a master

of detail, never overlooking one, never forgetting its importance, Stewart makes details serve the large and steadily seen ends with which he began. As historian or novelist, anthropologist or pundit of place-naming, he is consistently an expositor and defender of the human capacity for cooperation and organization and long memory which flowers as civilization. His books teach us who we are, and how we got to be who we are.

WALTER
CLARK'S
FRONTIER

Max Westbrook's little book on the writings of Walter Van Tilburg Clark—a book whose perceptions I often agree with though its metaphysical terminology and its Zen-and-Jung dialectic leave me pretty confused—begins with an anecdote told by Walt Clark himself. He said he was once introduced to a lady in the East as the author of *The Ox-Bow Incident*. She was incredulous. "You wrote *that*? My God, I thought you'd been dead for fifty years. You know, Owen Wister and all those people."

It is an instructive story. For one thing, it demonstrates the swiftness with which *The Ox-Bow Incident* made its way onto the small shelf of western classics. It further suggests that a book on that shelf is somehow embalmed: it has no contemporary reality to the ordinary reader, it is not something written by a modern writer or relevant to modern men and women, it escapes out of time, it acquires the remoteness and larger-than-life simplicities of myth and of certain kinds of folklore. And finally, as Westbrook points out (it is his principal reason for repeating the anecdote), the lady made a common but serious error in relating

The Ox-Bow Incident to *The Virginian*. It is like *The Virginian* in only superficial ways. Its purpose is not the celebration or even the definition of the cowboy hero whom Wister and Remington, between them, self-consciously created. To link it with Wister's belated chivalry is like comparing Conrad with Captain Marryat because both wrote about sailors. In fact, *The Ox-Bow Incident* is a novel that Henry James, that "historian of fine consciences," had more to do with than Wister did.

It is one of Westbrook's premises that Clark has been generally misread by the critics. I agree. It seems almost a statement of the standard condition of novelists of the West, who are a little like the old folks in the Becket play, continually rising up out of the garbage cans to say something, and continually having the lids crammed down on them again. We may want to speak to the nation or the world, but often, by the condescending assumptions of critics who cannot or will not read us, we are allowed to speak only to our own back alley or within the echoing hollow of our own garbage can. Walter Clark's western materials no more limit the depth and relevance of his fiction than the barbarous backwoods setting of *Huckleberry Finn* or the scruffiness of Yoknapatawpha County limit the validity of Mark Twain or Faulkner.

So Walter Clark was not simply a regional writer. Now that he is untimely dead, it is entirely appropriate that readers and seminars and groups should be discussing and analyzing how much more he was. But I add my bit to the discussion diffidently, for I am not a critic, and I do not want to contribute another misreading. Neither do I want to exploit his writings, as one would exploit some natural resource, for the making of a critical by-product. That is too much like cutting down redwoods to make Prestolite fireplace logs out of the sawdust. I only want to revisit him, and I welcome the opportunity to remind myself of the things in him that I always admired and envied, and to see what a new look will reveal.

My responses are personal, not only because I knew and liked

Walter Clark, but because in many ways our careers have been parallel. We were almost exact contemporaries—he was six months younger than I—and we grew up in the same part of the world, he from the age of eight in Reno, I from the age of twelve in Salt Lake City. The Great Basin is a unifying force; wherever you live in it, you flow toward every other part. Without knowing it, Walt and I shared much, even a passion for basketball and tennis. We may have played each other in one tournament or other, though if we did I do not remember. His name would have meant nothing to me then; and anyway I tend to forget people I played against forty or more years ago, especially if they beat me, as he probably would have. But the cultural geopolitics of the Great Basin was and is a reality even if it never brought us together, and it eventually did let Walt and me flow together into the same desert sink.

I had known him as a splendid novelist from *The Ox-Bow Incident*, but it was not until I read *The City of Trembling Leaves* that I recognized a blood brother. Shared responses to a shared reality are more important in literary communication than are shared ideas. If literature speaks to temperament, as Conrad said, then it speaks to experience simultaneously. I recognized myself in Tim Hazard and, I thought, in Tim's creator. We spoke the same language; we held attitudes that even when they differed were compatible. That sense of cultural affinity, of a shared and recognized youth, led me to look Walt up the next time I drove through Nevada, and my wife and I spent a long afternoon and evening of beer and talk with him and Barbara in the Carson Valley.

That was the beginning of a valued but not close friendship. I never saw as much of him as I should have liked; we were together a total of hardly ten days in more than twenty years. Though I once hired him to teach at Stanford, I hired him to replace me, and I was in Denmark all the time he was in Palo Alto. We corresponded off and on, saw each other occasionally. But from that first meeting we were friends and more than friends—allies, members of the same tribe, inheritors of the same western estate. Maybe the estate was meager, maybe we were the Diggers of literature, but the mysteries we pretended to were mutual, shared, ours. He taught me a lot about who I was. He was the kind of mirror which, because of isolation and the peculiar newness and poverty of my cultural traditions, I had never had a chance to look into.

I have just reread him, all except the early poems and a few ephemeral essays. It was a too-brief pleasure, for he was a novelist for only one decade, from *The Ox-Bow Incident* in 1940 to *The Track of the Cat* in 1949, and from posterity's point of view he wrote only four books. I should like to reflect a little on what his books mean to me, where they elude me, and how they are related to and how they differ from my own attempts in a similar direction. The cultural circumstances that breed likeness are not strong enough to breed identity. Though in many ways we were alike, in at least one major circumstance we were different, and that difference had something to do with a difference in the books we wrote.

We were alike in our response to country. We were Westerners in what desert, mountains, weather, space, meant to us. He was something of a mystic, as I am not, and if Westbrook is to be believed, he had a conscious intention of dramatizing Jungian archetypes and finding objective correlatives for sacredness within a profane culture. That goes over my head. Certainly I never felt the watchful gods of nature in quite Walt's way—I was probably content with their objective correlatives—but almost as much as he, I think, I felt an awe in the presence of unhumanized nature, I wanted to belong in the natural world and be part of it and be *right* with it, as in dozens of places Walt demonstrated that he did. Almost as much as he, but later in my life, I grew to hate the profane western culture, the economics and psychology of a rapacious society. I disliked it as reality and I distrusted it when it elevated itself into the western myths that aggrandized arrogance, machismo, vigilante or sidearm justice, and the oversimplified good-guy/bad-guy moralities invented mainly by East Coast dudes fascinated by the romantic figure of the horseman, and happily appropriated by a lot of horsemen and sidearm Galahads as self-justification. Those myths have made an impervious shield for all kinds of Western-ers, drugstore as well as authentic cowboys, in the dangerous wilderness of moral irresponsibility. I think Walt and I both felt that, strongly. I sense a fellow moralist in him.

We were both, however, to some extent products of the western experience and culture, in both good and bad and neutral ways. We were both squarer, I imagine, than boys our age in so-called sophisticated places. We accepted the tradi-tional western sexual mores, the division of women into good women and bad women, and a whole lot about the male obliga-tions of protection, chivalry, and, when called for, adoration. We accepted the prevailing athleticism of our place and time, and wanted to excel in competitive sports. We did not think of competition as evil in itself; we wanted sound minds in sound bodies; we wanted to play the game as clean as a hound's tooth, and all that. Put to the test, we respected self-reliance, and when we made literary moves we made them in the spirit of exploration and pioneering. We wanted to go out into our native deserts and mountains and bring back gold; we wanted to help our infant civilization to places as high as we ourselves sometimes felt we went. Our literary quest was a version of the dream of the Garden of the World; we wanted as much as any Mormon elder to make the desert blossom, though with differ-ent fruits. In a way that many deculturized and future-shocked moderns will never understand, there was a civilization-building impulse somewhere in our ambitions.

But I was far more radically a product of the young West than Walt Clark was. The civilized tradition of books, ideas, poetry, history, philosophy, all the instruments and residue of human self-examination, all the storage-and-retrieval possibilities of human experience, I knew only in school, and most imperfectly. It was all a foreign culture superimposed on my barbarism, and entirely foreign to my home, my family associations, my native conditioning. If at school I was part of the age of polished stone, and beginning to be literate, at home I was paleolithic and without the alphabet. No member of my family had ever attended high school, much less college: my father had left school after the eighth grade, my mother after the sixth. During our years in Salt Lake City, our household was at what I tend to think of as the Amos and Andy level of culture, and it had attained to that only after years at the Davy Crockett level, on the crudest of frontiers where we saw people few and seldom and books hardly at all. I have written about that cultural poverty in *Wolf Willow,* and it has no place here except to indicate the way in which Walt Clark and I differed fundamentally and from the beginning. I was a western boy who came hungrily toward civilization from the profound barbarism of the frontier, and was confronted with the fairly common task assigned would-be American writers—that of encompassing in one lifetime, from scratch, the total achievement of the race. Walt was luckier: he was a western boy who possessed civilization from childhood.

He grew up in a cultivated house, and his translation westward at the age of eight was not a move toward deprivation. His father was highly educated, the president of the University of Nevada; his mother was a gifted musician. Books, music, and ideas that I discovered late and by accident, or never discovered at all, were Walt's from birth. He really *had* the two worlds of civilization and the West, where I had only the West, and became a kind of pretender, or at best a seeker, every morning when I left for school. My school life affected my home life hardly at all, and it was a long time before pure accident gave me the notion that it might be possible for *me* to be a writer. Writers were people from elsewhere, or long ago. And when I began writing, I began by simply trying to report. It was another good while before I realized that I was writing primarily toward a much more personal life, up toward the higher intellectual ledges that I knew about from school. It was a little like trying to make Alley Oop, and Alley's dinosaurian concerns, relevant and significant to the National Academy. I had to discover, and in part create, a history and an identity for myself, and then climb from that foothold.

Walt knew very early the terms of his division. He was light-years ahead of me in self-knowledge and awareness. When he sat down to write about the West he was not, like me, limited to writing about scrub oak or sagebrush and wishing that they were the silver apples of the moon. He was self-consciously trying to graft the silver apples onto the sagebrush rootstock.

Many western novels, both realistic and mythic, have been on the side of the wilderness against the vulgarizing tendencies of settlement. The result has been sometimes nostalgia, sometimes bitterness, depending on whether the novelist looks hardest at past or present. You may see one or the other, or both, in all sorts of books, from Willa Cather's *A Lost Lady* (or for that matter Cooper's *The Pioneers,* the ancestor of hundreds of western novels) to Larry McMurtry's *The Last Picture Show.* We began to regret the wilderness almost before we invaded it, and to yearn for the past before we had one. For those who conceive the American dream romantically, its inevitable corruption is disgusting. "Lilies that fester smell far worse than weeds."

It is Walter Clark's distinction that he was never that simplistic, and became neither bitter nor nostalgic. He was on the side of the primal wilderness, but his wilderness was never Eden; its gods were both benign and destructive. He was opposed to the profane and exploitive and despiritualized culture of the settlement, but not to the point of repudiating it utterly, dropping out or copping out or shouting at it from a safe literary sniping post. He consistently tried to make the past, including the spiritually healthy but discarded past of the displaced Indians, relate to the present. He repudiated the machismo that won, and half ruined, the West, but did not repudiate its energy. He wanted it reinformed with spirituality, art, respect for the earth, a knowledge of good and evil. He wanted it to become a true civilization, not a ruthless occupation disguised as a romantic myth.

In Clark's last novel, *The Track of the Cat,* Curt and Curt's mother seem to represent a misguided exploitive harshness, a rigidity or sterility of mind and act, and the Paiute, Joe Sam, seems to represent a primitive nature mysticism victimized and debased. The drunken father is a casualty, as are, in their own ways, his children Arthur and Grace. Of the whole Bridges family, only the youngest son, Hal, has in him the possibilities of growth, reconciliation, and redemption. And there too, I realize on rereading the book, I recognized myself in Walt Clark's writing. Because I was a sort of Hal, without knowing I was. Rereading Walter Clark made me go back and glance through a book of my own, *The Big Rock Candy Mountain,* which I published a half dozen years before *The Track of the Cat.* On the very last page, in the last two paragraphs, I found my own more personal and more agonized statement of Walter's persistent theme. My character Bruce Mason, who is as close to myself as Tim Hazard is to Walt Clark, is ruminating at his father's funeral, after a quarter of a million words of turmoil, effort, bad guesses, mistakes, violence, and cross-purposes:

> It was good to have been along and to have shared it. There were things he had learned that could not be taken away from him. Perhaps it took several generations to make a man, perhaps it took several combinations and re-creations of his mother's gentleness and resilience, his father's enormous energy and appetite for the new, a subtle blending of masculine and feminine, selfish and selfless, stubborn and yielding, before a proper man could be fashioned.

He was the only one left to fulfill that contract and try to justify the labor and the harshness and the mistakes of his parents' lives, and that responsibility was so clearly his, was so great an obligation, that it made unimportant and unreal the sight of the motley collection of pallbearers staggering under the weight of his father's body, and the back door of the hearse closing quietly upon the casket and the flowers.

"You can't mean that ending," an eastern friend told me. But I did, and I think Walt Clark would have understood what I meant—something more than personal to me or my characters—something about the West's difficult becoming, something about its mistakes and crimes, something about its spiritual birthright sold for a mess of pottage, something about its hope. For he could not forget, and neither can I, that the western experience is more than personal; it is part of the process of civilization-building. It was precisely that perception that moved Willa Cather to describe her Bohemian farm girl Ántonia Shimerda as "a rich mine of life, like the founders of early races."

I think the attitude is characteristically western. We feel more affinity with Romulus and Remus than with Nero. We are still busy founding Rome while in New York they fiddle to celebrate its burning.

Civilization is Walter Clark's theme; the West is only his raw material. What else is the burden of *The Ox-Bow Incident*? That novel is a long way from being a simple reversal of the vigilante stereotype or an ironic questioning of vigilante justice. It is a testing of the whole blind ethic of an essentially false, imperfectly formed, excessively masculine society, and of the way in which individuals, out of personal inadequacy, out of mistaken loyalties and priorities, out of a fear of seeming womanish, or out of plain cowardice, let themselves be pushed into murder.

We live mainly by forms and patterns, the novel says. If the forms are bad, we live badly. We have no problem telling where good and evil dwell when we are dealing with the Virginian and Trampas. But here you cannot tell the good from the evil by the color of their hats. Neither the lynchers nor the lynched are all good guys or bad guys. Many of the lynchers would rather not be there and have not known how to say so. The hanged men are a greenhorn, an old senile man, and a Mexican whose criminal record is by no means clean. The terrified greenhorn, once he has accepted his situation, dies better than the Mexican, who was at first bold and unafraid. Davies, who opposed from the beginning the lynch mood of Tetley, failed to stop him because, quite simply, Tetley had more guts than he did. The preacher's morality is not binding because it is imported, almost irrelevant. Evil has courage, good is sometimes cowardly, reality gets bent by appearances.

The book does not end with the discovery that the hanged men are innocent and that lynch law has been a profound mistake. It goes on examining *how* profound a mistake. The moral ambiguities reverberate through the town. We begin to know the good guys from the bad guys by the way they deal with their own complicity in a tragic error. And the moral questioning, the first stage of conscience, goes on in the mind of that most Jamesian cowboy Art Croft, very much as it goes on in the consciousness of the nameless I/we narrator of *The Nigger of the "Narcissus"* after the crew comes ashore.

The Ox-Bow Incident was misread, as Westbrook says. It still is. I hate to think so, but I suspect that its unchallenged place on the shelf of western classics is due not to its being comprehended and appreciated, but to its being persistently misread as an example of the kind of mythic western that Walt Clark was all but parodying. Look at the blurbs on the Signet paperback, and at the summary of the book on the first inside page. To Signet and Signet's readers it is a novel of excitement and suspense and nervous trigger fingers. They do not read it as the report of a failure of individual and social conscience and nerve, an account of wrong sanctioned and forced by the false ethics of a backward folk-culture. They do not read it as a lamentable episode of a civilization in the throes of being born.

Clark's adaptation of the western makes use of its machinery but substitutes a complex and ambiguous moral problem for the blacks and whites of the genre. His version of the *Kunstroman* is equally desimplified. I call *The City of Trembling Leaves* a *Kunstroman;* I could as well call it a spiritual autobiography, for there are unquestionably autobiographical elements in it, such as the preoccupation with the Tristram cycle, with tennis, with the purifications to be found in the mountains, the awareness of the watchful gods.

Never mind. Biography or autobiography, *The City of Trembling Leaves* belongs in the pigeonhole with *A Portrait of the Artist as a Young Man, Look Homeward, Angel, Wilhelm Meister, The Hill of Dreams,* and more somber books such as *Jude the Obscure,* and especially some American portraits of the artist such as *The Song of the Lark.* It chronicles the development of a sensitive adolescent into an artist. It is preoccupied with the relationship between art and life, that obsessive theme of Thomas Mann's, and it explores that relationship not only through Tim's music and through the painting and sculpture of Lawrence Black, but also through the several variations on artistic adjustment made by Tim's musician friends in Carmel. It reveals a skinless sensibility in its mystical feeling for Pyramid Lake, the Sierra, and the desert. It weds Tim Hazard to the physical universe by a rite of passage and a symbolic skinny-dip straight out of Frazer's *Golden Bough,* or if you follow Westbrook, out of Jung. These are all fairly standard elements of a literary genre at least a hundred years old before Walt Clark took hold of it—a genre, one should note, much favored by self-obsessed romantics.

But if Tim Hazard is romantic, the book is not. It is steadily cauterized by irony. And the element of repudiation and compulsive self-exile, almost standard among spiritual autobiographies, is absolutely missing. Tim Hazard, this sensitive youth with musical aspirations and a high cultural potential, grows up in Reno and is never at war with it. It does not frustrate him. He hardly notices it, in fact. He is absorbed with school, and girls, and running, and tennis, and playing in dance bands. He accepts—and so did I—the standards of his time and place and tries to star in what they value; or if he cannot accept them, he ignores them. His father and his brother are not his kind, but he does not think of them as his enemies or threats to his spirit. Reno in its double aspect of middle-class town and jackpot center is not for him the threat that Dublin was to Joyce, or Asheville and his mother's boardinghouse to Thomas Wolfe, or Wellington, New Zealand, to Katherine Mansfield, or America to Ezra Pound.

Most important, the end of Tim Hazard's long struggle to be an artist is not flight or exile, as in so many lives and books, but reconciliation with his town and his past. Art, you might say, leads him not away from the limited western American town but deeper into it. He adds music to Reno without obliterating the traces of Reno that are left in himself. He is not led, as his friend Lawrence Black is, to a self-destructive perfectionism, either. He does not think of himself as contaminated by moving from jazz bands to symphonies, from folk music to composition, and back again—by the divergencies of taste between himself and his town. Some things he outgrows, as he outgrows his adolescent adorations and excesses, but they have strengthened him rather than harmed him. And that makes *The City of Trembling Leaves* unique in its genre. Clark has not justified himself at the expense of his surroundings, if we may take Tim to represent Clark. He has tried to use them to grow from, and in.

One must admit flaws in the book. For me, at least, there is an excess of philosophical abstraction. In trying to marry ideas pertinent to a sophisticated culture to the daily life of a western town, Clark has sometimes let the ideas blur the town. In trying to present Tim's adolescent adorations sympathetically but ironically, and at the same time not be ironic about the ultimate seriousness of Tim's efforts to make a unity of his divided heritage, he is sometimes overlong and unduly detailed, as if he feared the realistic boy might get lost under the symbolic artist. It is, in fact, an almost impossible task he set himself, at this stage of the West's history, and it reminds me of another long, imperfect novel about an artist born in a little western town, Willa Cather's *The Song of the Lark*. Cather assumed that the American artist must escape his or her birthplace and be a kind of stranger on the earth. When Clark lets Tim Hazard, after many failures, achieve his "Symphony of the Leaves," he has dared to suggest that there is a possible reconciliation among serious art, the ordinariness of a little western city, and the primal gods of the earth. It is something I should like to believe.

The City of Trembling Leaves appeared in 1945, the same year in which Clark's short story "The Wind and the Snow of Winter" received first prize in the O. Henry awards. The story is an absolutely first-rate achievement. But in terms of what it attempts, in the importance of what it says, it is almost insignificant beside the ambitious novel that most reviewers dismissed as an autobiographical self-indulgence.

In *The Ox-Bow Incident* Walter Clark had suggested that the values of the frontier society were narrow, false, only half formed, and he had planted a civilizing seed of conscience and doubt and unrest—and hence of youth—in the mind of the sensitive cowpuncher who was one of the lynchers. In *The City of Trembling Leaves* he had suggested that a native western boy, given adequate motivation, might become an artist even in the unlikely arena of the Biggest Little City in the World, and make his commonplace origins serve his art.

In *The Track of the Cat* he came at his theme of civilization, of the evil of the exploitive and profane white culture, and the possibility of reconciliation between that culture's energies and the watchful primal gods of the earth, in quite another way. A lot of reviewers were irresistibly reminded of Melville's white whale, and the book had a mixed reception. On rereading it, I find myself willing to grant some of their objections, but not willing to grant that the flaws are fatal. *The Track of the Cat* may be in some ways Walter Clark's best book.

The realistic objections are valid enough. Mountain lions do not act that way, do not hunt men, probably could not break the neck of a two-year-old steer, much less a bull, much less two or three steers and a bull in one flurry. Only a lion given a heavy injection of literary evil would act that way, and some readers would have been less uneasy if Walt had made his symbolic beast an old rogue grizzly, the only animal native to the Sierra Nevada that *could* break the neck of a steer, and *might* stalk his hunter. Once more, never mind: Keats said Cortez, Shakespeare put a seacoast on Bohemia. The beast is animate (and in good part imaginary) evil, and if the evil is made real to me, I am willing to suspend my disbelief in its objective correlative.

Some sticklers for realism, George R. Stewart for one, have objected that there is a fairly constant violation of the point of view—that Arthur, for instance, wakened by the bellowing of the attacked steers, would not be likely to hear it "like muted horns a little out of tune." Stewart would say that simile came out of Walt Clark, not out of Arthur Bridges.

Yes, sure. I would probably question that little technical impropriety myself in a student's story. But Walter Clark was no student, and what he had to say was important. His Arthur is endowed with some of the prophetic mysticism and second sight of Joe Sam, the family's Paiute hired man. Moreover, it is only by peering over the shoulders of his characters and nudging us with his own voice that Clark is able to steer us through all the tensions of the story and suggest the conflicts between Curt and Joe Sam, Curt and Arthur, Gwen and the mother, the drunken father and all the others, love and hate, good and evil. And I keep remembering that one of Walt's abiding intentions was to naturalize subtlety, sensitivity, spirituality, modulated and even ambiguous ideas, in his realistic western setting. He chose not to be limited, like some phonographic naturalist, by the verbal and spiritual vocabulary of probability. So far as I am concerned, it is legitimate if he gets away with it. He does.

Especially in the early sections, *The Track of the Cat* is a slow, tense drama, melodramatically lighted. I have used it for years as a magnificent illustration of how to achieve suspense by eyestrain. The characters are never overexplained; they reveal themselves in speech and act, and if their creator's need to make them symbolic as well as real sometimes strains them toward some monomaniac excess, they are actually less strained in that way than some of the characters (the preacher, say, or Tetley) in *The Ox-Bow Incident,* or the wonderful, manic musician Knute Fenderson in *The City of Trembling Leaves.* If we grant his panther a little legitimate heightening, we should not deny the same privilege to the human characters.

Symbolic, all of them, but for the most part persuasively real too. There is a real lion loose in the mountains, but the black painter of evil lives in the ranch house, in Curt, as dominating and arrogant as the worst of the *Ox-Bow* lynchers; and in Curt's mother, harshly pious, capable of suffering but invulnerable to understanding; and to some lesser extent in Curt's weak and evasive father. Their evil has already defeated the gentle brother, Arthur, long before Curt finds his broken-necked body in the snow. The same family evil—and I think we realize very soon that it is a social evil, a regional evil, a national evil, an evil of attitude like the cowardice and mob impulse in *The Ox-Bow Incident*—has completely destroyed the sister, Grace. The only person capable of resisting it, the only one of them besides defeated Arthur who can make contact with the Paiute Cassandra and primitive survivor Joe Sam, is Hal, the youngest son. I have already admitted to identifying with Hal and feeling his role as my own. It is hard to resist the temptation to be a culture hero. But Hal's in-between position, his hopeful stance as combiner and reconciler, is the essential stance of Art Croft, too, and of Tim Hazard, and of Walt Clark.

Perhaps strangely, I respond less to Curt's disintegration than to the tension in the ranch house. I feel it as a necessity of the plot rather than as a realistic or even philosophical probability. My experience with the Curts of the world does not lead me to think they are ever touched by the primal gods, that they ever comprehend good and evil, that they are very often visited by poetic justice. For me, Curt at the end is out of Eugene O'Neill, the Great God Brown in chaps, a literary figure, whereas the others, heightened or not, are authentic. But I will put up with both him and the black painter—excesses of the literary and symbolizing imagination—to know the believable, complex human torments of that ranch family in a crisis.

All of Walter Clark's novels were written from ideas, I believe, especially from a preoccupation with problems of good and evil within the context of the real West. He was a little like Hawthorne in knowing all the time what he wanted to say. The characters he created to say it through, whether historical or contemporary, have most of the time a solidity and realism that are altogether admirable. If he had a weakness, it was that sometimes his ideas outran their objective correlatives, and he steered them, or talked about them, rather than letting them act. Not often. And when the symbolic, larger meanings emerge, as so often, directly from something as solid as a log, when we meet and recognize the substance before we are asked to look at the shadow, then I follow him with my hat in my hand. He was not quite, like Hawthorne, trying to develop a usable past, or not that alone; he was trying rather to marry sensitivity and philosophical ideas to the half-primitive western life he knew. He kept trying to do the impossible, and he never missed by far. From 1949 on, many of us were waiting for the book that would outdo the three splendid earlier books and cap the career. It never came. Why?

Some have guessed that teaching distracted him, and certainly he was a teacher incredibly generous with his time. But he was a teacher all his life—at Vermont, in the Cazenovia high school, at Montana, at San Francisco State, at Nevada, with shorter stints at Stanford, Connecticut Wesleyan, and perhaps other places. He wrote all his books between the demands of teaching, and I cannot believe that it was teaching that stopped him. More than that, he told me in the early 1960s that he wrote all the time, and kept throwing away what he wrote. That was long after *The Track of the Cat.*

So did he after all fall victim to the perfectionism that he specifically repudiated in his character Lawrence Black? It is possible. What he had written had been widely misunderstood. His clash of belief and attitude with Leslie Fiedler at Montana might have made him determined to say it in some way that even Fiedler could understand, and he might have become discouraged with the difficulty, first of saying it, and then of making it audible beyond the garbage can and the alley. Without knowing how he felt, I suspect that the dramatization of his difficulty, through the association with Fiedler and the challenge embodied in such essays as "The Montana Face," would have made him more self-critical. And yet he was always self-critical; I cannot conceive that mere difficulty would have silenced him or led him to destroy his work.

What then? I wish I knew. But the fact that from 1962 onward he devoted much of his creative time to the editing of the papers of a pioneer named Alfred Doten suggests, if not an answer, some of the parts of an answer. To turn from fiction to history has been the tendency of scores of American writers who were reared on the thinly civilized frontiers. We have all done it, and it started nearly a hundred years ago, with Edward Eggleston in Indiana. Once we have written the books that deal with the early settlement years of our region, or with our own growing up to identity and awareness, we are likely to find neither the present nor the past rich enough to nourish the fictional imagination. For one thing, the western past has been sanctified by myth, and so cut off. For another, both present and past are too new. The apparent maturity that comes with the creation of valid literature about a new region is apparent only. Culturally the first literature, even the finest, may be premature, the product of applying a seasoned and organic tradition to an unseasoned place and society. And the growing of a native tradition takes generations.

This is speculation only. I was speculating in those terms years ago, and about others besides Walt Clark. I had in mind myself, too. I looked at Bernard DeVoto, and Paul Horgan, and Bud Guthrie, and H. L. Davis, and a lot of good western writers, and I found them slipping away from fiction and into history, as if at a certain point in their careers they found that they had done what their circumstances permitted, and had now to start digging the foundations for the real cultural house that would come with time. In a sense, that is the history of American literature, not merely of western literature. The kind of cultural deprivation that Hawthorne and Henry James lamented is not fatal, as witness their own careers; neither is it fatal in the West, in a newer time, as witness the achievements of Walter Clark.

But without a more developed and cohesive society than the West, in its short life and against all the handicaps of revolutionary change and dispersion, has been able to grow—and without a *native* audience for its native arts—there may come a time in a writer's career when the clutch of the imagination will no longer take hold on the materials that are most one's own.

If those things are true, or partly true, then it is understandable that Walter Clark's career as novelist should have been short. The remarkable thing is that he rendered his own divided inheritance with such subtlety and skill. His books are on the permanent shelf, and I do not mean the shelf of mythic, easy, deluding westerns. His theme was civilization, and he recorded, indelibly, its first steps in a new country. He naturalized the struggle between good and evil in Nevada as surely as Robinson Jeffers naturalized tragedy on the Big Sur coast.

HAUNTED BY
WATERS:
NORMAN
MACLEAN

The writing career of Norman Maclean is a phenomenon. A retired English professor from the University of Chicago at the age of seventy begins, secretly and almost shamefacedly, to write down the stories of his youth that he has told his children. He produces three stories of such unfashionable length and kind—among other defects, "they have trees in them"—that no magazine or trade publisher is interested. Through the influence of friends, they are finally brought out by the University of Chicago Press, which had never published any fiction before that and so far as I know has published none since.

This slim book, virtually without reviews or advertising, finds its way into hands that pass it on to other hands. Fly-fishermen discover it first, with delight, but others besides fishermen respond to it. A little group of admirers forms and spreads. A second printing is needed, then a third, then a paperback edition. By word of mouth a reputation is born. Now, ten years after his first and only fictions saw print, this author of three stories is an established name, an authentic western voice, respected and imitated, and books are being written about him.

Why? How? Every writer and publisher wishes he knew. The usual channels of publicity and criticism had virtually nothing to do with it. Neither did literary fashion, for that, along with the orthodoxies of contemporary short story form, is simply ignored in these stories.

For one thing, they are "realistic," and realism, as everyone knows, was long since left to the second-raters. For another, they are about the West, an environment of broad hats and low foreheads, a place traditionally short of thought and with only rudimentary feelings. For still another, they are about a *historical* West, Montana in the years during and just after World War I, a West that was less a society than a passing phase of the frontier; and they contain some of the mythic feeling and machinery, the crudeness, the colorful characters, and the ox-stunning fistfights made all too familiar by horse opera.

Don't look here for the economy and precision that have marked the short story at least since Joyce and in some ways since Poe. The characteristic modern short story starts as close to its end as it can. It limits itself to a unified action, often a single scene, and to the characters absolutely essential to that action. It covers the time and space required, no more, and picks up the past, insofar as it needs it, in passing. Ibsen perfected that "uncovering" technique in his plays a hundred years ago, rediscovering for both drama and fiction Aristotle's three unities.

But two of Maclean's stories spread across whole summers, and the third contains an entire life. In all three the action moves around—mountains to town, town to the Big Blackfoot to Wolf Creek, camp to café, café to bar. Instead of a rigidly limited cast of characters, whole communities inhabit these tales: rangers, cooks, dynamiters, packers, pimps, whores, waitresses with and without freckles, bartenders, barflies, family, in-laws, small-town doctors, horses, and coyote-killing dogs. Around their discursive actions a world grows up. Inclusion, not exclusion, is the intention; amplitude, not economy, is the means.

Furthermore, this writer talks to his readers, guesses at the motivations of characters, sums up, drops one-liners of concentrated observation and wisdom. He is garrulous and personal. The puppeteer shows his hands and feet. No wonder he couldn't find an orthodox publisher.

It is instructive to note what is not in the stories, but more so to note what is. All three, even "Logging and Pimping," the first written, shortest, and least satisfying, grow on rereading. The two longer ones grow a great deal. Things missed or only half seen edge out into the open. Things that looked only reported turn out to have been *rendered*. Throwaway lines reveal unexpected pertinence, discursiveness that we first forgave as naïveté has to be reappraised as deep cunning. Maybe Maclean knew fully what he was doing, maybe he moved only by instinct sharpened through years of studying literature, maybe his hand was guided by love and nostalgia for places and people long left behind. However he did it, he made a world.

The Montana of his youth was a world with the dew on it. Perhaps the time of youth always has dew on it, and perhaps that is why we respond to Maclean's evocation of his. But I lived in Montana, or close to it, during those same years, and it was a world younger, fresher, and more touched with wonder and possibility than any I have since known. After seventy years, I still dream it; and when it is revived by these stories it glows with a magical light, like one of those Ansel Adams photographs that are more magnificent than the scenes they pretend to represent.

The remembered and evoked world of barely touched wilderness and barely formed towns has, for all its primitiveness, violence, and freedom, an oddly traditional foundation. A raw society, it offers to growing boys mainly a set of physical skills— riding, shooting, fishing, packing, logging, fire-fighting, fist-fighting—and a code to go with them. The hero, the admired and imitated person, is one who does something superlatively well. To fail at a skill, if you try your best, is unfortunate but respectable; to fail in nerve or trying is to merit contempt.

It is absolutely right that the seventeen-year-old Norman Maclean of "USFS 1919" should model himself on Bill Bell, the best ranger, best packer, best all-around mountain man, and best fighter in the Bitterroot country. It is right that in "Logging and Pimping" a grown-up Norman Maclean should half kill himself keeping up with the sadistic logger-pimp Jim. It is right that in "A River Runs Through It" he and his brother, trained by their father in fly-fishing and its mysteries, should reserve their deepest contempt for bait-fishermen. Skill is both competitive and proud. As the basis of a code, it can be harshly coercive on attitudes and conduct.

Also, it is not enough. Unaccompanied by other more humane qualities, skill can produce a bully like Jim or a tinhorn like the cook. The code goes beyond skill to character; for those who subscribe to it, it defines a man. A man for young Norman Maclean is neither mouthy nor finicky; he is stoical in the face of pain; he does not start fights but he tries to finish them; he does what his job and his morality tell him to do. But he cannot get by on mere skill. He needs something else, some decency or compassion that can only be learned from such sources as the boys' preacher father. In the beginning, he reminds his sons, was the Word.

I knew a few preacher kids in my youth. Most were Scottish. All had to learn to reconcile the harsh, limited, demanding code of their frontier society with the larger codes in which grace and personal salvation ultimately lie. Norman Maclean learned that. His brother, Paul, with more skills, with every advantage except the capacity to transcend the code of his place and time, did not.

I speak as if the stories were about real people. I think they are. Maclean gives us no reason to make a distinction between real and fictional people. The stories are so frankly autobiographical that one suspects he hasn't even bothered to alter names. The only thing that has happened to young Maclean's experience is that it has been recollected in tranquillity, seen in perspective, understood, and fully felt. The stories are a distillation, almost an exorcism.

The Maclean boys grew up in a world "overbearing with challenges" and dominated by the code. Sent to the fire-watch station on Grave Peak, sure that he has been sent off as punishment for his dislike of the cook, young Maclean responds by trying to do the job so well, in spite of rattlers, grizzlies, and lightning storms, that Bell will have to admit he has been unjust. (Bell doesn't; he takes the performance for granted.) Pulling all day on the end of a seven-foot crosscut whose other end is in the hands of a bully determined to put him down, Maclean would die on the saw rather than admit he was even tired. Told to go for the money if a fight breaks out, he goes for it, though he knows he will get his face busted. Commanded to take his impossible brother-in-law fishing, he and Paul do, though they would rather drown him.

In every case the reward for faithfulness is acceptance. The logger-pimp Jim learns enough respect for Maclean to make him a "pal." Bill Bell, making up for the whole unsatisfactory summer, asks him to join the crew again next year. And the women caretakers of the impossible brother-in-law let him know without saying it (they are no more mouthy than their men) that he has done his duty, that the failure is not his.

These rites of passage through observance of the code, these steps toward a simplistically understood manhood, dominate both "Logging and Pimping" and "USFS 1919," and are present in "A River Runs Through It." But they are not enough to account for the astonishing success of Maclean's little book. The fact is, the title story contains everything that the other two do, and far surpasses them, transcends them. It flies where they walk. Where they are authentic, humorous, ironic, observant, and much else, "A River Runs Through It" is both poetic and profound.

In the other stories the skills under discussion are work skills from a half-forgotten time. They are re-created as lovingly as Melville re-creates the boats, the gear, the tryworks, and the rest of his cetology. They pack the crevices of the narrative with a dense exposition of *process*. Getting up from reading, we could make a pass at fighting a forest fire or balancing the load on a mule.

But fishing with a dry fly, which is the skill that gives both meaning and form to "A River Runs Through It," is not labor but an art, not an occupation but a passion, not a mere skill but a mystery, a symbolic reflection of life.

Fly-fishing renounces the pragmatic worms and hardware of the meat-fishermen. It is truly an art, "an art that is performed on a four-count rhythm between ten and two o'clock." It calls for coordination, control, and restraint more than for strength. To do it right you need not only skill but the imagination to think like a fish. It has its rituals and taboos and thus is an index to character like the code, but far subtler. There is no clear distinction between it and religion. It takes place in wild natural places, which for Maclean mean awe, holiness, respect; and in water, which he feels as the flow of time.

Like the lesser skills, fly-fishing has its arrogance. Witness Paul's response to Izaak Walton's *Compleat Angler:* not only is Walton a bait-fisherman but the sonofabitch can't even spell "complete." The pride of a supreme artist, plus an unswerving adherence to the code, is a recipe for disaster, a fatal flaw. Despite his artistry and his grace, Paul is one who cannot be helped because he will not accept help. Some saving intelligence, a capacity to see beyond or around the code, saves Paul's brother, but his brother cannot save Paul.

So is this a story of *hubris* in the Bitterroots, of a young god destroyed by pride? If it is, why all that other stuff the story contains—all that tawdry story of looking after the incompe-tent, mouthy brother-in-law, all that bawdy farce of the whore Old Rawhide and the sunburned backsides? If this is a story of pathetic or tragic failure, why is it cluttered up with so much exposition of the art of fishing, so many stories of fishing expedi-tions, so many homilies from the preacher father, so many hints about the relations of Norman Maclean with his wife's family? An impressive story as it stands, would this be even more impressive if it were cleaned up, straightened up, and tucked in?

I will tell you what I think. I only think it, I don't know it; but once when I suggested it in Norman Maclean's presence he didn't deny it. Perhaps, like Robert Frost, he thinks a writer is entitled to anything a reader can find in him. Perhaps I per-suaded him of something he hadn't realized. More likely, he knew it all along.

The fact is, or I think it is, that this apparently rambling yarn is made with the same skill that Paul displays while fishing the Big Blackfoot, the same deliberation and careful refusal to hurry, the same reading of the water. "It is not fly fishing if you are not looking for the answers to questions," the author says, and this is big water demanding every skill.

Listen to how Paul fishes (this is early in the story, and may be taken as a forecast of what is to come):

> The river above and below his rock was all big Rainbow water, and he would cast hard and low upstream, skim-ming the water with his fly but never letting it touch. Then he would pivot, reverse his line in a great oval above his head, and drive his line low and hard downstream, again skimming the water with his fly. He would complete this grand circle four or five times, creating an immensity of motion which culminated in nothing if you did not know, even if you could not see, that now somewhere out there a small fly was washing itself on a wave. Shockingly, immensity would return as the Big Blackfoot and the air

above it became iridescent with the arched sides of a great Rainbow.

He called this "shadow casting," and frankly I don't know whether to believe the theory behind it—that the fish are alerted by the shadows of flies passing over the water by the first casts, so hit the fly the moment it touches the water. It is more or less the "working up an appetite" theory, almost too fancy to be true, but then every fine fishermen has a few fancy stunts that work for him and for almost no one else. Shadow casting never worked for me. . . .

But if shadow casting never worked for the fisherman Norman Maclean, it works marvelously well for the fictionist. He fills the air with flies that never really settle, he dazzles us with loops of glittering line, he keeps us watching Old Rawhide, who does not matter at all, and the brother-in-law, who matters only in that he demonstrates the lack of everything that makes Paul special, and he keeps us from watching Paul, who does matter. Then, on page 102 of a 104-page story, the fly settles, and we strike at what we have been alerted to but have not been allowed to anticipate.

Bluntly, brutally, in a few hundred words, the important part of the story is ended with Paul's life; the shadow falls suddenly on a tale that has been often sunny, even farcical. Time comes down like a curtain, what has been vibrantly alive is only remembered, we are left hollow with loss, and we end in meditation on the Big Blackfoot in the cool of the evening, in the Arctic half-light of the canyon, haunted by waters.

The ending is brought off with such economy only because it was earlier obscured by all the shadow casting. A real artist has been fishing our stream, and the art of fishing has been not only his message but his form and his solace. An organ should be playing Bach's "Es ist vollbracht."

"A River Runs Through It" is a story rooted in actuality, in

known people and remembered events. But it is a long way from a limited realism. It is full of love and wonder and loss, it has the same alternations of sunshine and shadow that a mountain stream has, and its meaning can be heard a long way from its banks. It is an invitation to memory and the pondering of our lives. "To me," Maclean remarks in his introduction, "the constant wonder has been how strange reality has been." Fisherman or not, who is not haunted by waters?

THE SENSE OF PLACE

If you don't know where you are, says Wendell Berry, you don't know *who* you are. Berry is a writer, one of our best, who after some circling has settled on the bank of the Kentucky River, where he grew up and where his family has lived for many generations. He conducts his literary explorations inward, toward the core of what supports him physically and spiritually. He belongs to an honorable tradition, one that even in America includes some great names: Thoreau, Burroughs, Frost, Faulkner, Steinbeck—lovers of known earth, known weathers, and known neighbors both human and nonhuman. He calls himself a "placed" person.

But if every American is several people, and one of them is or would like to be a placed person, another is the opposite, the displaced person, cousin not to Thoreau but to Daniel Boone, dreamer not of Walden Ponds but of far horizons, traveler not in Concord but in wild unsettled places, explorer not inward but outward. Adventurous, restless, seeking, asocial or antisocial, the displaced American persists by the million long after the frontier has vanished. He exists to some extent in all of us, the inevitable by-product of our history: the New World transient. He is commoner in the newer parts of America—the West, Alaska—than in the older parts, but he occurs everywhere, always in motion.

To the placed person he seems hasty, shallow, and restless. He has a current like the Platte, a mile wide and an inch deep. As a species, he is nonterritorial, he lacks a stamping ground. Acquainted with many places, he is rooted in none. Culturally he is a discarder or transplanter, not a builder or conserver. He even seems to like and value his rootlessness, though to the placed person he shows the symptoms of nutritional deficiency, as if he suffered from some obscure scurvy or pellagra of the soul.

Migratoriness has its dangers, unless it is the traditional, seasonal, social migratoriness of shepherd tribes, or of the academic tribes who every June leave Cambridge or New Haven for summer places in Vermont, and every September return to their winter range. Complete independence, absolute freedom of movement, are exhilarating for a time but may not wear well. That romantic atavist we sometimes dream of being, who lives alone in a western or arctic wilderness, playing Natty Bumppo and listening to the loons and living on moose meat and moving on if people come within a hundred miles, is a very American figure but he is not a full human being. He is a wild man of the woods, a Sasquatch.

He has many relatives who are organized as families—migrant families that would once have followed the frontier but that now follow construction booms from Rock Springs to Prudhoe Bay, or pursue the hope of better times from Michigan to Texas, or retire from the midwestern farm to St. Petersburg or Sunshine City, or still hunt the hippie heaven from Sedona to Telluride to Sand Point. These migrants drag their exposed roots and have trouble putting them down in new places. Some don't *want* to put them down, but at retirement climb into their

RVs and move with the seasons from national park to national park, creating a roadside society out of perpetual motion. The American home is often a mobile home.

I know about this. I was born on wheels, among just such a family. I know about the excitement of newness and possibility, but I also know the dissatisfaction and hunger that result from placelessness. Some towns that we lived in were never real to me. They were only the raw material of places, as I was the raw material of a person. Neither place nor I had a chance of being anything unless we could live together for a while. I spent my youth envying people who had lived all their lives in the houses they were born in, and had attics full of proof that they *had* lived.

The deep ecologists warn us not to be anthropocentric, but I know no way to look at the world, settled or wild, except through my own human eyes. I know that it wasn't created especially for my use, and I share the guilt for what members of my species, especially the migratory ones, have done to it. But I am the only instrument that I have access to by which I can enjoy the world and try to understand it. So I must believe that, at least to human perception, a place is not a place until people have been born in it, have grown up in it, lived in it, known it, died in it—have both experienced and shaped it, as individuals, families, neighborhoods, and communities, over more than one generation. Some are born in their place, some find it, some realize after long searching that the place they left is the one they have been searching for. But whatever their relation to it, it is made a place only by slow accrual, like a coral reef.

Once, as George Stewart reminded us in *Names on the Land,* the continent stretched away westward without names. It had no places in it until people had named them, and worn the names smooth with use. The fact that Daniel Boone killed a bear at a certain spot in Kentucky did not make it a place. It began to be one, though, when he remembered the spot as Bear Run, and other people picked up the name and called their settlement by it, and when the settlement became a landmark or destination for travelers, and when children had worn paths through its woods to schoolhouse or swimming hole. The very fact that people remembered Boone's bear-killing, and told about it, added something of placeness.

No place is a place until things that have happened in it are remembered in history, ballads, yarns, legends, or monuments. Fictions serve as well as facts. Rip Van Winkle, though a fiction, enriches the Catskills. Real-life Mississippi spreads across unmarked boundaries into Yoknapatawpha County. Every one of the six hundred rocks from which the Indian maiden jumped to escape her pursuers grows by the legend, and people's lives get lived around and into it. It attracts family picnics and lovers' trysts. There are names carved in the trees there. Just as surely as do the quiet meadows and stone walls of Gettysburg, or the grassy hillside above the Little Big Horn where the Seventh Cavalry died, even a "phony" place like the Indian maiden's rock grows by human association.

In America the process of cumulative association has gone a good way by now in stable, settled, and especially rural areas—New England, the Midwest, the South—but hardly any way at all in the raw, migrant West. For one thing, the West has been raided more often than settled, and raiders move on when they have got what they came for. Many western towns never lasted a single human lifetime. Many others have changed so fast that memory cannot cling to them; they are unrecognizable to anyone who knew them twenty years ago. And as they change, they may fall into the hands of planners and corporations, so that they tend to become more and more alike. Change too often means stereotype. Try Gillette, Wyoming, not too long ago a sleepy cowtown on the verge of becoming a real place, now a coal boomtown that will never be a place.

Changing everywhere, America changes fastest west of the 100th meridian. Mining booms, oil booms, irrigation booms, tourist booms, culture booms as at Aspen and Sun Valley, crowd out older populations and bring in new ones. Communities lose their memory along with their character. For some, the memory can over time be reinstated. For many, the memory too will be a transient, for irrigation agribusiness from California and Arizona to Idaho has by now created a whole permanent underclass of the migrant and dispossessed, totally placeless people who will never have a chance to settle down anywhere, who will know a place briefly during the potato or cantaloupe or grape harvest, and then move on.

As with life, so with literature. Except in northern California, the West has never had a real literary outpouring, a flowering of the sort that marked New England, the Midwest, and the South. As I have noted elsewhere, a lot of what *has* been written is a literature of motion, not of place. There is a whole tradition of it, from Mark Twain's *Roughing It* to Kerouac's *On the Road.* Occasionally we get loving place-oriented books such as Ivan Doig's *This House of Sky* and Norman Maclean's *A River Runs Through It,* but even while we applaud them we note that they are memorials to places that *used* to be, not celebrations of ongoing places. They are nostalgic before history has taken its second step, as much a looking-back as *Huckleberry Finn* was for Mark Twain.

And that is a curious phenomenon, that nostalgia that has marked American writing ever since Irving and Cooper. From our very beginnings, and in the midst of our perpetual motion, we have been homesick for the old folks at home and the old oaken bucket. We have been forever bidding farewell to the last of the Mohicans, or the last of the old-time cattlemen, or the last of the pioneers with the bark on, or the vanishing wilderness. Just at random, read Willa Cather's *A Lost Lady* or Conrad Richter's *The Sea of Grass* or Larry McMurtry's *Horseman, Pass By,* or even William Dean Howells's *The Rise of Silas Lapham,* with its portrait of a businessman possessed of an antique and doomed integrity. We have made a tradition out of mourning the passing of things we never had time really to know, just as we have made a culture out of the open road, out of movement without place.

Freedom, especially free land, has been largely responsible. Nothing in our history has bound us to a plot of ground as feudalism once bound Europeans. In older, smaller, more homogeneous and traditional countries, life was always more centripetal, held in tight upon its center. In Ireland, for example, Yeats tells us, "there is no river or mountain that is not associated in the memory with some event or legend. . . . I would have our writers and craftsmen of many kinds master this history and these legends, and fix upon their memory the appearance of mountains and rivers and make it all visible again in their arts, so that Irishmen, even though they had gone thousands of miles away, would still be in their own country."

America is both too large and too new for that sort of universal recognition. It was just the lack of such recognitions and acceptances, the lack of a complex American society rooted in richly remembered places, that led Washington Irving to transplant European legends to the Catskills, and Hawthorne to labor at creating what he called a usable past. The same lacks drove Henry James, later, to exploit his countrymen not as dwellers in their own country but more often as pilgrims and tourists abroad, hunting what their own country did not provide. When native themes, characters, and places did emerge, they were likely to be local-colorish, exploiting the local picturesque and probably mourning its passing, or expressions of our national restlessness, part of the literature of the road.

Indifferent to, or contemptuous of, or afraid to commit ourselves to, our physical and social surroundings, always hopeful of something better, hooked on change, a lot of us have never stayed in one place long enough to learn it, or have learned it only to leave it. In our displaced condition we are not unlike the mythless man that Carl Jung wrote about, who lives "like one uprooted, having no true link either with the past, or with the ancestral life which continues within him, or yet with contemporary human society. He . . . lives a life of his own, sunk in a subjective mania of his own devising, which he believes to be the newly discovered truth.''

Back to Wendell Berry, and his belief that if you don't know where you are you don't know who you are. He is not talking about the kind of location that can be determined by looking at a map or a street sign. He is talking about the kind of knowing that involves the senses, the memory, the history of a family or a tribe. He is talking about the knowledge of place that comes from working in it in all weathers, making a living from it, suffering from its catastrophes, loving its mornings or evenings or hot noons, valuing it for the profound investment of labor and feeling that you, your parents and grandparents, your all-but-unknown ancestors have put into it. He is talking about the knowing that poets specialize in.

It is only a step from his pronouncement to another: that no place is a place until it has had a poet. And that is about what Yeats was saying only a moment ago.

No place, not even a wild place, is a place until it has had that human attention that at its highest reach we call poetry. What Frost did for New Hampshire and Vermont, what Faulkner did for Mississippi and Steinbeck for the Salinas Valley, Wendell Berry is doing for his family corner of Kentucky, and hundreds of other place-loving people, gifted or not, are doing for places they were born in, or reared in, or have adopted and made their own.

I doubt that we will ever get the motion out of the American, for everything in his culture of opportunity and abundance has, up to now, urged motion on him as a form of virtue. Our tradition of restlessness will not be outgrown in a generation or two, even if the motives for restlessness are withdrawn. But after all, in a few months it will be half a millennium since Europeans first laid eyes on this continent. At least in geographical terms, the frontiers have been explored and crossed. It is probably time we settled down. It is probably time we looked around us instead of looking ahead. We have no business, any longer, in being impatient with history. We need to know our history in much greater depth, even back into the geology, which, as Henry Adams said, is only history projected a little way back from Mr. Jefferson.

History was part of the baggage we threw overboard when we launched ourselves into the New World. We threw it away because it recalled old tyrannies, old limitations, galling obligations, bloody memories. Plunging into the future through a landscape that had no history, we did both the country and ourselves some harm along with some good. Neither the country nor the society we built out of it can be healthy until we stop raiding and running, and learn to be quiet part of the time, and acquire the sense not of ownership but of belonging.

"The land was ours before we were the land's," says Robert Frost's poem. Only in the act of submission is the sense of place realized and a sustainable relationship between people and earth established.

A LETTER TO
WENDELL
BERRY

Greensboro, Vermont
July 25, 1990

Dear Wendell,

It has taken me a long time to write you about your latest
book,* and I know exactly why. I want to praise not only the
book but the man who wrote it, and it embarrasses my post-
Protestant sensibilities to tell a man to his face that I admire him.
If I know you, what I want to say will embarrass you too, but
we will both have to stand it.

Obviously I have not got through a long life without praising
people—their houses, their gardens, their wives, their children,
their political opinions, quite often their writing. But though I
have liked a lot of people and loved a few, I have never been
much good at telling them so, or telling them why. The more
my admiration goes out to a man or woman personally, and not
to some performance or accomplishment, the harder it is for me

*What Are People For? (San Francisco: North Point Press, 1990).

to express. The closer I come to fundamental values and beliefs, the closer I come to reticence. It is a more naked act for me to tell someone I am impressed by his principles and his integrity than to say that I like his book or his necktie.

Nevertheless, though I admire this book as I have admired all of yours since you read the last chapters of *Nathan Coulter* in my Stanford classroom more than thirty years ago, and though I am touched by the inclusion of a friendly essay on myself, I want to say something further, whether it embarrasses us both or not. I acknowledge you as a splendid poet, novelist, and short story writer, and as one of the most provocative and thoughtful essayists alive, and I am not unaware that as a writer you make me, one of your "teachers," look good. My problem is that I can't look upon your books simply as books, literary artifacts. Without your ever intending it, without the slightest taint of self-promotion, they are substantial chunks of yourself, the expression of qualities and beliefs that are fundamental, profound, and rare, things that not even your gift of words can out-dazzle.

That gift, as Conrad says somewhere, is no such great matter: a man is not a hunter or warrior just because he owns a gun. When I quote you, as I often do, I am paying tribute to your verbal felicity, which is always there, but I am really quoting you for qualities of thoughtfulness, character, integrity, and responsibility to which I respond, and to which I would probably respond if they were expressed in pidgin.

Those qualities inform every page of *What Are People For?* They are fleshed out in the people you approve, such as Nate Shaw, Harry Caudill, and Ed Abbey. They are documented in your stout preference for the natural over the artificial or industrial, the simple over the complex, the labor-intensive over the labor-saving, a team of Belgians over a tractor, manure over chemical fertilizers, natural variety over man-managed monocultures. You reaffirm, in "Writer and Region," the respect for place that was evident in *A Place on Earth, The Unsettling of America, A*

Continuous Harmony, The Long-Legged House, and other books. In humorously repudiating the speed and ease of the word processor you repeat your lifelong distaste for technical innovations that elevate the mechanical and reduce the human. In "The Pleasures of Eating" you carry your belief in natural wholesomeness from the production to the consumption of foods, and emphasize your sense of the relatedness of the agricultural and the cultural.

Some people have compared you with Thoreau, probably because you use your own head to think with and because you have a reverence for the natural earth. I am not sure the comparison can be carried too far, though it is meant to be flattering. Thoreau seems to me a far colder article than you have ever been or could ever be. He was a triumphant and somewhat chilly consummation of New England intellectualism and Emersonian self-reliance. Emerson himself said he would as lief take hold of an oak limb as Henry's arm. You are something else. The Nature you love is not wild but humanized, disciplined to the support of human families but not overused, not exploited. Your province is not the wilderness, where the individual makes contact with the universe, but the farm, the neighborhood, the community, the town, the memory of the past and the hope of the future—everything that is subsumed for you under the word "place." Your "ruminations," as you call them, most often deal with matters that did not engage Thoreau's mind: human relations, love, marriage, parenthood, neighborliness, shared pleasures, shared sorrow, shared work and responsibility. Your natural move is not inward toward transcendental consciousness, but outward toward membership, toward family and community and human cohesion. Though you share with Thoreau a delight in the natural world and the pleasures of thought, I think you do not share his austerity, and I doubt that you will end, as he did, as a surveyor of town lots.

What has always struck me as remarkable about you, and hence about your writing, is how little you have been influenced

either by the fads of *Tendenzliteratur* or by the haunted and
self-destructive examples of many contemporary writers. You
may well have learned from the Delmore Schwartzes, the John
Berrymans, the Randall Jarrells, the Sylvia Plaths, but I can't
conceive of a time, even in your most erratic youth, when you
were in danger of following them down. You never had a
drinking problem or a drug problem; you have been as apparently immune to the *Angst* of your times as you have been
indifferent to contemporary hedonism and the lust for kicks.

By every stereotypical rule of the twentieth century you
should be dull, and I suppose there are some people, especially
people who have not read you, who think you are. By upbringing and by choice you are a countryman, and therefore a sort
of anachronism. The lives you write about are not lives that
challenge or defy the universe, or despair of it, but lives that
accept it and make the best of it and are in sober ways fulfilled.

We have grown used to the image of the artist as a person
more notable for his sensibility than his balance. We might go
to that artist for the flash of insight, often achieved at terrible
cost to himself, but not for sober wisdom. I don't disparage
those Dionysian writers; they have lighted dark corners for all
of us, and will continue to. But I find your example comforting
because it restores a lost balance—one doesn't *have* to be crazy,
or alcoholic, or suicidal, or manic, to be a legitimate spokesman
to the world, and there is more to literature, as there clearly is
to life, than aberration and sadomasochism. Your books *seem*
conservative. They are actually profoundly revolutionary, and I
have watched them gain you an increasingly devoted following
over the years. Readers respond to them as lost dogs in hope of
rescue turn toward some friendly stranger. The thought in your
essays is so clear and unrattled that it reassures us. Your stories
and poems are good like bread.

I say that your books are revolutionary. They are. They fly
in the face of accepted opinion and approved fashion. They
reassert values so commonly forgotten or repudiated that, reas-

serted, they have the force of novelty. In *What Are People For?*
you quote some correspondents who are dumbstruck at your
refusal to use a word processor, and your explanation of your
refusal is as revolutionary as it is sane: you don't *want* the speed
and ease of a word processor. You already, you say, write too
fast and too easily. (You don't, but that is partly because you
understand that a degree of difficulty is as necessary to prose as
a scythe stone is to a scythe.) You don't want very many of the
speed-and-ease facilitators of industrial life. You want, as many
others of us do, to be able to work even if the power is down.
You understand such things as word processors as the fences and
walls that can collectively imprison us. You prefer to be free and
at large, with your pad and pencil. But you want to be free in
the place you have chosen, in the society of which you are a
voluntary member.

From the time when you first appeared as a Fellow in the
writing program at Stanford in 1958, I recognized you as one
who knew where he was from and who he was. Your career
since has given not only me but a large public the spectacle of
an entirely principled literary life, a life not merely observant
and thoughtful and eloquent but highly responsible, a life in
which aesthetics and ethics do not have to be kept apart to
prevent their quarreling, but live together in harmony. During
the thirty-two years since we first met, plenty of people have
consciously or unconsciously tried to influence the direction of
your life. You tried the wider world for a few years, at Stanford,
in New York, on a year's Guggenheim in Italy, and eventually
you concluded that you belonged back in Kentucky, where you
had come from.

That was a move as radical as Thoreau's retreat to Walden,
and much more permanent. I am sure that people told you you
were burying yourself, that you couldn't come into the literary
world with manure on your barn boots and expect to be welcomed, that you owed it to yourself and your gift to stay out
where the action was. I was myself guilty of trying to persuade

you against your decision, for sometime in the 1960s I alighted at your Kentucky River farm and tried to talk you into coming to Stanford on some permanent basis. Fortunately, I got nowhere. And you and I both know of a more dramatic instance when you refused an opportunity that many writers would sell their souls for. You refused it because you felt that it might obligate you or impede your freedom of mind. Some might have called you stubborn, or perhaps too timid to risk yourself in deep water. I learned to think of you as simply steadfast.

It has been a robust satisfaction to me that, incongruous as you are in post–World War II America, little as you reflect the homogenized and hyperventilated lives of termite Americans, stoutly as you rebuff the blandishments of technology and progress and the efforts to make life effortless, you have won a large and respectful audience. You have established yourself as a major figure in the environmental movement, even though the environmentalism you promote is really stewardship in land use, and has less popular appeal than the preservation of wilderness, parks, and recreational land. You look upon the earth not mystically but practically, as a responsible husbandman, but your very practicality has made you one of the strongest voices against land abuse.

Those who read you devoutly—and this letter is an indication that I am one of them—find something else in you that their world too much lacks: the value, the real physical and spiritual satisfaction, of hard human work. We respond to your pages as victims of pellagra or scurvy respond to vitamins. You may lack readers among agribusinessmen and among those whose computers have already made unnecessary both the multiplication tables and the brains that once learned them, but you are a hero among those who have been wounded and offended by industrial living and yearn for a simpler and more natural and more feeling relation to the natural world.

And you give us all this with such directness and grace. "Grace" is a word that in fact I borrow from you, and it is the only word that fits. In an essay you comment on two fishing stories, Hemingway's "Big Two-Hearted River" and Norman Maclean's "A River Runs Through It," the one "a feat of style" that deals with mystery and complication by refusing to deal with it, the other a work of art that ultimately "subjects itself to its subject." I like that distinction, for it helps to clarify your own performance. None of your writings that I know, and I think I must know almost all, can be dismissed as a feat of style. Everything you write subjects itself to its subject, grapples with the difficult and perhaps inexpressible, confronts mystery, conveys real and observed and felt life, and does so modestly and with grace. In the best sense of the word, your writing is a by-product of your living.

I should add that you wouldn't be as good a man as you are if you were not a member of Tanya, and she of you.

Yours,
Wallace Stegner

THE LAW OF
NATURE
AND THE
DREAM OF MAN:
RUMINATIONS
ON THE ART
OF FICTION

Once, when I was young and trying to learn to write, I used to study the manuals, hopeful that there was a *way,* and that it could be learned. I remember once going to a lecture entitled "How to Write a Short Story Though Ignorant." Knowing my own ignorance, though not especially humble about it, I thought that a humorous man who started from right where I was should be able to teach me something.

Vain hope. The ignorance in the man's title was a come-on. He knew exactly how to write a story. He had a bottle into which he could pour any mixture, and over the years he had confirmed his confidence in the method by selling the entire product of his bottling works to *The Saturday Evening Post.*

For him, a story was made, not born or discovered or achieved, and if it began as something discovered in life, it was not a story until it had been tugged and pulled to fit his pattern. Every story began with a carefully constructed situation with the seeds of conflict in it. Two men were rivals for a girl, or a gold mine, or control of a corporation. They were evenly matched, and only the most tenuous and sometimes deceptive clues told a reader which one was the good guy and which the bad. First one held the advantage, then the other, a seesaw game; but a smart writer dropped hints calculated to mislead the reader so that the outcome would arrive as a surprise. At the point of greatest complication it should seem that the bad guy, by now suspected and disliked, would win. Then, as swiftly and economically and plausibly as possible, something was introduced or revealed that turned things around. Bad guy went under, good guy came out on top, as in *Cinderella* and many other basic plots that could be looked up in Polti's *Thirty-six Dramatic Situations*. By the time the dénouement was reached, a reader would realize that he had been hoping for this inevitable solution all along.

Since seeking instruction from that ignorant lecturer I have written a few dozen short stories and a dozen or more novels, and I am willing to grant that his method of the plotted story, of the complication resolved, which is as old as story-telling itself and as out of fashion as the Prince of Wales–inspired 1920s pants known as Oxford bags, can still be effective and artful in the right hands and the right circumstances, and when informed with real passion. Conflict is still the essence of drama, no matter how we attenuate or etherealize it. Winning and losing, as football and basketball and baseball games demonstrate, are still endings that people care about, and last-minute winnings and losings are the most dramatic and satisfying of all.

Reversal of expectation is basically foolproof, as TV and the movies prove every day; and even stories that seem to avoid entirely the calculated manipulation implicit in reversals can be seen, when we look closely, to be still reversals. Look at John Cheever's "Torch Song," which, after leading us through the career of a woman who seems tender, compassionate, and humane, turns the last page and shows us necrophilia.

Listening to that lecturer long ago, I didn't grant any validity at all to his traditional formulas. I was offended that he tried to sell me the tired old routine carpentry of story-telling. Though I might have granted that conflict is still the essence of drama, I disliked the contrivance that conflict seemed to demand. For in the 1920s I was a modern young man, and had read Chekhov and Kafka and Mansfield and Joyce and Hemingway, who had dispensed with formula plots and found better ways. In the post-Modernist 1990s the ways they found may be common-place or even anachronistic, but in the twenties they were revelation. In place of winnings and losings, they all dealt in nuances, illuminations, epiphanies. Often nobody won and nobody lost. Often there was no resolution, but only a revealing— sometimes sudden, sometimes, as in Chekhov, as gradual as a slow dawn. Sometimes, as in Kafka, stories never ended at all, but simply raveled away like dreams that we awaken from and lose even as we grope to recover them.

My distaste for that lecturer stemmed partly from the fact that he was commercial, and I was above *that,* and partly from his carpenter's-rule method, but most of all, I finally concluded, from the fact that he had nothing *but* method. He wrote from an unvarying blueprint. He pulled prepackaged frivolous sur-prises out of his sleeve to elicit a gee-whiz response. There was no fire in his belly, no passion or vision or doubt in his mind, no penetration or challenge in what he wrote. He illuminated nothing, opened no windows, left no worm of wonder working in his readers' heads. He had nothing to say, and nothing to ask beyond the questions to which he had just precooked the an-swers.

The writers I admired, and still admire, were not carpenters but sculptors. Their art was and is a real probe of troubling human confusions. They spurned replicas, they despised com-mercialized entertainment. They were after the mystery im-plicit in the stone.

By now I am prepared to guess that any method that lets a writer lay bare a moment of that mystery is legitimate. Skill is whatever works. Different skills will work for different writers, and upon different readers, but any skill must work *toward* something. We are not creating machines that will do nothing but run. Moreover, the eye is not a Xerox copier; it must add something to what it sees. The late Donald Barthelme, when he said that he was in love with fragments, probably spoke his true mind. But he forgot to add that he added something to his fragments, and that the best of them are thus not fragments at all, but illuminations.

One page or six hundred, a fiction is more than a well-carpentered entertainment. It is also more than the mirror in the roadway that Stendhal said it was. Because a good writer is not really a mirror; he is a lens. One mirror is like another, a mechanical reflector, but a lens may be anything from what is in your Instamatic to what makes you handle your Hasselblad with reverence. Ultimately there is no escaping the fact that fiction is only as good as its maker. It sees only with the clarity that he is capable of, and it perpetuates his astigmatisms.

It should make me nervous, and does, to talk about my own writing when both the writing I talk about and the things I say about it may reveal optical opacities or incapacities of which I am totally unaware. That sounds as if I were afraid of being found out, as if my fictions were either personal confessions or *romans à clef*, and that when an ''I'' character speaks in a Stegner novel or story he is to be read as W. Stegner, sneakily expressing W. Stegner's attitudes and feelings from behind a mask.

Which of course is irritating nonsense. No novel, even one meant to be autobiographical, can be read in so naïvely literal a fashion, though it is evident from my mail that people do it all the time. Writers are far more cunning than the credulous reader supposes. We are all practiced shape-shifters and ventriloquists; we can assume forms and speak in voices not our own. We all have to have in some degree what Keats called negative capability, the capacity to make ourselves at home in other skins. Shakespeare had it supremely; he could speak with utter persuasiveness out of the mouth of Hotspur or Shylock,

Iago or Hamlet or Juliet. Faulkner, too, had it supremely. You could no more reconstruct William Faulkner's life or personality from his fiction than you could reconstruct Shakespeare from his plays. On the other hand, some writers have, or use, that capacity hardly at all. The fictions of Hemingway, Thomas Wolfe, and Katherine Anne Porter, for three, are haunted by recurring characters who look like clones of their authors.

The differences between those extremes of "objectivity" and "subjectivity" are obvious but not critical. Some writers want to expose themselves, some to disguise themselves, some to efface themselves. Some who appear to expose themselves are distorting themselves for reasons of their own. There is more than one way to impose order on your personal chaos; but since good writers write what is important to them, they are bound to be in there somewhere, as participants or observers or ombudsmen.

You do not see many autobiographies by fiction writers. Unlike soldiers and statesmen, they do not seem to be driven at a certain age to set it all down in print. The reason may be that most fiction writers have already written their autobiographies piecemeal, overtly or covertly, and go on doing it every working day. "I envy you," somebody said to me once. "It must be nice to be able to write your life instead of having to live it." He had it a little wrong: it isn't a substitution, but a succession. You have to live it first. But once you have written it, or parts of it, you find that you have used up your autobiographical principal as fictions.

If there is a sense in which every piece of fiction is autobiographical, it is just as true that every autobiography is a fiction. A couple of years ago I had the disturbing experience of writing a brief autobiography for a reference book, and I noticed three things. One was the difficulty of getting my precious life into ten thousand words; the second was that I constantly had the feeling that I had written all this before; and the third was that on every page I had to restrain myself from inventing, elaborating, straightening, going around and around myself like a fussy mother getting her sixteen-year-old daughter ready for her first formal dance. I was running a sack race, leg-bound by facts, whereas when I had rendered some of the same experiences as fiction I could be cavalier with them even while, in the interest of general truthfulness, I felt the impulse to tell them truly. And I don't know which version is truer.

As an example of how close autobiography and fiction can be, and how their related methods interweave, consider Philip Roth's *The Facts*—which is not the facts at all. The book purports to give the true dope on the life of Philip Roth, as distinguished from the life of his creation, alter ego, and stooge, Zuckerman. But in *The Facts,* Zuckerman, a fiction, enters unbidden (well, no, not unbidden—invited, rather) and from the sidelines emits challenges, ironic comments, and Bronx cheers as his author goes through the charade of telling his true life story. *The Facts* is as surely a novel posing as an autobiography as *Zuckerman Unbound* is an autobiography masquerading as a novel.

Chaos, Henry Adams said in his *Education,* is the law of nature, order is the dream of man. Both fiction and autobiography attempt to impose order on the only life the writer really knows, his own. Once at a literary meeting I heard someone ask John Cheever why he wrote. He replied without hesitation, "To try to make sense of my life." That is the best answer I can conceive of. The life we all live is amateurish and accidental; it begins in accident and proceeds by trial and error toward dubious ends. That is the law of nature. But the dream of man will not accept what nature hands us. We have to tinker with it, trying to give it purpose, direction, and meaning—or, if we are of another turn of mind, trying to demonstrate that it *has* no purpose, direction, or meaning. Either way, we can't let it alone. The unexamined life, as the wise Greek said, is not worth living. We have to examine it, if only to persuade ourselves that we matter, and are in control, or that we are at least aware of what is being done to us. Autobiography and fiction are variant means to the same end.

Neither one should be wrapped in any straitjacket of method. The method becomes paramount only when it becomes an end in itself, a formula for arriving at prepackaged answers and evading the real questions, or, conversely, a formula for over-turning existing formulas. The guts of any significant fiction—or autobiography—is an anguished question. The true art of fiction, in which I include autobiography, involves putting that question within a plausible context of order.

When we invent fictional characters, as when we invent gods, we often invent them in our own image: we create the unknown out of the materials of the known. The worlds that novelists create, even the fantasy worlds of space and backward or forward time, are made out of the details of the world we were born into. Invention and method here fuse. The writer may play games of distortion, double exposure, deliberately blurred focus. He may focus upon himself focusing, as John Barth and others have done in making fiction out of the act of making fiction. Ingenious as it often is, that gets a little Alexandrian for my taste. I do believe the real world exists, and that literature is the imitation of life, and I like to keep my categories recognizable. Sleight of hand is not enough, and distortion can be a method with real dangers in it.

Thus the admirable artist Flannery O'Connor said that she dealt in the grotesque because when speaking to the hard-of-hearing one must shout. That remark rather offends me as a reader. I don't think I am hard-of-hearing; and anyway, with the truly deaf, shouting doesn't help, it only confuses and annoys. I like O'Connor's stories better than her justification of them, because her justification of them seems to me doctrinaire. Having no such spiritual certainties as she had, I have to make do with spiritual uncertainties; and having besides a temperamental aversion to the hyperboles of distortion, I have had to clarify the life I know in the only way I know. My life challenged me to make sense of it, and I made fictions. But I wanted the fictions to be recognizable and true to the ordinary perception, deaf or otherwise, and I thought I could best achieve that aim with a method that was direct and undistorted.

Ansel Adams, trying to explain what his photographs were about, borrowed a word from his idol Stieglitz, the word "equivalent." The photographic image was an equivalent of the feeling the photographer had when he created it, a form of transferable currency. I will accept that notion for fiction, too; and like Adams and Edward Weston and Imogen Cunningham and the others of San Francisco's *f64* group, I prefer to avoid the double exposures, the imitation of painting, the tricky lighting and artful composition, and rely, insofar as I am able to, on found objects, natural lighting, and the clear statement of the lens.

Literature is a function of temperament, and thank God there are many kinds of temperament and therefore many kinds of literature. I can speak only for my own, and after considerable acquaintance I have determined that my temperament is quiet, recessive, skeptical, and watchful. I don't like big noisy scenes, in fiction or in life. I avoid riots and mass meetings. It would embarrass me to chase fire engines. I have a hard enough time making sense out of what my life hands me, without going out to hunt for more exciting events.

Thirty years ago, in London, I got into a discussion with Martha Gellhorn, whom many will remember as Hemingway's third wife. She told me with admirable frankness that though I wrote like a bird, I didn't write about anything that interested her. She had just returned from reporting events in the Sinai and the Gulf of Aqaba, and she thought I ought to go down there, or someplace like it, someplace where things were *happening,* so that I could apply my talents to subjects worthy of them. I offended her, I am afraid, by saying that I thought that would be a kind of slumming. Not for her, since she was a journalist, but for me. I didn't think then, and I don't think now, that going out and committing experience in order to be able to write about it is the best way of making sense of my life. Unless I was irresistibly drawn to the Arab-Israeli conflict, unless I had some personal stake in the outcome or some plan for bringing about a settlement, I thought I ought, in sheer sympathy, to leave that desert to those whose commitments led them to shed their blood there.

So long as I am saying what doesn't interest me, I may as well fill out the list. As I wouldn't be tempted to exploit the battles or troubles of strangers for my own purposes, or play innovator for the sake of being in on the latest fad, so I have never been driven to thump what Mencken called the booboisie, or foam in rage at the middlebrows, or speak in thunder on this morning's headlines. Not in fiction. Fiction is too important to be abused that way. In fiction I think we should have no agenda except to try to be truthful. The shouters in thunder roar from their podiums and pulpits; I squeak from my corner. They speak to the deaf, but it takes good ears to hear me, for I want to be part of the common sound, a not-too-dominating element of the ambient noise.

I am old enough to have watched a lot of bright innovations and passionate causes fade out into ex-fads, just as in my childhood I watched a lot of hopeful shortgrass homesteaders fade out and disappear before the drought and hot winds. My family was among them. We turned tail and disappeared, and I never got over the faint residual shame of quitting. I admired the stickers, and I still do. Perhaps that is why, if I had three wishes, or only one, even, I would choose to be the author of *Tom Jones* rather than of Lyly's *Euphues*. Or, to make the comparison fairer, of *Tristram Shandy*.

These attitudes I have grown into slowly. I started, as I just said, with the revolutionary and iconoclastic attitudes of the twenties, the time when I was in college. I vorted with the

Vorticists and imaged with the Imagists, and if I had been able to get to Paris I would probably have babbled with the Dadaists in the direction of total intellectual, artistic, and emotional disaffiliation. But there was one trouble. I had grown up a migrant, without history, tradition, or extended family, in remote backwaters of the West. I never saw a water closet or a lawn until I was eleven years old; I never met a person with my surname, apart from my parents and brother, until I was past thirty; I never knew, and don't know now, the first names of three of my grandparents. My family could tell me little, for neither had finished grade school, and their uprooting was the cause of mine. My mother was sympathetic and affectionate—a saint—but she hadn't the tools to help me in many of the places where I needed help.

And so, though I was susceptible to the dialectic of those who declared their independence of custom and tradition and the dead hand of the past, I had no tradition to declare myself independent of, and had never felt the dead hand of the past in my life. If the truth were told, and it now is, I was always hungry to feel that hand on my head, to belong to some socially or intellectually or historically or literarily cohesive group, some tribe, some culture, some recognizable and persistent offshoot of Western civilization. If I revolted, and I had all the appropriate temptations, I had to revolt away from what I was, and that meant *toward* something—tradition, cultural memory, shared experience, order. Even my prose felt the pull of agreed-upon grammar and syntax. Eventually, inevitably, I was drawn to what I most needed.

I have been trying to make natural chaos into human order, trying to make sense of an ordinary American life, for a long time now, more than fifty years. The West, in which I have spent most of my life, is not simply a retarded culture, though for a time it was. It is also a different culture from that of the literary capital, a different culture with different drives and assumptions and prides and avenues of opportunity. School and college do sandpaper the roughness of the frontier, but the frontier leaves its tracks. My first fifteen years were migrant and deprived, my next fifteen aspiring and academic and literary and deprived, my last fifty-odd academic and literary and not so deprived. It is progress, of a sort, I suppose; but I am still the person my first fifteen years made me.

Without consciously intending to, I have written my life. *The Big Rock Candy Mountain* and *Wolf Willow* cover the years of frontier transience in the Dakotas, Washington, Saskatchewan, Montana, Utah, and Nevada. *The Preacher and the Slave,* about the IWW martyr Joe Hill, and *Recapitulation,* a growing-up-in-the-twenties novel, utilize the milieu of Salt Lake City, where I attended high school and college. About that place I have also written histories, biographies, essays, and short stories. My forty-five years in California are reflected in *A Shooting Star, The Spectator Bird, All the Little Live Things,* some stories, and *Angle of Repose,* all of them utilizing houses and communities we have lived in, and all of them inevitably revealing fragments of myself. *Angle of Repose* escapes the personal—I borrowed a set of ancestors entire—but because I chose to tell that story in the first person, a lot of people have mistakenly recognized me in Lyman Ward's wheelchair.

Of all the books I ever wrote, *Crossing to Safety* is in some ways the most personal. It is, in fact, deliberately close to my own experience, opinions, and feelings, which are refracted through a narrator not too different from myself. If *The Big Rock Candy Mountain* was an exorcism, and it was, *Crossing to Safety* is an attempt to understand and make sense of an important relationship in the lives of my wife and myself, a friendship that was rich and rewarding but that left us fumbling for meanings and unsure of our emotional ground. I could also say, though I wouldn't push this, that it is an attempt to make the commonplace memorable, to communicate through the story of essentially uninflected lives all the pain, anguish, confusion, affection, sacrifice, the spontaneous pleasures and the unanticipated catastrophes, of the kind of living that most of us experience.

It was a risky book to set before a reading public accustomed to spicier fare. There is not a murder, a divorce, an illicit weekend, a gun, a liaison, a drug dream, a hot sex scene, even a wild party, in it. It deals with academics, who by definition are said to be tepid and undramatic. Two young couples meet during the Depression in Madison, Wisconsin. One pair is rich, well endowed, well connected, and ambitious. The other is poor, orphaned, unconnected, and ambitious. The two men face similar problems, similar crises of promotion and tenure. The wives are both pregnant. Nothing there to strain the acting powers of Clint Eastwood or Cher. Over the course of thirty years these couples have children, suffer disappointment and illness, make do, put one foot after the other, survive, and are bent but not broken by their experience.

Very different in their personalities, they remain close friends, as some people do. They don't always approve of one another—in fact, all three of the others have difficulty accepting the dominating personality of Charity Lang—but friendship outlasts disapproval, irritation, and matriarchal rigor. At the end of the book, and for that matter at the beginning, since the front-stage action lasts only a day, Charity is on her way out of the lives she loved and supported and dominated, and the others are left to survive, each according to individual nature and condition, relying on whatever it is that in a long life they would not part with. The themes of the novel are love, friendship, and survival. The villains are willfulness, polio, cancer, and blind chance. The tensions are the tensions between and among people who love each other at least as much as they resist each other. It is all very quiet. I intended it to be true. I wrote my guts out trying to make it as moving on the page as it was to me while I was living and reliving it.

My reason for writing that novel was not literary, in the usual sense, at all. We once had such friends as Sid and Charity Lang, and I tried to put them on the page without distortion, exaggeration, or heightening, because I kept trying, even after they were both dead, to understand them. I wanted to work out iconically the deepest and most troubling relationship of our lives, and the most rewarding. I wanted to comprehend how a woman as charming as Charity, a woman with every grace and every opportunity, affectionate, generous, thoughtful, intending only good, could at the same time be a domineering matriarch, a willful putter-downer of her husband, a tyrant sometimes to the children whose every first word and first tooth and first illness she lovingly preserved in the family records; a woman who could say in anguish, at the end, "My God, I have done so much harm!" when all she had intended was affection and aid. I wanted to understand how it might have been to be Charity's husband—by what combination of love, forgiveness, and self-deception Sid Lang could have submitted to a lifetime of humiliating henpecking. I knew how it was to be Charity's friend, alternately baffled, angry, and disarmed. Only by writing her as straight as I knew how could I get a clue to how it felt to be a member of her family. I suppose I wanted to justify their lives, bring them together, lay their ghosts.

In that effort I wrote very close to memory and fact. I resisted whenever I felt myself wanting to adjust or improve or straighten out. I adopted a narrator who, though not myself, was not unlike me—a western orphan, upwardly mobile, making his way. I used episodes from our actual experience because, better than any invented episodes, they evoked the quality of our relationship. I reported the scene of Charity's going off to the hospital to die exactly as my wife, who was present, reported it to me. I relied on memory for many scenes—the birth of Sally Morgan's child, the sailing mishap on Lake Mendota in Madison, the walking trip in the Green Mountains, the dinner party at which the four first became friends.

Nevertheless, I was not running a sack race. I was not tightly bound, as I would have been in a history or biography or autobiography, by the explicit facts. I could expand or contract, omit or amplify, according to some interior stabilizer that told me what was right, here, for this book, and what was not.

What I wrote was a labor of love and bafflement, so close to the facts that at first I thought I would not try to publish it. But I had made more unconscious changes than I knew, and members of Charity's family helped persuade me that what I had written was a novel, not a case history or a memoir. I did not emerge with answers, prefabricated or earned. I emerged with as many questions as I had had when starting out. I still don't understand Charity Lang, or Sid Lang, who loved and endured her. But maybe something has changed. Once I wrote them, they achieved a sort of inevitability. There they were, in a book, characters made permanent, irrevocably what they were, and even I, who put them in that book, feel them somehow more substantial and less troubling than when they existed only in my life or my memory.

Back where we began. How to write a story, though ignorant or baffled. You take something that is important to you, something you have brooded about. You try to see it as clearly as you can, and to fix it in a transferable equivalent. All you want in the finished print is the clean statement of the lens, which is yourself, on the subject that has been absorbing your attention. Sure, it's autobiography. Sure, it's fiction. Either way, if you have done it right, it's true.

AFTERWORD

T. H. Watkins

In the prologue to his biography of Wallace Stegner, Jackson Benson wrote of his conversations with his subject, "Although he was very candid and forthright, he did project a sense of reserve, friendly and kind, but never too close."

That reserve would not have surprised anyone who knew Stegner. He was a man of rectitude, with regard to himself as well as others. In the twenty-seven years I knew him, I never heard him succumb to common gossip, and in responding to inquiries about his personal history he would, as often as not, refer the questioner to his fiction as the best guide to his origins and experiences. But even in *The Big Rock Candy Mountain* and *Recapitulation*—the two novels most closely tied to his own life—his fiction is not always a particularly reliable guide to the man, as Stegner knew perfectly well. "You break experience up into pieces," he told an interviewer, Richard Etulain, "and you put them together in different combinations, new combinations, and some are real and some are not, some are documentary and some are imagined. . . . It takes a pedestrian and literal mind to be worried about which is true and which is not true. It's all of it not true, and it's all of it true."

This is some of what we know to be true: Born in Iowa in 1909, he grew up poor in a rootless and spectacularly dysfunctional family in which learning was hit-or-miss and stability never more than a vague dream. His childhood was a hegira that took the family from Iowa to a North Dakota farm town, out to the lumber camps of Washington State, back to Iowa, up to a futile homestead in southern Saskatchewan, then down to the wrong side of town in both Great Falls, Montana, and Salt Lake City, Utah, where the family moved from house to house but never moved up. His father, George Stegner, a handyman, erstwhile entrepreneur, and sometime bootlegger, was an erratic provider and a physically and emotionally abusive man who seemed to single out his somewhat delicate son for special cruelties. Stegner would spend much of his life trying to exorcise the pain his father had caused him by using literature as therapy—"writing him out of my system," as he once put it. By the end of his life, he thought he had managed to do it; I'm not so sure he had.

His mother, with whom he was very close, did her best to protect him, though she was all but helpless in the face of the father's relentless personality. Still, her attempts to soften the harshness of the boy's environment were a legacy he carried in his heart for the rest of his life and gave him, I am convinced, an uncanny sensitivity to the needs and feelings of women in general; this is certainly reflected in his fiction, in which women play a larger and more central role than in the work of any other male writer I know about. Her death from breast cancer while Stegner was a graduate student at Iowa was an almost unendurable blow. It was Wallace who nursed her in her final days, since the father could not abide the presence of death. The experience fed the fire of the young Stegner's anger at his father and at the same time gave him an understanding of the bitter implacability of fate that never really left him. This was echoed again and again in his later life, as cancer seemed to haunt many of the women closest to him, including his wife, Mary. This, too, he dealt with in his writing, most notably in *All the Little Live Things* and in his final novel, *Crossing to Safety*.

His mother's death left him with a shrinking family circle. His older married brother, Cecil, had died of pneumonia at the age of twenty-three. He did keep in touch with his aunt Min Heggen, his mother's sister, who lived in Minnesota with her family. He was particularly close to her son Tom, who would eventually write *Mister Roberts* under his guidance. The possibility that Wallace and his father could ever have reconciled was slim at best, and that possibility vanished when, not long after his mother's death, George died by his own hand.

Out of this wreckage, Stegner built a life fired by his determination to overcome his bleak and lonely upbringing—not by pursuing the main chance, like his father, but through learning. Learning was a ladder to respectability and stability, to all that his childhood and youth had lacked, and it must be said that he succeeded magnificently. The boy who had learned to read almost in spite of his childhood education, who had once been trapped in a seemingly inescapable vortex of poverty and instability, scrabbled his way through two universities and achieved three degrees (this in the heart of the Great Depression). He became one of the most respected writers and thinkers of the twentieth century—and in the American West, which he did as much to define and defend as any writer in that century, he was nothing less than an icon.

He would teach at the Universities of Utah and Wisconsin, Harvard, and Stanford, where he founded the Stanford Creative Writing Program in 1946 and headed it up until his retirement in 1971. Many of the more than one hundred writers who passed through that program went on to produce enduring and even important work: Eugene Burdick, N. Scott Momaday, Tillie Olsen, Wendell Berry, Larry McMurtry, Edward Abbey, and Harriet Doerr, among many others. He taught at the Bread Loaf Writers' Conference every summer, beginning in the late 1930s and continuing throughout his Harvard years, cheek by jowl with such luminaries as Robert Frost (who became a close friend), Bernard DeVoto (who became an even closer friend), Archibald MacLeish, and Louis Untermeyer.

His twenty-eight books would include three short-story collections, three collections of essays, thirteen novels, two biographies, three histories, and one historical commentary; he was the editor of an artful and effective conservation polemic, *This Is Dinosaur,* of John Wesley Powell's classic *Report on the Lands of the Arid Region of the United States,* and of DeVoto's *Letters;* as World War II was drawing to a close he wrote *One Nation,* a groundbreaking investigative report on race and religious prejudice in America, and, thirty-six years later, he published *American Places,* a collection of essays on the natural human landscapes of the country written with his son, Page. His short stories were selected for inclusion in seven annual volumes of *The Best*

American Short Stories and four *O. Henry Awards* anthologies—and he and his wife, Mary, served as the editors of one O. Henry volume. He wrote both fiction and nonfiction for most of the major magazines of his time; he was the editor in chief of one magazine (*The American West*) and contributed in one editorial capacity or another to several more, including *Saturday Review.* He and Mary were for many years the West Coast editors for Houghton Mifflin. He won both the Pulitzer Prize (for *Angle of Repose,* also selected by the Modern Library as one of the one hundred best novels of the century) and the National Book Award (for *The Spectator Bird*). He received three Guggenheim fellowships; was a Fulbright lecturer in Europe and the Middle East; taught a session at the University of Toronto; had a collection of honorary degrees; and was a card-carrying member of the National Institute and Academy of Arts and Letters, the American Academy of Arts and Sciences, and Phi Beta Kappa.

In short, as a man of letters, Stegner was himself a significant contributor to what he called "the great community of recorded human experience" and one of this country's few genuine "belletrists," as his Stanford friend and colleague Nancy Packer described him. It was a career, said his friend the critic Malcolm Cowley, that was "unequaled in this century," and for that alone his story is worth the telling.

So is the story of his role as a citizen agitator in the cause that remained closest to his heart for some forty years—conservation. He never accepted my characterization of him as one of the central figures in the modern conservation movement, but I got no arguments from anyone else. He founded one organization, the Committee for Green Foothills; served for a time as advisor to Interior Secretary Stewart Udall; sat on the National Parks Advisory Board, the board of the Sierra Club, and the governing council of the Wilderness Society; and was emotionally and often directly involved in most of the major conservation issues from the postwar years until his death. Most important in this context, of course, was his writing. He joined a body of environmental writers whose influence, for the first time in our history, was a major force in shaping public policy across a wide variety of conservation issues, from the building of dams in the Grand Canyon to the threatened disposal of the nation's public land system, from species preservation to the Wilderness Act of 1964. What is more, he gave voice to the emotional content of the environmental movement as no one else did, particularly in "Wilderness Coda," in which lies a literary moment, like Thoreau's "In wildness is the preservation of the world," whose echoes will reverberate a generation later and will probably be felt for generations to come: "We simply need that wild country available to us, even if we never do more than drive to its edge and look in. For it can be a means of reassuring ourselves of our sanity as creatures, a part of the geography of hope."

A good part of who Stegner was, I think, resides in that passion, for the concern was the inevitable by-product of years of searching. Stegner spent much of his life trying to find his place—not so much his intellectual or social place (though that, too, was important to him), but his actual physical and spiritual place in the world, a way to see the world and himself in it. When I first was given a tour of the little plot of land around his and Mary's home in Los Altos Hills, California, I was struck by the tender sense of intimacy his idle conversation about the place conveyed. Every tree and bush—most of which he had planted forty years before—seemed as real a part of his being as his own internal organs. He had always envied those with their feet and their traditions firmly planted in one place. So he found his hilltop in Los Altos Hills in 1948 and built a house upon it and surrounded it with growing things, the root of each tree and shrub a spike nailing him down. On the other side of the continent, in Greensboro, Vermont, he and Mary did much the same with another house, another plot of ground for the summer months, and while Wally was dead by the time I got to see it, it took no great leap of imagination to sense his presence in the maples and ferns of this bosky dell just as profoundly as in the golden hills dotted with oaks in Los Altos Hills. If you can't be born to a place where you can stay, then make one—or two.

I think that hunger for place informed his entire life, even when he did not know it. It was what gave his memory its precision and his words their grace in such works as *Wolf Willow,* and it colored almost everything he wrote. The need to know his place in both the natural and social world gave him an eye for and a sensitivity to all places in which he found himself, even as a transient. There are few novelists or short-story writers in our literature whose work is more completely wedded to natural landscapes, whether the action unfolds deep in the dark, almost claustrophobic forests of New England or under the lidless sky of Montana. It was almost as if he could not imagine writing something without that kind of linkage, and I believe that sense of connectedness is the key to both the man and the work.

Here is an excerpt from one of Wally's letters, sent to me from Greensboro on September 5, 1989:

> Now that Labor Day has passed and the hordes of weekenders have departed, silence begins to fall on these woods, and as silence falls, little flames of red and yellow begin to lick up out of the green. A couple of cold nights like last night and we will be living in the middle of something like the Yellowstone fires—all happily unfought. . . . We walk a couple of gentle miles a day, and I have built a railing on the porch of my workshack/thinkhouse so that I won't fall off and break something, and I write little ruminations and introductions and feel autumnal but not bad. They mought of killed us but they ain't whupped us.

———

T. H. WATKINS was the first Wallace Stegner Distinguished Professor of Western American Studies at Montana State University at the time of his death in 2000. He had been an editor at *The American West* and *American Heritage* and, later, vice-president of the Wilderness Society and the editor of its magazine, *Wilderness,* until it was discontinued.

Watkins wrote twenty-eight books on history, the environment, and nature. The best known was *Righteous Pilgrim,* a biography of Harold Ickes, which won a *Los Angeles Times* Book Award.

Watkins loved the red-rock country of the American Southwest and backpacked in the Escalante Wilderness Area almost every fall. Recognition and awards came his way over the years, but he often said that one of his most meaningful achievements was his long and close friendship with Wallace Stegner.

THE MODERN LIBRARY EDITORIAL BOARD

Maya Angelou
•
Daniel J. Boorstin
•
A. S. Byatt
•
Caleb Carr
•
Christopher Cerf
•
Ron Chernow
•
Shelby Foote
•
Stephen Jay Gould
•
Vartan Gregorian
•
Richard Howard
•
Charles Johnson
•
Jon Krakauer
•
Edmund Morris
•
Joyce Carol Oates
•
Elaine Pagels
•
John Richardson
•
Salman Rushdie
•
Oliver Sacks
•
Arthur Schlesinger, Jr.
•
Carolyn See
•
William Styron
•
Gore Vidal

A Note on the Type

The principal text of this Modern Library edition
was set in a digitized version of Janson, a typeface that
dates from about 1690 and was cut by Nicholas Kis,
a Hungarian working in Amsterdam. The original matrices have
survived and are held by the Stempel foundry in Germany.
Hermann Zapf redesigned some of the weights and sizes for
Stempel, basing his revisions on the original design.

MODERN LIBRARY IS ONLINE AT
WWW.MODERNLIBRARY.COM

MODERN LIBRARY ONLINE IS YOUR GUIDE TO CLASSIC LITERATURE ON THE WEB

THE MODERN LIBRARY E-NEWSLETTER

Our free e-mail newsletter is sent to subscribers, and features sample chapters, interviews with and essays by our authors, upcoming books, special promotions, announcements, and news.

To subscribe to the Modern Library e-newsletter, send a blank e-mail to: sub_modernlibrary@info.randomhouse.com or visit www.modernlibrary.com

THE MODERN LIBRARY WEBSITE

Check out the Modern Library website at
www.modernlibrary.com for:

- The Modern Library e-newsletter
- A list of our current and upcoming titles and series
- Reading Group Guides and exclusive author spotlights
- Special features with information on the classics and other paperback series
- Excerpts from new releases and other titles
- A list of our e-books and information on where to buy them
- The Modern Library Editorial Board's 100 Best Novels and 100 Best Nonfiction Books of the Twentieth Century written in the English language
- News and announcements

Questions? E-mail us at modernlibrary@randomhouse.com.
For questions about examination or desk copies, please visit
the Random House Academic Resources site at
www.randomhouse.com/academic